The Book of
Bramford

A Suffolk Parish and its People

Bramford Local History Group

HALSGROVE

First published in Great Britain in 2003

British Library Cataloguing-in-Publication Data
A CIP record for this title is available from the British Library

ISBN 1 84114 231 X

HALSGROVE

Halsgrove House
Lower Moor Way
Tiverton, Devon EX16 6SS
Tel: 01884 243242
Fax: 01884 243325
email: sales@halsgrove.com
website: www.halsgrove.com

Frontispiece photograph: *Shoeing a horse at the forge in The Street, c.1930.*

Printed and bound in Great Britain by CPI Bath Press, Bath.

CONTENTS

Bramford Street looking north with The Angel on the left, c.1900.

Bramford Works, early 1920s. A view from the east clearly showing the equipment needed to manufacture sulphuric acid.

ACKNOWLEDGEMENTS

When the members of Bramford Local History Group were approached by Halsgrove with a view to producing a history of the village, it seemed an almost unmanageable task. However, once word of the project spread throughout the community, material was contributed by a large number of residents, both past and present. The Local History Group would not have been able to produce this book without the help of these people and would like to offer its sincere thanks. The members hope they will enjoy reading the results.

Bramford Local History Group would like to thank the following people who have contributed to this book:

Jean Austin, Les Beckett, Brian Blomfield, Gwen Boston, Wynne Browes, Angela Brown, John Bugg, David Chappell, Canon Ronald Christian, Charles Clarke, Miss Coupland, Colin Davis, Jack Dodman, Barry Earthy, Ronald Earthy, Nicholas Fiske, Peggy Ford, Dane Garrod, Jeane Gedge, Don Golding, Louise Gynn, Veronica Hall, Sylvia Harvey, Malcolm Hood, Mary Hughes, Janet Jackaman, Peter Jackaman, Michael Jackson, Pat Jarman, Mary Jolly, Bert Keeble, Joyce Keeble, Michael Kinsey, Pat Lait, Christopher Leathers, Derek Mayhew, Hazel Mayhew, Wendy McGinty, Joan Mills, Jenny Milverton, John Newman, W.G.T. Packard, Dennis Page, Elizabeth Palmer, Dick Pegg, Derek Porter, W.A. Prentice, Bernard Purbrick, Mick Russ, Olive Simpson, Beryl Sims, Marilyn Smith, Jim Thacker, Caleta Thomas, Bob Wakeling, Margaret Warton, Margaret, Pauline and Gordon Watkins, Roger Whittell, Jackie Willis, Margaret Woollard, Ronald Wright.

The group would also like to thank the following people for their help with information about the church bells, the tower and bell-ringing: Janet Southgate, for permission to include part of her husband Robert's memoirs; George Pipe, for researching the Norwich Diocesan Association Reports for Bramford references; David Salter, for retrieving the Felstead peal records for Bramford from the internet; and others whose memories were exercised for information.

There may be other people who have lent photographs and information; we hope they will accept our thanks for their contribution and accept the sincere apologies of the group if their names have been omitted.

Our grateful thanks are extended to staff at the Suffolk Record Office in Ipswich for their patience and assistance, the *East Anglian Daily Times*, Suffolk County Council and the Unit for Landscape Modelling at Cambridge University for use of the aerial photographs in 'Early History'. Also thanks to Fisons Photographic Studios and Michael Jackson for the aerial photographs in 'Farms and Farmers'.

Information has been obtained from *Bramford Manor et Soke in 1251, Ipswich's once Regal Neighbour* by J.T. Munday, published privately by Bramford Parochial Church Council in 1981, and *Early Country Motoring* by John F. Bridges.

With such a rich and varied history, it would have been impossible to include every fact and every family. The Local History Group has done its best to cover as many subjects as possible, and the authors hope they will be forgiven for any omissions.

Above: *A very early photograph of Bramford Street before the first Post Office was built, c.1860. The small cottages on the right are where the Co-op store is now.*

Left: *An old painting of Bramford Street where Walnut Tree Close and Place are now. Date and artist unknown.*

Bramford water meadows, 1996. This photograph was taken from Hazel Wood looking north with Bramford Parish Church in the distance.

ONE
❧❧❧
EARLY HISTORY

FROM THE ICE AGE TO DOMESDAY

The parish of Bramford straddles the River Gipping close to its lower reaches and this valley, which contains one of the major waterways in south-east Suffolk, has formed a focus of settlement and an important route across East Anglia since prehistoric times. The Bramford Parish area has therefore seen a gathering concentration of human activity since the end of the last ice age some 30,000 years ago.

When the ice melted it left behind several large boulders known as sarsen stones and there are a number of these dotted around the village; one was used as a bucket rest at the water pump in Bramford Street for a number of years and is now in a private garden. Another stone has recently been brought from a field boundary to stand outside Cherryfields in the aptly named Gipping Stone Road. Two more are in the south wall of the chancel of Bramford Church, and a very large one survives inside supporting the tower.

Worked flints found in both the Blood Hill Pit to the west of the river and Coe's Pits to the east provide evidence of Palaeolithic and Neolithic occupation.

The sand and gravel terraces along the river and the heavier clay soils of the valley slopes have seen

Sarsen stones in the south wall of Bramford Church.

some 4,000–5,000 years of agricultural use and thus no ancient monuments are visible. However, aerial surveys and the collection of worked flints, pottery shards and metal artefacts from the surface of ploughed fields tell a different story.

Towards the end of the Neolithic (or New Stone) Age, c.2000BC, there was an advance in technology with the emergence of copper alloys which in turn saw the beginning of the Bronze Age. As society grew more complex, monuments began to appear in the landscape. These monuments are the round barrows, or tumuli, which are formed by piles of earth being raised over Early-Bronze-Age burial sites as a mark of respect and a symbol of status. In addition, these mounds are probably marks of a tribal or familial ownership which would indicate a person's association with a particular area.

These Bronze-Age round barrows do not survive in a form visible from the ground, but aerial photographs have recorded their characteristic ring ditches at eight points along the River Gipping in Bramford. Of particular note at this site is a group of three ring ditches close to Acton Road, which were visible prior to the development of the area in the late-twentieth century. While these Early-Bronze-Age monuments were unfortunately not investigated before the developments, the aerial photographs do indicate the presence of a substantial farming community in the locality.

There has been little systematic survey of the Bramford area and thus archaeological records for the later prehistoric period are sparse. However, metal-detector finds do hint at continued settlement. A Late-Bronze-Age metalworker's hoard, dated c.800BC, of old and scrap copper-alloy artefacts ready for recycling, has been found in the Bramford Tye area. A subsequent Iron-Age presence is then attested by finds of Celtic coins, from around 50BC, close to Paper Mill Lane.

Archaeological evidence of the Roman period in Bramford Parish is far more abundant. At least five or six foci of probable Roman origin have been

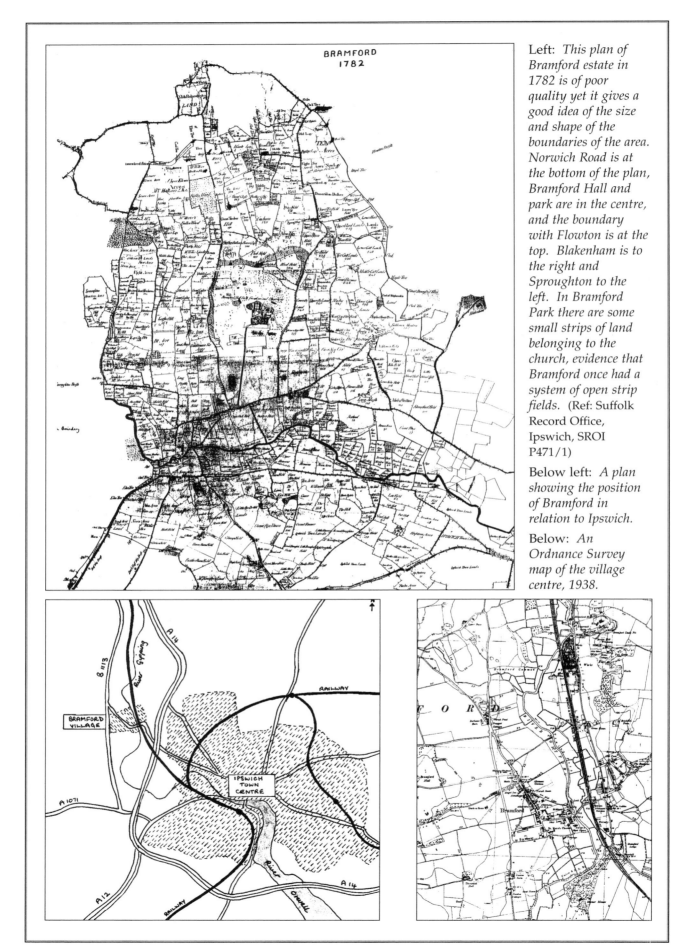

Left: *This plan of Bramford estate in 1782 is of poor quality yet it gives a good idea of the size and shape of the boundaries of the area. Norwich Road is at the bottom of the plan, Bramford Hall and park are in the centre, and the boundary with Flowton is at the top. Blakenham is to the right and Sproughton to the left. In Bramford Park there are some small strips of land belonging to the church, evidence that Bramford once had a system of open strip fields. (Ref: Suffolk Record Office, Ipswich, SROI P471/1)*

Below left: *A plan showing the position of Bramford in relation to Ipswich.*

Below: *An Ordnance Survey map of the village centre, 1938.*

identified from pottery and metal finds across the area of the parish, indicating a dense settlement pattern of prosperous farms. These sites are generally located along the crest of the slope overlooking the valley bottom, and above the main Roman road in this part of Suffolk, which is known as Loraine Way. This road, called the B1113 in modern times, is more of a local route, but during the Roman period it was the main link between London, Colchester and Caistor-by-Norwich, via the small market town of Combretovium, which is located only a mile or so north of Bramford between the modern-day villages of Baylham and Coddenham.

There is little historical evidence of events in East Anglia following the period of Roman habitation. However, settlement of the region clearly continued, albeit on a reduced level, and by c.AD500–600 a prosperous local community had taken to burying their deceased in pagan splendour with weapons and personal jewellery on the Boss Hall estate – historically part of Bramford Parish. Later Saxon activity was also revealed at Boss Hall in the discovery of a particularly wealthy woman's grave dating from c.AD700. In addition, evidence of settlement from the eighth century until at least the eleventh century has been uncovered on the White House Industrial Estate, again in the historic area of Bramford Parish. It is likely that late-Saxon settlement developed close to the Parish Church and it would have been during this period that the parish structure of today emerged.

The main settlement of Bramford developed around the river crossing – the name of the village suggests that this was a ford, which was probably on the south side of the present church. 'Bram' might refer to the growth of brambles close to the river which may have been used as a reference point. A bridge was probably not built until medieval times.

Many aspects of the evolution of a village are influenced by its geography and underlying geology, and Bramford has a rich variety of both. It is served by a substantial river which provides power, transport and the means to enrich adjacent meadowland. Bramford is bounded east and west by slopes which contain a mixture of soils conducive not only to the production of a variety of crops, but also to supplying the raw materials for several industries.

The particular combination of natural materials and water-power found here has helped create an industrial area extant since the mid-medieval period in the north-eastern extremity of the parish, adjacent to its boundaries with Claydon and Blakenham.

During the mid-eleventh century Bramford

Anglo-Saxon burial urn, now in Ipswich Museum.

emerged into historical records with mention of a large royal estate, previously owned by Edward the Confessor and taken over by William the Conqueror. The presence of a royal estate marks Bramford as a prosperous parish in a mainstream area, close to historic and prehistoric communication routes and favoured by good land. Therefore it is not surprising that a dense settlement pattern of farms and cottages continued into the medieval period.

EARLY SURVEYS

The entry for Bramford in the Domesday Survey compared numbers of people and animals, etc. in the area at the time of King Edward the Confessor, the time of the Conquest, and the time of the survey:

In the Hundred of Bosmere, King Edward held Bramford as 12 carucates of land and as a manor. Then as now 40 villeins (unfree landholders) *and 8 bordars* (also unfree but a lower class) *and 1 slave* (the lowest class). *Then and afterwards 1 plough, now half. Then as now 18 ploughs belonging to the men. 30 acres of meadow. Then as now 1 mill. A church with 80 acres of free land and 1 plough. Then 10 pigs, now 12. Then as now 30 sheep. Then it was worth £… (blank) now £15. It is 1 league long and 1 league broad.*

Also included in Bramford jurisdiction was land in Ipswich and Hemingstone. In Samford Hundred Stigand held a manor with ten carucates of land with men and ploughs, but this may possibly refer to Sproughton which is not mentioned in the survey. After the Conquest all land belonged to King William, either directly or indirectly. Bramford was held directly and was therefore a royal manor.

William granted the manor of Bramford to provide income for the establishment of Battle Abbey in thanks for his defeat of Harold. In 1130 it was granted by Henry I to the Church of St Mary in York, and this was confirmed by Richard I in 1189. In 1250 the manor was held by the Bishop of Ely and so it remained until the Dissolution of the Monasteries by Henry VIII. In 1250 the rectory was transferred to the Bishop of Ely, who became the rector, and a detailed survey of all the property in the village was carried out. Revd Munday, who lived in Fraser Road, wrote a small booklet about this survey.

The survey records farmland of over 231 acres, meadow of over 18 acres, 27 acres of fen or pasture, and almost 6 acres of common grazing land. It mentions roads at Faukendon, Goldpeces, Bulherne, Seven Acres, Brokholes, Benhey, and refers to

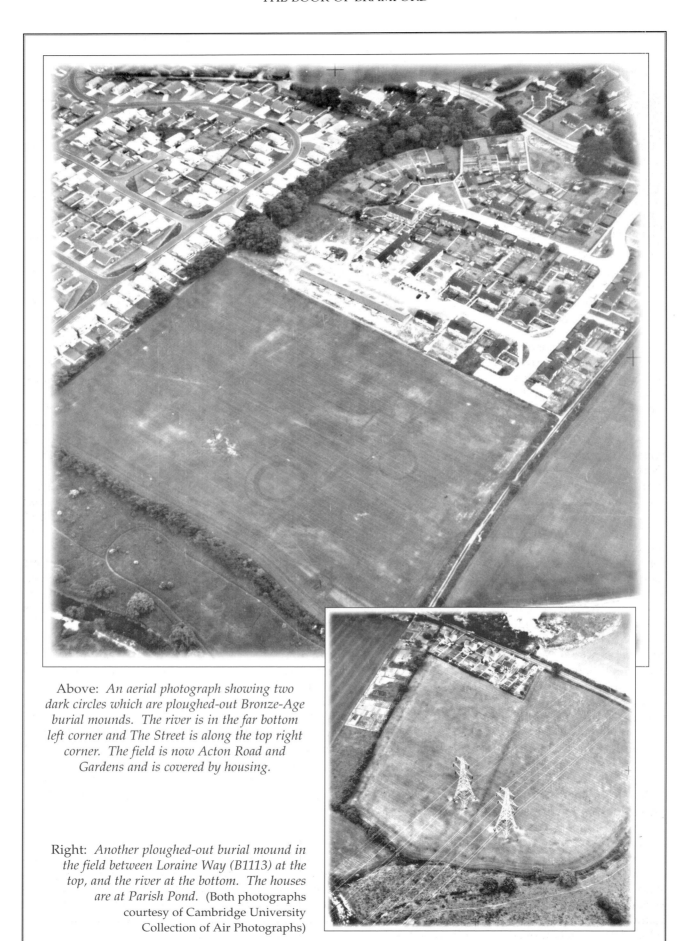

Above: *An aerial photograph showing two dark circles which are ploughed-out Bronze-Age burial mounds. The river is in the far bottom left corner and The Street is along the top right corner. The field is now Acton Road and Gardens and is covered by housing.*

Right: *Another ploughed-out burial mound in the field between Loraine Way (B1113) at the top, and the river at the bottom. The houses are at Parish Pond.* (Both photographs courtesy of Cambridge University Collection of Air Photographs)

Coe's Chalk Pit, Paper Mill Lane, showing geological formations. There is a railway track at the bottom of the pit. (This image is taken from *The Geology of the Country Around Ipswich*, P.G.H. Boswell, published by His Majesty's Stationery Office, 1927.)

Sampson's house, Robert Mete's house and the house of Juliana at the Tye. (It is very likely that Bulherne is the old spelling of Bullen, referring to the road now called Bullen Lane, and that the road to the Tye is almost certainly now Tye Lane.) Even as late as the twentieth century some of these field names were still in use in a modern form. Also in the village were two water-mills, woodland, a stream called Burgord and a fishery. There were settlements at Blood Hill, Bramford Common, Holm Field, Ducklemere and Scotdoune, though there were obviously people living at the Tye, and no doubt near the bridge as well.

Tenants had landholdings of various sizes. The largest was held by Roger de Lovetot with 200 acres for which he paid 50s. annually. Other principal landholders were: Alda de Shrubbelonde (the miller), Eustachius Aletaster, Agnes de Aldefeld, Loveday Olone, Peter son of Christian, James le Norman, Cristiana de Ponte (bridge), John de Quentone, Roger de la Grene, Hubert Mori, Alex de Reymes, John Maynard, Roger and his brother Geoffrey de Flosford, Juliana de la Tye, Thomas Rodland, Cristina de Cattelond, Gregory de Polstede, Cristiana the widow of Odems, Norman son of Peter, Roger Calmodin and Wakelin de Calva. In total there were 129 people named in the survey, which, apart from listing their landholdings, also stated their rights and privileges on the manor.

Some of the other trades mentioned apart from miller were smith, carpenter, carter, weaver, tailor, horse doctor, vine dresser, wheelwright and trader.

In the *Taxatio Ecclesiastica* of 1291, which was an account of income from all parishes in Suffolk, Bramford was the second richest in the county, with an annual value of over £46, while Framlingham with its castle was worth just £43. Bramford was certainly the richest in the Hundred of Bosmere, followed by Barking at £40 – the original settlement which later largely moved to Needham Market.

At some point a second manor of Lovetofts was established. It was granted to the Tibetot family by Edward I as a reward for their services in subduing the Welsh during the late-thirteenth century. This was based at Lovetofts Hall, the site of which is now in Ipswich beside the later Lovetofts Drive. Originally the parish extended east towards Ipswich as far as the Norwich Road, to include the later White House and Whitton Crown.

The Bishop of Ely possessed many estates in East Anglia and appointed stewards to control them and collect taxes from the local people. At least ten Bramford men were involved in the so-called Peasants' Revolt of 1381. The steward, William Fraunceys, was one of the few men killed during the uprising (though not in Bramford), showing just how much the 'establishment' was hated. Although the men were punished, they do not appear to have suffered unduly and several started their own sub-manors following the revolt. However, it was the beginning of the end for the manorial system, and although it continued in name for several more centuries, in practice the local people gradually became more and more independent.

It is evident that during the thirteenth century Bramford was a thriving community with quite a large population. Each of the 129 people named in the survey no doubt had other family members living with them.

A further survey was carried out in 1568, possibly for the purpose of the Tax Subsidy produced in that year. The wealthiest men in the village were required to pay tax assessed on the value of their land or goods, so the entire village was examined.

The plan overleaf shows the centre of Bramford bounded by Bullen Lane, Mill Lane, the river, Vicarage Lane and Fitzgerald Road across to what is now Loraine Way. It shows the buildings and land as they were described in 1568.

The 1568 survey is written in medieval Latin. It describes 800 plots of land and identifies who held each plot, the acreage, whether it was leasehold or freehold, what manor it was in and what the land was used for. It also notes any buildings on it, who the previous recorded tenants were, and where that plot of land stood in relation to the plots around it to the north, south, east and west. The first bearings are obtained by features such as the river and roads which appear in the survey descriptions. The survey works in a sequence around the village. Using the survey and imposing it on a modern map incorporating the named features, the compass bearings and the land area, it has been possible to reconstruct the village houses standing in the mid-1500s, but the plot shapes can only be approximate because of the way the survey expresses the information. Taking Plot 2 (near the church) as an example, the survey provides the following interesting information:

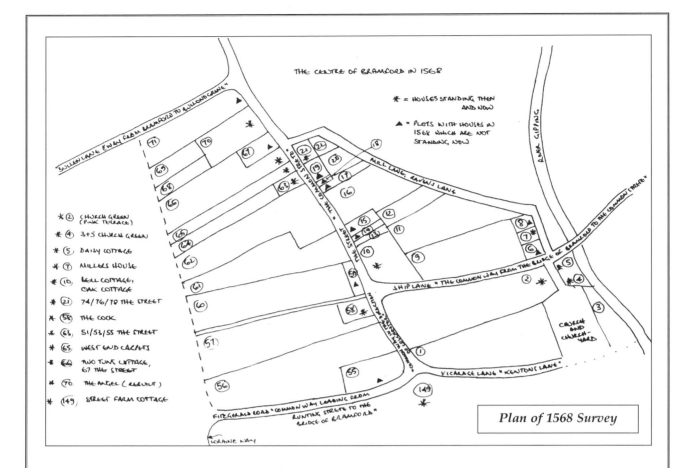

Plan of 1568 Survey

The oldest houses in the centre of Bramford, still standing today, are as follows (plot numbers taken from the 1568 Bramford survey translation as drawn on the above map):

Plot 2 The pink cottages with exposed timber framing situated on Church Green. There was a building called Beverlies here in 1471, but the present properties may have been built after 1522 for William Betts, as they were referred to in the survey as 'the capital tenement now built'.

Plot 4 3 and 5 Church Green were one property owned by William Betts, which existed by 1568.

Plot 5 Daisy Cottage, Church Green, near the bridge. The earliest court rolls mention was in 1526.

Plot 7 The miller's house was first identified in the 1568 survey.

Plot 10 Bell Cottage and Oak Cottage were mentioned in 1518, and had three successive owners prior to 1568.

Plot 21 74, 76 and 78 The Street. Despite the appearance of two of these three houses, the building was once a timber-framed house, now converted into three terraced houses. By 1568 there had been two previous owners.

Plot 58 This was a half-acre site and may have accommodated the present Cock pub. If so, it was the tenement owned by John Cocke in 1568 and first mentioned in the court rolls of 1461.

Plot 63 51, 53 and 55 The Street had one previous owner by 1568, William Betts.

Plot 65 This is now the carpet shop, much altered from 1498 when it was first in the court rolls.

Plot 66 Two Tuns Cottage and 67 The Street, formerly Three Tuns Cottage, first mentioned in 1568.

Plot 70 The Angel, also once owned by William Betts, existed on this site in 1505 but was rebuilt after the 1750s.

Although the 1568 survey of Bramford confirms which buildings were standing at that date, many of them can be traced back to earlier court rolls, and the earliest reference to them may be later than their date of construction. Equally, the buildings listed above are not exactly as they would have appeared in 1568, and other 'originals' may be concealed behind the façades of later additions, waiting to be discovered.

William Betts holds freely in the manor of Lovetoft the tenement of Beverleys with a croft adjacent now with the capital tenement built on it, lying between lands once of Sir Philip Bothe on the south, and the common way leading from the bridge of Bramford to the common street there on the north, and abuts on the common way in the direction of Colchester and the common street on the west, and against the waste or common way next to the bridge there on the east, and contains by estimate 4 acres.

This is the building now painted pink with its timber frame exposed on Church Green. It was formerly the manor-house of Beverleys, and stood in four acres of land, part of which is now occupied by St Mary's Close.

The survey is proof that certain houses were standing in Bramford in about 1568 and more information about some of them can be obtained by reference to the manorial records which date back to c.1400. On the plan, plots 2, 4, 5, 7, 10, 21, 58, 63, 65, 66 and 145 are buildings which were extant by 1568 and are still standing in 2003. Plot 70, The Angel, has been rebuilt.

Houses and buildings were constructed on freehold land, but other land was leasehold. There are a few examples in the survey which show a continuance of the old practice of working for the lord of the manor in exchange for land. One tenant had to pay the lord rent of 12d. and also perform eight days' labour for him in the autumn, providing his own food, as well as giving the lord two hens and a cockerel.

One piece of land had a strange rent attached to it – Newhay Wood was held for the rent of 1lb of pepper a year. Otherwise all land was subject to annual money rent payable to the lord of the manor.

There is little evidence of the enclosure of land. Headlands marked the different plots, in a similar way to present-day paths between allotments. There were few strip fields left by this time. The survey confirms that the land was used for grazing and growing crops, and in some cases plots had alternative uses, suggesting the beginning of a market economy. Much of the land was damp and there were osier beds, a mere, water meadows, marshes and alder groves. Construction materials were extracted from some of the land, from clay, chalk and lime pits. There was also a brick kiln and a tile lodge.

Many pieces of land had names, including Blasts, Le Whart, Brodearse, Shortbutts, Catlands, Mousebrook, Wrens Park, Goryland, Bloodhill and Gallowlands.

Bramford was a network of field paths, common ways, lanes, royal highways, paths to the church and dominical ways reserved for the lord of the manor. There were causeways over marshy areas and, in 1568, three bridges – Bramford Bridge, Bishops Bridge and Ewyns Bridge. There was also a forded crossing over the river called Kentons Watering, which was beyond the end of Vicarage Lane.

The information from the survey can be compared with the Tax Subsidy, which states the value of the lands and goods of those men in Bramford who were wealthy enough to pay tax. It seems that the survey and Tax Subsidy were carried out at a time when the relative importance of the landed gentry was declining and the merchant classes were rising in significance. Roger Payne of Street Farm Cottage paid almost as much tax on his goods as his very rich neighbour, Thomas Bacon, paid on his land.

It is quite likely that the majority of Bramford villagers who worked on the land did not go far beyond the village, but the rich merchants no doubt had connections in London. They would have travelled down the original Roman road to Colchester and London. Meanwhile the landholders continued working the fields, pastures, orchards, meadows and woodlands of Bramford, engaged in growing barley, wheat, rye, oats, peas, hops and occasional hemp, keeping pigs and poultry, horse breeding, dairying and grazing animals, and producing building materials using the earth and trees around them.

MANORIAL COURT ROLLS

The division of the country into manors, each ruled by a manorial lord who controlled the villagers and presided over courts, saw administration begin in earnest in the form of manorial records or court rolls.

Extracts from the manorial records for Bramford during the period from 1400 to 1600 provide a fascinating insight into the lives of people in the village, and also the development of society.

The manor records were written in medieval Latin on long pieces of parchment which were eventually sewn together at the top, rolled up and stored as court rolls. Each roll formed a collection of court records relating to the reign of successive monarchs. Even though the ink on the oldest of Bramford's records is over 600 years old, it is mostly still legible.

The court rolls record the petty crime in the manor, the transfer of property on death or sale, and how the manor gained its income. They do not give any indication of what else was happening in the country at the time. The crimes recorded were those which inconvenienced the inhabitants in general, signalled a minor breakdown in social order, or harmed the manor's finances. Fines were imposed and tenants could be at risk of losing their tenancy. Here is an example of unacceptable social behaviour:

Erasmus Nicholls, gentleman, throws out through the gutter of his new mansion house into the highway there excrements and filthy earth to the nuisance of his neighbours.

William Uffet ploughed up with his wagons 'le Churchpathe' and the market way across the Holme Pightle leading into the Mill Lane.

In 1356 there was obviously some kind of neighbourly dispute:

William Mentil broke into the premises of Margery Cooke.
Margery raised hue and cry on William.
Alice the wife of William drew blood from Margery maliciously.
Margery did the same to Alice maliciously.

And again in 1376:

William Pod drew blood from Alex Byg maliciously.
Margaret Byg raised hue and cry on William Pod.
John the son of John Bacon drew blood from William Pod.
William Pod drew blood from John Bacon maliciously.
John Pecock did the same.
William Pod drew blood from John Bacon maliciously.
John Bacon did the same to William Pod.

Women could be property owners in their own right and it is recorded that 'Margaret Weyland sold her land and tenement in Bramford in 1421.' The rolls contain various snapshots of village life:

Anna Battell, singlewoman, came into the town of Bramford and there gave birth to an illegitimate son. (1529)
Anna Battell, singlewoman, staying in Bramford is of ill repute causing a nuisance to her neighbours. (1530)
Geoffrey Garland placed dung on the King's highway, to the nuisance of his neighbours.
Richard Betts and John Kenton are common players of prohibited games, and they also lurk about, grimacing and annoying their neighbours.

Houses could be sold freehold but because they were within the manor a payment similar to ground rent had to be made to the lord of the manor as well as a fee for leaving the land and a fee for entering it as new owner – these charges were known as 'onfare' and 'offare'. In addition, a special Bramford custom existed whereby the lord of the manor took a fee for all pieces of land every 21 years, irrespective of whether it had changed hands.

Another special custom of Bramford manor concerned 'fallen women'. The following example dates from the 1590s:

The jurors present that a certain Susan Ellis gave birth to an illegitimate child in this manor, therefore by custom of this manor, the lord of the manor confiscated

an outer garment from her. There existed a waistcoat which was taken to the court, and the court officers who were appointed to assess the penalties valued it at 12d.

On 21 April 1597 there was an inquisition into a death in Bramford recorded in the court rolls. The body of Mary Goldingham, spinster, was inspected by the jury. William Wagger had reported that a female was hanging in his barn, the cause of death being 'a string of hemp valued at 2d.'. She was suspended from a roof brace at one end of the barn with both her feet weighted down to the straw. According to the jury a felony, slaughter or murder had been perpetrated.

For those people in Bramford who died before 1533, when the burial registers began, a mention in the court rolls may have been the only written record of their life. For Mary Goldingham the only other mention of her name was in the register and as there were no other people in the village with the same name she was almost certainly a newcomer. It appears that Anna Battell stayed in the village as the name occurs in the registers throughout the seventeenth and early-eighteenth centuries.

Following the Dissolution of the Monasteries by King Henry VIII, Bramford passed into private hands. In 1596 one of the lesser manors was purchased by William Acton. He was a clothier from Ipswich and following his death his son had a monument erected to him in the church of St Mary Elms in Ipswich. At this time traders were not considered to be gentlemen so it was necessary to purchase estates in the country to become accepted into society. William Acton purchased other manors with large areas of land in Bramford and the surrounding parishes, and this was continued by his descendants. His grandson John probably built the first hall on a site overlooking the village between the Tye and Bullen Wood. There may have been an earlier manor-house on the main street opposite the end of Bullen Lane, next to where the Methodist chapel is now.

By the time Bramford Hall was built c.1631 the family were well established in the county, with at least one Acton becoming High Sheriff. After 200 years the family name died out and the estate passed through the female line into the Broke family of Nacton. Because Bramford Hall was a small house compared with their other estates, the family did not live in the parish and tenants were found for the hall and land.

At the end of the nineteenth century the estate passed once again through the female line into the Loraine family. When this family died without heirs the estate was broken up and the hall demolished, a story which continues in a later chapter.

TWO

PLACES OF WORSHIP

THE CHURCH OF ST MARY THE VIRGIN

The Church of St Mary was built to the north of the original river crossing. There was, no doubt, an earlier wooden building on or near the plot, which was probably built to incorporate a site of pagan worship, hence the use of sarsen stones in the foundations. Early documents also mention a church or chapel dedicated to St Albert, or Albrightstone, which stood near the present junction of Sproughton and Bramford roads, but this has long since disappeared.

Parts of the church date back to the thirteenth century: the chancel contains a piscina, priest's door, and sedilia, where the deacon and sub-deacon sat during services. The main body of the church dates from the fourteenth century and contains some fine features, the most notable of which are the finely-carved font cover and the stone rood-screen.

In the floor of the church there are tablets dedicated to deceased landowners such as Sicklemere (now Sycamore). The walls contain memorials to members of the Loraine and Packard families, and to the young men of the village who died during the First and Second World Wars. At the eastern end of the north aisle there is a plaque dedicated to Eliza Mee who was born and grew up in the village. She became the organist in the church in spite of her blindness.

Many of the columns are marked with graffiti, mostly carved during the seventeenth century; no doubt frowned on at the time, it is fascinating to see today. Two columns hold alms boxes (no longer in use), one of which bears the inscription:

Graffiti in Bramford Church dating from the sixteenth and seventeenth centuries.

*Remember the poore the Scripture doth record
What to them is given is lent unto the Lord*

White's Directory of 1884 described the windows:

The chancel window represents the Crucifixion, and at the west end of the north aisle is a three light window representing the Ascension, which was erected in 1869, to the memory of Rev. William Bedford, a late vicar. At the east end of the north aisle is a window representing the Parable of the Sower, which is in memory of Robert William Mumford, Esq., who died in 1870, under which is a brass memorial to Mrs. Mumford who died in 1881. (This window was destroyed by a bomb during the Second World War; a painting of it by Wilfred Hurry has been given to the church by his family.) The tower window, representing Faith, Hope and Charity, is in memory of the late Lady Middleton. The stained glass window behind the altar was given to the church by Mr. Fullbrook-Leggatt of Bramford House and commemorates the Leggatt family connections. The three centre panels depict St. Lawrence (the parish in Ipswich where they owned property and where members of the family were buried), the Virgin Mary in the centre (to whom the church is dedicated) states their connection with a church of this name in Reading, Berkshire, as does the next window dedicated to St. Giles. The two outer windows are dedicated to St. Edmund, and St. Etheldreda the founder of Ely Abbey. The window was dedicated in January 1905. Members of the Leggatt family are buried just inside the north gate of the church.

Above: *The Church of St Mary the Virgin, Bramford,
from the north, 1997.*

Inset above: *Eliza Mee, blind organist.*

Right: *The alms
box.*

The medieval stone rood-screen at the flower festival, July 2002.

Left: *Bramford Bridge and Church, c.1900.*

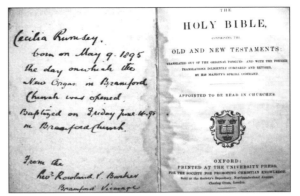

Above: *The front page of Celia Rumsey's Bible.*

Below: *Bony Bob's Bouncing Bell-ringing Band at the Suffolk Guild Striking Competition, Woolpit, 1969. The Bramford team won. Left to right, back row: Robert Southgate, Mervyn Bewley, Alan Walters, Martin Whittell, Neville Whittell, Lawrence Pizzey (curate), Simon Christian; front: Roger Whittell, Jennifer Andrews, Christine Leech, Margaret Brown, Susan Abbott, Penny Smithson, Sandra Cunningham.*

Above: *An early vicarage was set back from the lane, from a painting by an unknown artist, c.1800.*

Above: *A drawing of the church interior with box pews and choir loft.*

Right: *Martha Leggatt, c.1890*

VICARS OF BRAMFORD

1299	Geoffrey de Horwode	1474	Henry Whiterat
1327	John Fenton	1487	Bartholemew Nerthem
1327	William de Herleston	1487	William Knyght
1329	John de Brightewaltone	1517	John Pylkington
1354	Robert Henning	1541	Adam Taylor
1355	Roger de Chesthonte	1567	Richard Snow
1364	John Ful de Armenton	1578	John Harte
1387	Simon de Heuchem	1583	John Carter
1408	Edward Barbeur	1623	Daniel Heron
1410	Walter Stoning	1631	Edward Brasier
1413	John Stapelaw	1661	Anthony St George
1427	John Newlye	1686	Francis Dade
1444	John Newlye	1722	Henry Darby
1459	Thomas Beccles	1723	William Shaw
1460	John Smith	1744	Robert Mawson
1469	Walter Mareys	1760	Robert Hudson

1788	Edward Barker
1795	George Naylor
1854	Spencer Woodfield Maul
1859	William Bedford
1869	Henry Ed. Cruso
1894	Rowland Vectis Barker
1904	Arthur W. Payne
1908	Fred Burstal Butler
1920	William Herring Lillie
1932	A.J. Treloar
1936	Arthur W. Evans
1940	Christopher Harford
1949	T. Bernard Beal
1956	Ronald Christian
1992	Roger Dedman

There have been a number of changes to the church over the centuries. In 1641 the Puritan William Dowsing, acting on the orders of Parliament, caused all images in the church to be destroyed, including the removal of all the angels' heads in the roof. The ringers' gallery at the rear of the building was removed after being badly damaged in a fire caused by a spark from the brazier used for heating. The date of the fire is not known, but it may have been in 1875 when the churchwarden's accounts show a bill for over £300 for repairs to the tower. The font was moved to the back of the church from its original position and the box pews were replaced in a Victorian restoration. A vestry and altar screen were later additions at the end of the nineteenth century and the organ was moved during the 1900s.

When churches and parishes were established, each family had to pay tithes – one tenth of their produce – in order to support the church. These were paid to the rector who either lived in the parish or appointed a vicar in his stead, as in the case of Bramford where the rector has never been resident in the parish. As late as 1846, when the tithes were commuted to a payment of money instead of goods, there were still strips of land belonging to the church in the large fields. This is evidence of the original system of farming in Bramford in the form of strip fields, where all families were allocated their own strips to cultivate.

In 1677 the Glebe Terrier for Bramford, held in the Suffolk Record Office in Ipswich, listed the village properties which were owned by the church: 'Item: One vicaridge house and a parcel of grownds adjoining unto that, containing by estimation two acres.' The villagers had to pay tithes of 8d. per acre for meadow, 16d. for every cow with calf, 4d. for every milk cow, 3d. for every bullock, 4d. for every orchard, 12d. for every colt, one egg for every hen, two eggs for every cock, one lamb in ten, and one pig in ten.

In 1716 the church possessed one pewter flagon, one silver plate, one chalice, one carpet, four cushions, one cloth for the communion table, two surplices, one cushion for the pulpit, two common prayer books, one large Bible, a book of homilies, 'one booke of Marters that's old', five bells and a bier.

In 1723 the parsonage house, which stood in what is now the garden of the Glebe House in Vicarage Lane, was described as the site of the vicarage with one mansion house, one stable, one back-house, two other small buildings, a barn and an orchard. There was also the remains of the old town clock and a sundial on the south side of the steeple. The vicar was paid £60 per annum in four instalments.

In 1763 land at Stowupland was mentioned for the first time. This was a small farm purchased with money left to the village in the will of William Acton. The farm's income was to help support the poor people of the parish. A further £5 was to be distributed amongst the poor from a legacy left by Francis Brook, together with the interest from an investment of £10 to be given monthly in the form of bread.

By 1794 the vicarage barn had been demolished and moved, and in 1804 more details about the house were given. It covered an area of 1,881 sq.ft. and was built of lath and plaster with a tile roof. By 1845 it had been enlarged or rebuilt to cover an area of 2,492 sq.ft with a stucco finish and a slate roof. The vicar was still receiving £60 per annum, but the church also employed a clerk and a sexton, paid £5 and £2 per annum respectively.

In 1903 the church also owned Springfield Cottage in Ship Lane, which was left for the use of the curate in the will of Miss Martha Leggatt of Bramford House. This later became the vicarage but is now a private house once more. Miss Leggatt also left £200 for deserving widows, £200 for church expenses, £200 for school repairs and £50 each to the Bramford Coal and Bramford Clothing Clubs.

THE CHURCH TOWER

A traveller passing between Ipswich and Norwich through the Gipping Valley, either by road or by rail, is unlikely to miss the tower and steeple of Bramford Church reaching high into the sky. Constructed between 1330 and 1350, the church tower and stair turret, which reaches up to the last stage of the tower, were built as one. It was in the eighteenth century that the towering spire and weather-vane were added.

The material used in the construction, namely flint rubble, is common throughout East Anglia as there is little local stone available. Stone for the arches and buttress corners was usually imported from Northamptonshire. Where local stone was available it was employed and stones carried down by glacial action can be seen in the body of the church. In the case of the tower, the north-east corner stands on a massive sarsen boulder which may have been part of an earlier church building on or near this site. There has been some speculation as to whether the tower was vaulted at one time; corbels exist at a height greater than that of the old ringers' gallery, so it seems to be a possibility. The great height of the nave arch also gives credence to the theory.

Externally the tower is supported by eight corner buttresses, the eastern pair continuing down into the body of the church, partially blocking the western nave arches. These buttresses give the tower an appearance of strength but, because of the weight difference between the main body of the tower and the buttresses, this is not the case. Action was taken to strengthen the tower in earlier times, and clamp irons can be seen on the outside of the walls and in the ringing room inside. In the 1950s the north-west buttress collapsed and underpinning was carried out, but not on the other external buttress.

The church organ, April 2002. Peter Jackaman, the organist for 33 years, and Olive Thorne, a visitor from Canada whose grandparents, the Rumseys, were schoolteachers in Bramford. Her mother was born on the same day that the organ was dedicated.

THE CHURCH ORGAN

The organ in Bramford Church was built by Hunter and Son of Clapham. It was installed in May 1895 at the east end of the south aisle before being moved to its present position at the west end of the north aisle in 1950. It consists of two manuals and pedals of tubular pneumatic action.

Swell Organ		Great Organ	
Open Diapason	8'	Open Diapason	8'
Liebluh Gedact	8'	Viol D'Amour	8'
Salicional	8'	Stop Diapason	8'
Voix Celeste	8'	Flute	4'
Gamba	8'	Principal	4'
Principal	4'	Fifteenth	2'
Cornopean	8'	Twelfth	2'
Couplers		Pedal Organ	
Swell to Great		Bourdon	16'
Swell to Pedal		Flute Bass	8'
Great to Pedal		Three composition	
Sub Octave Swell		pistons to each	
Octave Swell		Manual	
Total number of speaking pipes			**802**

THE CHURCH BELLS

Nothing is known of the original four bells at Bramford Church which were recorded in the return of 1553. These were probably melted down when the bells were increased in number to five in 1632. The enthusiasm for change ringing at that time meant that many ancient bells were used for metal or older bells were added to. The bell-founder who cast the new bells in 1632 was Miles Graye of Colchester, regarded by many as the 'Prince of Bell-founders'. His most famous work is the tenor (the largest bell) at Lavenham, cast in 1605. The church of St Mary le Tower in Ipswich also has a bell cast by Miles Graye in 1605 of the same weight as the Lavenham bell, but the Ipswich example is the inferior product.

In Bramford the five bells produced by Miles Graye can be regarded as tonally average. Examination of the bells shows that the tenor has not been tuned and is a virgin bell, a common practice during that period. The others all exhibit some degree of tuning to bring them into accord with the tenor. The method of tuning was fairly crude, to sharpen or flatten the note pieces were either chipped off the lip of the bell or chiselled out from the waist of the bell on its inside. The bells at Bramford illustrate both of these methods of tuning. The smallest bell, the treble, was added to the older five in 1805. Without evidence to the contrary it would seem that this bell was put in to celebrate the great naval victory by Lord Nelson, an East Anglian hero, at Trafalgar. These six bells remain in the church at the time of writing and bear the following inscriptions: 'Thomas Mears and sons of London fecit

100 – NOT OUT!

From Ipswich Journal, 11th May, 1895

IMPROVEMENTS AT BRAMFORD CHURCH On Thursday a dedication service was held in Bramford Church, on the occasion of the opening of a new organ. There was a very large congregation present. The Rev H.E.T. Cruso, formerly the vicar, and who resided in the parish for about a quarter of a century, but now resident at Tunstall, in the diocese of Canterbury, delivered an admirable address on the subject of "Praise", advocating congregational singing. In the evening there was a still larger congregation, and at one time it seemed rather doubtful if all could be seated, but chairs were brought and with the excellent arrangement of able and courteous churchwardens order and comfort were the result.

The organ was built by Messrs. Hunter and Son, of Clapham, London. It has two manuals and built on the tubular system, with patent pneumatic coupling chamber, compass CC to G, 56 notes. The specification of the organ is as follows:- Great organ, CC to G: Open diapason, 8ft., 56 pipes; stopped diapason, 8ft., 56; Viol-d'amour, 8ft., 56; dulcians, grooved to No. 2, 8ft., 44; principal, 4ft., 56; flute, 4ft., 56; fifteenth, 2ft., 56. Swell organ: Open diapason, 8ft., 56 pipes; lieblich gadget, 8ft., 56; salcional grooved to No.9, 8ft., 44; voix celeste, 8ft., 44; principal, 4ft., 56; cornopean, 8ft., 56. Pedal organ: Bourdon, 16ft., CCC to F, 30 pipes; flute bass, 8ft., 30. Couplers: Great to pedals, swell to pedals, swell to great, subociave swell, octave swell, 3 composition pistons on great organ: 3 composition pistons on swell organ.

Mr B.H. Button very ably presided, but during the early part of the service there was some slight difficulty in obtaining the sound required, and a little attention from the builder was needed. It might be stated that the cost of the organ has been defrayed, but there remains a debt of about £30 in respect of improvements in the church. During the afternoon and evening service the church bells were rung by the following ringers:- E. King, first; W. Giles, second; S. Finter, third; H. Giles, fourth; W. Brown, fifth; J. Hardwick, tenor.

An article about the new organ.

Removal of the tenor bell for repair in 1965.

1805' on the treble and 'Miles Graye made me 1632' on 2, 3, 4, 5 and the tenor. The tenor has a diameter of 41ins and weighs 10cwt 3qr 6lb.

The bells in St Mary the Virgin Church have a particular distinction. Five of the bells, the heaviest, are of the same founder and date. No other church has a ring of bells with as many bells cast in the same year by Miles Graye. St Margaret's Church in Ipswich once had a complete six by Miles Graye dated 1630, but one bell was recast during restoration work in 1925.

When originally installed and augmented in 1805, the bells would have hung in a timber frame with timber wheels and fittings, this would have remained until the end of the nineteenth century. In 1906 the bells were rehung by the local Ipswich bell-founder and bell-hanger, Alfred Bowell, courtesy of Mrs Henderson. His firm had completed bell-hanging work throughout Suffolk and neighbouring counties and Bowell's bell-hanging technique and philosophy was simple. His designs were uncompli-cated, making his installations comparatively easy to maintain. Thus the bells at Bramford were rehung on a sturdy iron and steel frame, the bells hanging in plain brass bearings. The metal parts of the bell frame have since been protected against corrosion and regular attention has been given to the bearings, yet the bells 'go' as well now as when they were first rehung in 1906.

The bells had rung out over Bramford for over 300 years and it was not until the 1960s that the note of the tenor was percieved to be slightly peculiar. On examination it was found that the bell had become cracked in the sound bow, the portion of the bell where the clapper strikes, due to over-zealous sound-ing with a chiming hammer. In 1965 the tenor was removed from the tower and transported to Denmark where specialist repair work was carried out by the firm of August Nielsen.

At the time of writing the bells are in good condition but a problem with the north buttress of the tower prevents them from being used regularly. Until sufficient funds have been raised for repair the bells must remain silent for safety reasons.

25 YEARS OF CHURCH ACTIVITY 1975–2000

From the 1960s onwards great changes took place in the Church nationally and Bramford stood steady, adopting changing styles of worship up to and including the great revision of 1980 when *The Alternative Service Book* was adopted, and worship took on a radical new and 'modern' style. The church boasted a choir of boys and girls, ladies and even two men until the 1970s, when it continued with a good choir, ably trained by Peter Jackaman, resident organist since 1965.

In the 1950s a club known as The Ship Club was provided on a Saturday morning for junior school-children where model making, games and various activities took place. In 1973 the club held an event in support of a charity raising money for children in India. The curate at St Matthews Church in Ipswich, Revd Ampat Thomas George, who was born in India, came to an Indian evening in Bramford with his wife and a retired lady missionary to speak about India. Indian refreshments were served by the children dressed in Indian style. Unfortunately the club folded in 1975 due to a lack of willing helpers.

About this time, four Church Army members visited Bramford for two days and stayed with local people. Children's meetings were held at 6p.m. on the two evenings and the response was so over-whelming that a Church Army captain resident in the diocese was invited to hold a week's holiday club at a later date. The club was well attended by the children, who participated in the Sunday worship at the end of the week. More of these events were held over the next few years, but they ceased due to a lack of available Church Army personnel.

In 1977 a Parish Conference was held as a one-day event, commencing after morning service and continuing after a break for lunch. As a result the Mission Group was divided and re-formed as the Overseas Mission Group and Home Mission Group. The Home Mission Group subsequently met and three groups were organised along with the estab-lishment of Area Home Meetings. These meetings continued fortnightly for a while; on one occasion on a summer Sunday evening worship was held on the banks of the River Gipping with electricity for amplification supplied from Mr Baalham's premises in Mill Lane. Unfortunately, due to the movement of parishioners and lack of replacement leaders, these groups had all ceased by 1982.

In 1966 the vicar, Ronald Christian, gathered together a few younger members of his congregation who played the guitar, and one or two who didn't, to assist in the presentation of a folk service. The recep-tion of this was so encouraging that he announced further such services would be held on the third Sunday of each month at 6.30p.m. These events led to the formation of Bramford Folk – a small group of musicians and singers who dressed in dark blue and white, with blue hangings on their music stands. The band performed in other churches around Suffolk and once a month assisted in worship at an old people's home in Ipswich. But again, after several years the group was abandoned.

As a result of studies with the Methodist Church, it was agreed that once a quarter the Parish Church and the Methodist chapel would share each others normal pattern of Sunday evening worship. By the 1980s further joint activity had been introduced when worship with the Methodist chapel took place on one Sunday afternoon bi-monthly at Cherryfields, the senior citizen's home in the village. These initiatives continue at the time of writing.

Throughout the latter part of the twentieth century Bramford was faced with the age-old problem of restoring the church building – falling masonry, cracked walls and leaking roofs! Over the years flower festivals have been held in the church in order to raise funds and these still continue. However, in 1992 a new creature came on the scene – the Duck Race on the River Gipping. The event was held by the river bridge on Mr Church's land off Ship Lane and involved 1,000 ducks, a car boot sale and other activities. The day was a tremendous success. It was repeated two years later when 1,500 ducks took part and there were more activities on the picnic site, by kind permission of Suffolk County Council. The event was sponsored by the *Daily Star* newspaper, and ably abetted by 'Big Bill Stoddart', landlord of Bramford Cock. When the debt for the church roof was eventually paid, a celebration weekend was held with a flower festival in the church entitled 'A festival of flowers and thanksgiving'.

In the 1960s Bramford ecclesiastical parish had transferred into the Ipswich deanery, partly in anticipation of the expansion of Ipswich. This growth did not take place, but the ecclesiastical parish remained in Ipswich. At this time the Ecumenical Movement was gaining pace and Ipswich deanery formed two groups of churches of all denominations. Bramford became a member of the North West Ipswich Fellowship of Churches.

The growth of the village's population in the early 1960s led to overcrowding in village schools and subsequent reorganisation left the old junior school buildings in Ship Lane empty. Negotiations were put in hand and the church eventually obtained the use of a detached part of the school for church activities, it was called St Mary's Schoolroom. Sunday school was held here for many years, with children joining the service in church at the offertory. During the 'winter of discontent' in 1973, when power cuts were a regular occurrence, the old heating system was used over the weekends. It appeared to be a better system than the later electric heaters!

In more recent years the ownership of the schoolroom has passed to the Church, and many

DATE FOR YOUR DIARY!

BRAMFORD FUN DAY AND DUCK RACE

SPONSORED BY NATIONAL NEWPAPER THE DAILY STAR

ON

SATURDAY 28th MAY 1994

MORE TO SEE AND DO FOR THE WHOLE FAMILY

DUCKS WILL BE ON SALE SOON FROM –

THE BRAMFORD POST OFFICE	THE BRAMFORD BAKERY
THE BRAMFORD COCK	THE BRAMFORD FISH SHOP
JULIE LAST – THE VICTORY HALL	THE PAPER SHOP
PAULA – THE CORNER SHOP	BRIDGET – THE SCOUT HQ

'CANOE RACING'   'STALLS'
'BALLOON RACE'   'PUNCH & JUDY'
'WILD WEST SHOW'   'CAR BOOT SALE'

WATCH OUT FOR POSTERS WITH MORE INFORMATION

improvements have been made by a band of willing workers, mostly retired people who get together to enjoy the work, the company and a cup of tea. Many health and safety requirements have been incorporated and the building has been brought up to modern standards. It is available for hire when not required by the church.

Bramford has a large churchyard, which for a few years has been closed to burials – these instead taking place in the village cemetery. Over the years the grass in parts of the churchyard had grown to such an extent that some of the graves were difficult to find. A loyal band of three men, Colin Beck, Don Mayes and Norman Warne, managed to maintain the grass on the northern side, the main entrance to the church, and parts to the east and west. The great storm of 1987 saw debris blown off the trees and so in 1988 a working party was formed to clear a further area of long grass which was then maintained. A party of young offenders came to help and even more was cleared. At another time, a group of students from the nearby Otley Agricultural College came and layered part of the hedges – keeping alive ancient agricultural skills. Another hedge which had disappeared was replaced with new stock.

Eventually the Church Council decided to 'require' the Parish Council to take over the churchyard as a charge within the council's precept arising from Council Tax, and the grass is now cut twice a month during the growing season. The hedges also get an occasional trim. A recent benefactor has provided a seat from which to admire the south side of the church where Bramford's Millennium Yew has been planted.

In January 1991 Revd Canon Ronald Christian retired from full-time ministry as vicar of Bramford after 35 years, and the parish began a long interregnum. During this time the churchwardens were legally in charge of the church and the Church Council met regularly to decide such matters as preachers for the Sunday services. The incumbent in 2003, Revd Canon Roger Dedman, was licensed as priest-in-charge on 6 April 1992. It was then that further consideration was given to the position of Bramford Church – a rural parish in an urban deanery which was now effectively isolated from Ipswich by the new A14 trunk road along the entire eastern edge. Already, with parliamentary and local government boundaries having changed, a number of properties in the ecclesiastical parish of Bramford were within Ipswich Borough. After satisfactory negotiations with the neighbouring St Thomas Parish in Ipswich, a new ecclesiastical parish boundary was established along the line of the A14. The parish then removed from Ipswich deanery and returned to Bosmere deanery which it had left some 25 years previously.

Bill Stoddart, compère at the Fun Day in 1994.

THE PARISH REGISTERS

The parish registers for Bramford began in 1553 when it became necessary to keep a record of all the baptisms, marriages and burials which took place, and at times the documents shed some light on the lives of the parishioners.

Very little is known about the earlier vicars. The most interesting vicar appears to have been Anthony St George, who was appointed in 1661 and continued until he died in 1686. As these dates correspond almost exactly with the reign of King Charles II, and as the Acton family who owned the main manor at that time were Royalist, it is logical to suppose that St George was also a Royalist supporter. He was expelled from Queens College, Cambridge, in 1650, no doubt for that very reason.

His son William was born in Bramford in 1662, but his wife Alice died a few months later. He married his second wife, Marie Littlewood, at St Mary Elms Church in 1665, and it can be no coincidence that this was the church of the Acton family in Ipswich. Their daughter Mary was born in 1667.

Anthony St George noted interesting details in the registers, such as the great fire of London in 1666, and the storm of 1661, but his spelling was not the same as that currently used:

Memorandum there happened such a great and violent winde the 18th of February 1661 that the Personage Barne of Bramforde and allsoe many other barns in this towne fell downe by reason of the violencie of the winde, Likewise the spire of the Towne Steple of Ipswich fell downe and alsoe seaven score oake trees were blowen up by the rootes in my Lord of Herefordes Parke, this I was an eye witness of, his oculis vidi. This was entred in the Register booke by me the 24 of Februarye 1661.

About 140 oak trees were destroyed and Lord Hereford lived in the house we now call Christchurch Mansion in Ipswich.

Anthony St George also recorded deaths by misadventure and epidemics of smallpox, especially in May 1675 when the disease killed ten people. He also recorded notes about the vicarage and other events in the parish, for example in 1672 when Edward Mason of Bramford was employed to move the vicarage pump into the house.

In some cases it is possible to reconstruct families from the parish registers. For example, in the case of John Tanne who lost his first wife and two of his children in July 1601. He married again a few years later, only to lose his second wife and her two sons in the plague epidemic of 1610.

It was not necessarily the poor of the parish who died young; quite often the rich families fared no better. Mr Lawrence Mulleyner was described as 'Gent' in the registers and was lord of Lovetofts Manor. In the Hearth Tax Returns he was taxed for seven hearths, so he must have had quite a big house. Between 1670 and 1687 he and his wife had 14 children baptised in Bramford Church, but at least eight of these died before they reached the age of ten.

One man whose record stands out in the registers is Richard Wellam. He first appeared when his daughter Abigail was baptised in 1624, then three years later his wife was buried. Although it is not recorded in Bramford, he must have remarried, as he and his wife Elizabeth had four more children baptised between 1629 and 1640. Either he had never married Elizabeth (which is unlikely) or she died, as in 1644 he married another Elizabeth. It could have been a different Richard, but this is unlikely considering following entries. In 1657 Joan, wife of Richard, was buried. Then in 1661 more baptisms began, this time for Richard and Rachel – possibly a second or even third Richard? But then in May 1670 the burial took place of Richard Wellam 'an antient man', and seven months later in December 'Widowe Wellom, wife of old Richard' gave birth to twins – Richard and Rachel! If this was the same Richard, he was married at least five times and had at least nine children.

The Methodist chapel, June 2000.

The interior of the Methodist chapel, June 2000.

A memorial stone in the west wall of the chapel.

GUN EMPLACEMENT

At the north end of the churchyard, on the banks of the River Gipping, stands a concrete gun emplacement. It was installed in the early 1940s in case of enemy invasion. The gun was mounted in a special pit which offered some protection for the men of the Home Guard. The pits were known as Spigot Mortar Pits and were usually installed at places where enemy tanks would have to advance in single file, such as bridges or narrow lanes. Although the guns would not have been able to defeat an army, it was hoped that in the case of invasion they would have been able to delay the enemy long enough for the regular soldiers to take over.

ECCLESIASTICAL CENSUS, MARCH 1851

Church of St Mary
Given to Battle Abbey by William Rufus
Total sittings 300–500
Estimated number of persons at service – 100 in the morning, with 30 scholars, and 143 in the evening with 30 scholars.
George Naylor, Vicar

Methodist Chapel
Building 10 years old, sittings 44 + 40
Estimated number of persons – 50 scholars in the morning, 45 adults and 30 scholars in the afternoon, and 50 adults with 25 scholars in the evening.
E. Moulton, Minister

THE METHODIST CHAPEL

A chapel was built in the village in 1842 but the first mention of a specific building was in 1811, the date of the first Ipswich Circuit plan. The site of this first building is unknown but it is likely that before that date services were held in private homes, or even in the open air. *White's Suffolk Directory* indicates that a Wesleyan chapel, with seating for 84 people, was erected at the rear of 11a Ship Lane, Bramford, in 1842.

In 1810 the chapel had a membership of 12, which in the following year had grown to 18. The Ecclesiastical Census of March 1851 shows the number of persons attending the services as 'morning 50 scholars, afternoon 45 adults and 30 scholars, evening 50 adults and 25 scholars.'

By the late 1860s it was realised that the building was not big enough and a plot of land was purchased at the north end of Bramford Street. The present building, together with a small cottage for a caretaker, was built in 1873 for £450, and was registered as a place of worship on 14 March 1874. The foundation-stone was laid on 27 August 1873 by William Pretty, a woollen merchant from Ipswich.

*Methodist chapel outing, c.1930s. Alec and Vera Pryke are in front and
Harold Double is standing second from the right.*

The list of trustees included the architects and an engineer, William and Edward Pretty, three other men from Ipswich, two traders from Woodbridge, Revd Malpas the superintendent, and Henry Bumstead, a market gardener from Bramford. The architects were Cattermole and Eade of Ipswich, and the builder was John Fosdike of Woodbridge. The schoolroom upstairs was added and opened in 1878. After the new church was built, the old building in Ship Lane was converted into cottages.

The Methodist cause has had many ups and downs. Whilst the membership was never great, the work of the Sunday school was well maintained. Like so many village churches, finance was always a problem and the crisis came in 1965 when, with only six members and no Sunday school, the circuit considered closing the chapel. This was prevented by the announcement of a new housing development in the village which would increase the population.

In 1965 the building was renovated with money inherited from Annie Wiles who was a dedicated worshipper. She was born in 1879 and kept a sweet shop at 63 The Street. She was a teacher at the Sunday school and organist at the chapel. Later she lived at The Homestead in Duckamere, before her death in November 1957.

The cottage and land next to the chapel was sold and the money used for necessary safety work on the building, and redecoration both inside and outside. Electric heating was installed, the harmonium was replaced with a second-hand Reed organ from Castle Hill URC in Ipswich and new furniture was purchased for the schoolroom. The Sunday school recommenced in 1970 and membership of the chapel grew to a maximum of 39.

The chapel was modernised in 1992 when the pews were replaced by chairs, the electric lighting was renewed, the floor carpeted and an audio and loop system installed. Work was also carried out to facilitate access for the disabled. The Reed organ was replaced with an electronic instrument in 1994.

The membership of the chapel at the time of writing is more than 20. In keeping with the majority of churches today, the chapel is used for a wide variety of activities, both devotional and social, including many which are shared with members of the Parish Church. The latest venture is the formation of a computer club, which has proved very popular and encourages people from the local community to learn new skills.

Many social changes have occurred in the latter part of the twentieth century and continue into the twenty-first. This has had a major effect on all chapels and churches, and discussions are currently under way concerning the direction in which they are heading.

THREE
PRINCIPAL BUILDINGS

The following buildings have been listed by the Department of the Environment.

Grade I:
Church of St Mary, thirteenth–fourteenth century.

Grade II:
Daisy Cottage, Church Green, seventeenth century.
3 and 5 Church Green, mid- to late-sixteenth century.
2–8 Church Green, formerly the Ship Inn, early-sixteenth century.
6–10 The Street, formerly the Bell Inn, late medieval.
Royal Oak House, The Street, late-eighteenth century.
1 Ravens Lane and 74–78 The Street, mid-sixteenth century.
The Cock Inn, The Street, sixteenth century.
51–55 The Street, mid-sixteenth century.
Carpet Shop, The Street, late-fourteenth to early-fifteenth century.
65–67 The Street, late-fifteenth to sixteenth century.
Street Farm Cottage, Vicarage Lane, early-sixteenth century.
The Old School and School House, Ship Lane, 1860 with later extensions.
Bramford House and front wall, Ship Lane, 1693–94.

Mill House, Mill Lane, late-fifteenth century.
Millbank and gateposts, Mill Lane, around 1754.
Bridge House, Mill Lane, around 1850.
The Gables, Ipswich Road, seventeenth century possibly with earlier core.
Fidgeons Farm, Bullen Lane, early- to mid-seventeeth century.
Bullen Hall Farm, Bullen Lane, around 1600.
Grindle Farm, Grindle Lane, early-seventeeth century.
Runcton House, Loraine Way, fifteenth century with Crown Post in roof.
Sycamore Farm, Somersham Road, fifteenth and sixteenth century.
Dairy Farm, Somersham Road, early-sixteenth century.
Tye Farm, mainly seventeenth century.
Thornbush Hall, early-seventeenth century with later additions.
113–117 Paper Mill Lane (The Grove), early-nineteenth century.
North warehouse at Fisons factory, Paper Mill Lane, 1858–60

2–8 Church Green
A large timber-framed building presently divided into three dwellings. It may well have been a guildhall before the Dissolution of the Monasteries, but in the eighteenth century was known as the Ship Inn. It has been altered over the centuries, but retains a number of original features.

6–10 The Street
Currently divided into two dwellings, this very early medieval hall house was for many years the Bell Inn. It has been carefully restored and retains many original features.

Left: *An old drawing of 6–10 The Street, which used to be the Bell Inn.* (SROI Ref F s Ips 9)

A drawing of Church Green, the larger building was at one time the Ship Inn and the smaller building is now Daisy Cottage. (SROI Ref. FS353 Vol 5 No 149)

Two Tuns Cottage in The Street, 1990s.

Street Farm Cottage, 1990s.

The Cock Inn

This property has been an inn for nearly 500 years. The building is thought to date from the sixteenth century, although a number of alterations have been made since then. An extension at the front of the building was probably a lean-to butcher's shop added in the nineteenth century.

Two Tuns Cottage

Originally part of a larger dwelling known as Three Tuns, this property was owned for many years by the Kerridge family who were benefactors to Bramford Church, but was usually divided into several small dwellings and let to tenants.

Street Farm Cottage

This dwelling was built in 1522 as one of two wings attached to a house which was already standing in 1416. Every owner has been traced from 1416 to 2003.

In 1416 a house, probably a single-storey hall house with an open central hearth, stood on the site now occupied by Street Farm Cottage. It was owned by Robert Bolton, who became lord of the manor of Kentons and Boltons. It was later sold to John Gosnald who had connections with Otley Hall, but it reverted to the Boltons, and was then sold to Sir Thomas Russhe in 1518. In 1522, 'Boltons once Gosnald' was sold to William Betts. He added two

Dragon beam, Street Farm Cottage, c.1990.

wings to form a merchant's residence with an H-shaped plan. His initials 'W' and 'B' were carved onto the external oak corner posts as an advertisement of his wealth. The original hall house at the centre and the west wing collapsed or were burned down at a later stage, leaving only the east wing which is the present Street Farm Cottage, retaining the 'W' initial of William Betts on the corner post.

In 1537, the property was sold by Betts to Thomas Barker, then to Roger Payne in 1567, and subsequently to John Rust in 1579. It stayed in the Rust family until 1679 when it was purchased by the Mills family. They held it until 1794 when it was bought by Nathaniel Acton as part of his acquisition of most of the village.

The property was known as Peppers Pightle around 1800 and was in multiple occupation by farm tenants for many years. The Actons, succeeded by the Brokes, and their successors the Loraines, owned it until the estate was broken up in the early 1960s, when it was purchased by Richard Pinkney. The name Street Farm Cottage can be traced back to about 1945, but it has also been known as Street Barn Cottage. In 1976 it was sold to Barry Hall who added a new west-facing extension and who remains the owner at the time of writing.

In 2002 the main part of Street Farm Cottage was 500 years old. Despite its own fluctuating fortunes, the remaining part of the house has survived – a testament to the quality of the house, which has an oak frame.

Street Farm Cottage retains its individual character, although not its original appearance as a large house. Development has encroached towards it on two sides, but the house is perfectly at home in its old surroundings overlooking the fields and water meadows, some of whose boundaries are unchanged after many centuries.

The house was built at a time when East Anglia was very wealthy, but has survived through periods of poverty, like other Suffolk timber-framed houses. The property moved down the social scale over the centuries, as did many other Bramford houses which were subdivided and tenanted. However, the continued existence of these properties, now redecorated and maintained, contributes greatly to the character of the village.

Bramford House

This fine property was built in 1693 or 1694, but may have an earlier core. The land, along with several nearby buildings including a malt-house, was purchased from the Alston family of Lovetofts Hall in 1659 by John Warner.

In 1696 it was sold by John Brasier of Bramford to Edward Burton of Playford and described as:

A tenement, etc., and land lying between the Kings Highway leading from Bramford to Ipswich, land of Mr.

Left:
Bramford House in Ship Lane, c.1990.

Below:
Brick found in the wall of Bramford House during restoration in the 1980s.

Above:
Mill House in Mill Lane, 1988.

Right:
Millbank in Mill Lane, 1982.

Rowland to the west and north, and upon the gardens, mill house and Kilnhouse of John Brasier on the east.

During the early 1700s it passed through various hands until in 1742 it was in the occupation, but not the ownership, of William Leggett. In 1759 John Leggett bought additional land to the west on the condition that he erect a 'good brick wall to be a perpetual partition'. This wall is still standing, but is now the boundary between Springfield Cottage and 23 Ship Lane.

Above: *The Gables, before the conservatory was destroyed by a bomb in the 1940s.*

Below: *Grove House, Paper Mill Lane, formerly the home of the Packard family, since divided into three dwellings.*

Throughout the late-eighteenth and nineteenth centuries Bramford House remained in the hands of the Leggatt (now spelt with an 'a') family, until Miss Penelope Leggatt died in 1902.

The front wall of Bramford House is also listed and was probably built at the same time as the house. During restoration work in the 1980s an original brick was found bearing the engraving 'John How', presumably the name of the man who made it.

Mill House
Probably built by the miller for his own use, the house has an early-fifteenth-century core with many later alterations. One of these early changes was the installation of a 'priest's hole' which has subsequently been removed.

Millbank
The house and gateposts date from the mid-eighteenth century, probably 1754, although there may have been earlier buildings on the site. The deeds state that in that year Henry Rowning sold to Benjamin Rowning a 'Mansion House'. It was purchased by Revd Naylor in 1825 who only stayed there for six years. It was later bought by the Leggatt family of nearby Bramford House.

The Gables
Standing near the junction of the road to Ipswich, Ship Lane, Paper Mill Lane and Whitton Leyer, this house enjoys a prominent position. In the nineteenth century it belonged to the Mumford family. In the early-twentieth century the pump hall, formerly a brew-house at the rear of the property, was used as a small theatre. At the start of the Second World War the owner at the time, Mr Coupland, also built an air raid shelter. During the war a bomb destroyed the conservatory and windows on the front of the house. As a child the daughter of the house was very ill with scarlet fever and because she was confined to her room, her mother kept her amused by carving small birds and animals on a beam there. The house is currently divided into two dwellings, and a room in the south side is thought to be haunted.

The Grove
This building is now divided into three dwellings but was previously one owned by the Packard family. It was built to the east of Paper Mill Lane, but

Left: *Thornbush Hall before the 1930s extension. The Fiske family are pictured: Ethel, Helen, Edgar, Katie, Old Parker the gardener, mother and baby, c.1900.*

Rear view of Bramford Hall which shows the original part to the house, with the newer impressive frontage and conservatory, c.1900. (From the Vick Collection SROI Ref: K475/1-3)

Above: *A drawing of Bramford Hall in 1837 by H. Davy.* (SROI Ref: *Page's Suffolk Illustrated* Vol. 4.)

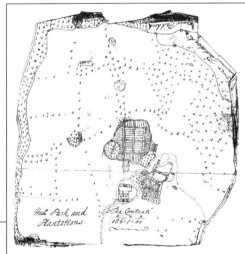

Above: *Plan of Bramford Park, c.1820.* (SROI Ref: HB8/5/58)

Left: *Bramford Lodge, the home of the Wainwright family, c.1900. It is now Clarice House.*

The nineteenth-century vicarage, now the Glebe House.

in the nineteenth century the lane was moved to run behind the house, between it and the farm buildings.

Grindle House

This farmhouse lies on land which was never part of Bramford Manor. It is on the southern boundary of the parish and the stream which runs alongside, 'The Grindle or Grundle', is an ancient boundary, not just between the parishes of Bramford and Sproughton, but also between the Hundreds of Bosmere and Samford. Grindle Lane was very likely an old route to Kersey as a map of 1771 names the lane Kersey Pack Way.

Thornbush Hall

An early-seventeenth-century house with some timbers reused from an older building, Thornbush Hall has been extended several times over the centuries but still retains some interesting features. It stands on an impressive site at the head of Thornbush Lane, and was quite possibly an early manor-house. It was the home of the Fiske family for many years.

Sycamore Farm

It is very likely that the first farm on this site was built by the Sicklemore family, who rose to prominence after the Peasants' Revolt of 1381. They apparently held land at Bramford Tye at the time, and may have been responsible for building the

farmhouse there too. Throughout much of the nineteenth and twentieth centuries Sycamore Farm was owned by the Jackson family, who took a leading role in village affairs.

Bramford Lodge

This building is not listed, but stands on a prominent site overlooking the village close to the boundary with Ipswich. It was a private house for many years and home to several influential families, including at one time Miss Isaura Loraine. In the 1980s it was converted into a restaurant, but at the time of writing is a centre for fitness housing a gymnasium, sauna, swimming-pool, hairdresser and other leisure amenities. It is known as Clarice House.

Glebe House

The Glebe House in Vicarage Lane is built on the site of the early dwellings of village vicars, except that it is much nearer the lane. The current building is Victorian and is not listed.

DEMOLISHED BUILDINGS

Bramford Hall

There is no doubt that had the structure still been standing today, Bramford Hall would have been the most important residence in the parish. It was built on the high ground overlooking the village, probably by John Acton in 1631. On an early plan the first hall

Lovetofts Hall before demolition in the 1940s.

The Old House on the corner of Ship Lane and Paper Mill Lane, c.1910. A cross marks the carved beam supporting the roof and the remains of the jettied ends of the 'Wealden' house can be clearly seen. At this time the house was divided into two dwellings but the name of the family is not known.

appears to have been built as four sides around a central courtyard, a popular style at the time. At some stage it was enlarged, probably by Nathaniel Acton II around 1745.

Over several generations the family expanded their landholding in this and other nearby parishes, until the last male heir died in 1836 and the estate passed through the female line to the Broke family of Nacton. After this date the building and shooting rights were let to various tenants. One famous visitor to a shooting party around 1900 was Sir Arthur Conan Doyle, author of the Sherlock Holmes mysteries.

During the Second World War the hall was used as quarters for officers, but being no longer required by the family, it was sold in 1956 and later demolished; part of it has survived as a modern dwelling.

Lovetofts Hall

It is possible that this hall was built on an ancient Anglo-Saxon site, as a burial-ground has been excavated nearby. It is another house which was once of great importance to the people of Bramford but no longer exists. The hall stood beside the present Lovetofts Drive in Ipswich and, until boundary changes in the 1930s, this road formed the perimeter between the village and the town. Lovetofts Manor was granted to members of the Tibetot family by Edward I as a reward for their help in subduing the Welsh in the late-thirteenth century and remained in their hands for several generations until passing to the Alston and Wentworth families.

During the twentieth century Lovetofts was owned by the Catchpole family, brewers from Ipswich, who lived at Whitton White House. At that time the hall was divided into two dwellings, one of which had an impressive staircase and many oak beams. After the Second World War the house and farmland were purchased by Ipswich Borough Council. The farm buildings were demolished in 1947 and the house a few years later. The land was used to build Whitehouse Estate and the parish boundary was moved further west to incorporate the whole site into Ipswich.

The Old House

This house stood at the junction of Ship Lane and Paper Mill Lane and, at the time of its demolition in the 1960s, was divided into two dwellings. It began life as a much larger building, in the style of a 'Wealden' house. This was a timber-framed property with three sections, the end two of which were jettied. Photographs of the house show the remaining central section with overhangs at the side where the jetties would have been and a carved lion's head beam supporting the roof.

The Round House

Built as a gatehouse to Bramford Hall, this small, single-storey roundhouse stood at the north end of The Street at the bottom of the long drive leading to the hall. At the start of the twentieth century the inhabitants were Mr and Mrs Parker. The house was demolished in the 1960s when it was no longer needed by the hall and had become derelict. Local people have retained very fond memories of the Round House which Bramford Local History Group has adopted as its logo.

The Round House in The Street, with The Angel in the background, c.1930.

Raw materials being unloaded by steam crane from a barge at Bramford Works, late-nineteenth century. The docking area can still be seen today near the railway bridge at the rear of the works. In front of the barge is the steam lighter m.v. Trent River which was used, with others, to tow barges between Ipswich and Bramford. Captain George Glading was skipper for more than 50 years. During his time aboard he rescued 12 people from the river, winning the Royal Humane Society's Bronze Medal in 1902, the Society's Bronze Clasp in 1905 and a Testimonial parchment from the same society in 1922.

A corner of Bramford Works laboratory in 1913. W.G. Mills is seated.

FOUR

❧☙

THE VILLAGE AT WORK

THE FERTILIZER INDUSTRY IN BRAMFORD

A fertilizer and chemical production works has been in existence alongside the River Gipping in Bramford for more than 150 years. It was located between the railway and Paper Mill Lane and finally ceased to be a manufacturing site as late as the summer of 2003.

It is impossible to contemplate chronicling the many different companies that have operated from this site over such a long period. Instead it is possible to provide a brief history of the companies and the activities and people involved over the years.

Why fertilizer production?
In 1840 Justus Von Liebig wrote:

The crops in a field diminish or increase in exact proportion to the diminution or increase of the mineral substances conveyed to them in manure.

Edward Packard, 1819–99, founder of Edward Packard and Company.

This scientist was the first to discover that phosphate of lime in bone-meal could be rendered more readily available to plants by treatment with sulphuric acid. Soon afterwards it was discovered that phosphate rock could be treated using the same reaction. Phosphate was also to be found in coprolites, the fossil excrement of the great lizards which once roamed the earth. Beds of this excrement were found in south-east England and, around 1840, scientists found that coprolites dissolved in sulphuric acid produced a product to which the name 'superphosphate' was given.

The value of superphosphate was quickly appreciated by the agricultural community and, as the process was a simple one, factories sprang up all over the country. England became the birthplace of the superphosphate industry.

In the 1850s two of these superphosphate pioneers, Edward Packard and Joseph Fison, built factories on a greenfield site in Bramford.

Edward Packard and Company
Edward Packard, born at Hasketon in Suffolk in 1819, was encouraged by the discoveries made at the time to start grinding and dissolving bones at Snape, Suffolk, in 1843. Before long he began dissolving coprolites in acid to make superphosphate and in 1847 moved the operation to Ipswich docks (Coprolite Street at the docks in Ipswich is still in existence today). However, the unpleasant fumes from the manufacture of this chemical upset the local residents in Ipswich, forcing his move to Bramford along the Ipswich to Stowmarket canal (the River Gipping). With rail communications available, Packard built a superphosphate factory and in 1854 a sulphuric acid plant, so bringing into operation the first complete superphosphate factory in Britain. The year 1878 marked another milestone in the history of the company with the construction of a phosphoric acid and concentrated superphosphate plant – the first plant for double or triple superphosphate to be erected in England. Edward Packard retired from the business in 1891 and died eight years later at the age of 80.

His sons Edward, later to become Sir Edward Packard, and Henry assumed responsibility for the company and they formed a limited company in 1895.

At home trade was good, but abroad it prospered even more, with large quantities of superphosphates

Left: *Joseph Fison, 1819–78, founder of Joseph Fison and Company, grandfather of Sir Clavering Fison.*

Below: *Doug Stephen, General Manager at Bramford Works in the 1960s and '70s. He was appointed to the Horticulture Division Board in 1978.*

Above: *Very early days of screening fertilizer. Dick Lay (left) and Charlie Keeble.*

Left: *Tomorite has been a brand leader since 1913 when Prentice Brothers bought the trademark from William Colchester. Originally it was in powder form but has long been supplied as a liquid.*

Right: *Eustace Carey Prentice, 1833–84, founder of Prentice Brothers.*

Men bagging Fison, Packard and Prentice granular fertilizer in the 1930s; note they are all wearing flat caps.

going to Russia and the West Indies. In 1901 the total sales of fertilizers was 20,000 tons, only 5,500 of which were for the home market. With added concentration on home sales, turnover and profit continued to improve.

In 1913 the Mills-Packard chamber, an improved sulphuric acid chamber, was designed by works foreman W.G. Mills, a Bramford man, and was quickly adopted by sulphuric acid manufacturers all over the world.

During the First World War the state control of the fertilizer industry caused competition to disappear, and the enforced co-operation with other fertilizer companies led to a decision to amalgamate with James Fison and Sons of Thetford in 1919.

Joseph Fison and Company

Joseph Fison, born in 1819, was the son of Lorimer Fison who, after learning the business of farming, milling and baking from his father James, moved to Stowmarket in Suffolk to set up on his own account. Lorimer Fison died in 1833 when Joseph was only 13 and at 16 the young boy entered the business himself. In 1840 he moved to Eastern Union Mills at Stoke Bridge, close to the docks in Ipswich, and in 1856 began to experiment with the manufacture of superphosphate, ingeniously using his stone flour mills for grinding the phosphatic coprolites. But, like Edward Packard, he seems to have been attracted by the advantage of canal and railway facilities at Bramford, and moved there in 1858 to a site right alongside that of Packards. Edward Packard seems to have raised no objection. This move sparked off Joseph Fison's entry into the field of compound fertilizers, for he quickly built up a trade in this area, and gained a reputation for products of excellent quality. Joseph died in 1878 at the age of 59, but the business continued in the hands of his two sons, James and Herbert. Manufacture was extended and mainly as a result of Herbert's love of travel, overseas agencies were opened up, particularly in South Africa.

A further landmark was reached in 1895 when a limited company was formed – in the same year that Packard's had also taken the same action. Business prospered and by 1914 exports had drawn level with home sales and the Bramford Works had been enlarged.

In 1919 the Board was strengthened by the addition of F.G.C. Fison, later Sir Clavering Fison. In the mid-1920s Herbert Fison's health began to fail and although he remained as chairman, the business of the company was largely conducted by Clavering.

Prentice Brothers

In 1856, not many miles from Bramford, at Stowmarket in Suffolk, the Prentice brothers, Eustace and Edward, had also set up a factory producing superphosphates. Like Packard and Fison, they too had adopted a policy of expansion.

However, in 1922, Prentice Brothers received a severe setback as a result of a disastrous fire at the Stowmarket Works and this, coupled with intense competition and the unchecked import of superphosphate, resulted in a slow recovery.

Fison, Packard and Prentice Ltd

By 1929 Packard, Fison and Prentice Brothers had become household names to East Anglian agriculturalists and were well known throughout Britain and in other parts of the world. Until that year they had been in keen, virtually cut-throat, competition with each other. However, the agricultural depression and the entry of strong competitors into the compound fertilizer field seriously weakened their positions. It was decided that the only way to gain the necessary size, strength and stability to defend themselves was to amalgamate. Agreement was reached to end competition among themselves and form a new company. So it was that Fison, Packard and Prentice Limited was born in Bramford in August 1929. Clavering Fison was elected chairman with W.H.T. Packard as vice-chairman.

By 1936 Fison, Packard and Prentice was becoming a name to be reckoned with – important to the country's economy and with many hundreds of shareholders dependant upon its success.

Early in 1937 the company doubled the size of its organisation with the purchase of Anglo Continental Guano Works Ltd in Silvertown, Essex.

Up until 1942 the numerous companies absorbed by Fison, Packard and Prentice continued, by and large, to sell their products under their own names and brands. In that year it was decided to change the name of the company to Fisons Ltd, and all the subsidiaries, with one exception, were incorporated into a central organisation.

At the height of the Second World War, Fisons was established at Bramford and a new advertising slogan was coined: 'It's Fisons for fertilizers'.

Fisons Ltd

It is reasonable to ask why the new company was named Fisons and not Packard or Prentice. Prior to 1942 representatives from Packard and Prentice rode bicycles to visit customers, whilst those from Fisons had cars, consequently making them known to more customers. Fisons folklore has it that it was this fact which decided the name of the new company!

Fisons continued to be a major international and much respected company for the next 53 years; it finally ceased trading in 1995. Although it began life as a fertilizer company, it ended as a major pharmaceutical company. In its heyday Fisons employed some 12,000 people worldwide. Its operations and influence spanned the globe and for more than 50 years Fisons Bramford Works manufactured quality chemical and fertilizer products for the garden, professional and international markets.

Left: *An aerial view of Fisons Bramford Works, mid-1970s. Modern warehousing and bulk intake buildings, complete with the latest handling systems, were constructed on the southern end of the site (bottom of photograph).*

Below: *Dennis 'Frip' Ford pictured in the summer of 1979 having completed 50 years' service with Fisons. Dennis started work with Fison, Packard and Prentice in July 1929. He considered the later introduction of free tea and coffee to be a retrograde step because he remembered the days when there was free beer!*

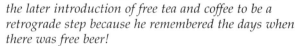

Left: *Support for the local community. A cash donation plus Greenmaster Autumn lawn fertilizer was made to the Bramford Playing-Field Management Committee in the 1980s. Left to right: Brian Blomfield (Fisons), Pat Jarman, Cyril Bird, Tony Fox (secretary), Peter Smith (kneeling).*

Above: *Fisons piece work gang, 1950s. Two hundredweight bags of raw materials had to be unloaded by hand right up to the end of the 1950s; only then did suppliers reduce the maximum size to 1cwt.* Left to right: *Ernie Bilner, Frank Allum, Russell Sparrow, Dougie Dodds, Russell Rivett.*

Below: *Alan Purdham presenting cash prizes to the winners of the Fisons Safety Draw in 1978 after Bramford Works had been accident free for 132,000 hours.* Left to right: *Mo Eley, George Beckman, Frank Allum, Gordon Burnside, Margaret Benstead, Alan Purdham, Steven Rickman, Colin Leach.*

Above: *Despatch Office staff at Fisons pictured in Bramford Works on the day of Alan Cooper's retirement, 1982.* Left to right: *Les Pryke, Brian Reynolds, Barry Roper, Russell Rivett (plant foreman), Angela Cadge, Arthur Scrivener, Alan Cooper, John Farrant, Katy Pilbrow.*

Above: *In order to beat the petrol shortage in 1957 bicycles were issued to horticultural shop representatives. Cars were used to take equipment to each main centre where the bikes would be unloaded. Fisons reps would then head out on their calls, carrying specially designed cases. The photograph shows Vic Marston ready for action.*

Right: *Vera Earthy attending to the number 3 carton line at Fisons Bramford Works, 1960s. In the background, operating the number 2 small packs line, are Spencer Lockwood (left) and Charlie Chittock (right).*

Left: *Fisons successful football team, late 1950s. At this time the company had other works in the Ipswich area. The players named below are Bramford Works employees. Left to right, back row: ?, Terry 'Wacker' Dedman, Dave Foreman, ?, ?, ?, ?, ?, ?, ?, Bill Robinson, Brian Blomfield; front: Barry Caley, Doug Upson, ?, ?, Fred Gee, Harry Cobb (manager), ?, ?, ?, Owen Roper, ?, Ron King.*

Right: *A proud Bramford Works team with the Fisons Inter-departmental Cricket Shield in 1960. Left to right, back row: Alan Pryke, Sid Taylor, Owen Roper, G. Clarke, Ernie Halls, George Risby, Eric Tate, Steve Turner, Trevor Seymore; front: Dick Howgego, Wilf Bullard, Barry Fowler, Sid Dowe, Tony Greengrass, Ron King.*

Below: *The Bramford Works team on the raft they built to compete in the annual Felixstowe Raft Race in the summer of 1982. Some of those on the raft are: Kevin Burch, John Randall, June Stannard, Val Stone, John Large, Colin Leach, John Carr, Paul Stannard, Brian Fayers, Mervyn Russen, Pat Dee, Paul Dobell, Ray Dobell, David Thurtell (standing) and Jim Lowe.*

Right: *Sir Edward Packard.*

When Fisons ceased trading in 1995, Bramford Works had been in continuous operation since 1851 and it would continue for another eight years.

Levington Horticulture

When Fisons ceased trading the Horticultural Division (of which Bramford Works was a part) was subject to a management buy-out, led by Phil Parry. The new company was named Levington Horticulture. The name was selected for two reasons: firstly because the village of Levington in Suffolk had been the major research centre for Fisons, and secondly because Fisons Levington Composts were major brand leaders in the market-place.

Scotts UK Ltd

In December 1997 Levington Horticulture was taken over by Scotts, which has its headquarters in Ohio in the United States. It claims to be the largest producer of horticultural products in the world. Bramford Works appeared to play a part in the overall plans of Scotts and, once again, continuity of operation seemed assured. Unfortunately this was not the case.

Gradually Scotts moved manufacturing facilities from Bramford to other parts of the UK and Europe and finally in the summer of 2003 Bramford Works closed down. The familiar sights and sounds of factory operation ceased and a valuable source of employment for the local community disappeared. The office block on the eastern side of Paper Mill Lane is still functioning but a future use for the production site has yet to be determined.

THREE KNIGHTS OF THE REALM

Three key players in the history of Bramford Works are Sir Edward Packard, Sir Clavering Fison and Sir George Burton. They were long serving, deeply committed to the business and had a constant concern for the welfare of their employees.

Sir Edward Packard KB

Edward Packard was born in Saxmundham, Suffolk, in 1843, and was educated at Bury St Edmunds Grammar School and Kings College, London, where he studied chemistry and engineering. Edward had a great sense of duty, and throughout his life was devoted to work for the public good. He was involved in the following local concerns:

Vicar's Warden, Bramford	*50 years*
Ipswich Fine Art Club	*50 years*
Ipswich Town Council	*50 years*
Harwich Harbour Board	*52 years*
Ipswich Dock Commission	*60 years*
Fertilizer Manufacturers Association	*60 years*
Woodbridge Conservative Association (chairman)	*until 1921*

Edward joined the prosperous phosphate-grinding and fertilizer-manufacturing business in about 1863. His brother Henry, who died in 1912, also entered the business at about the same time. Edward took a great interest in the works at Bramford and used his mechanical knowledge to install and erect the first steam crane to be used on the site. In 1886, at the age of 43, he became chairman of the family business. He remained chairman for 43 years until 1929, when Fison, Packard and Prentice Ltd was formed. In 1895 Edward was one of the leading men in the fertilizer industry and he remodelled the Fertilizer Manufacturers Association, of which he was elected president in 1926. When he retired from active business in 1929 he was made an honorary life member of the association.

Edward married Ellen Turner in 1867 and went to live at Grove House in Paper Mill Lane, Bramford, which was a five-minute walk from the works. He remained at Grove House until his death some 65 years later. Edward and Ellen had 12 children (six daughters and six sons) and 23 grandchildren, and Grove House was always the location for family gatherings.

During his life in Bramford Edward took the greatest interest in the parish and its inhabitants. It was his custom on Boxing Day to give a small sum of money to every widow in the parish who called at Grove House. In addition to being vicar's warden of St Mary's Church, he was chairman of the School Management Committee, and when it was first proposed that the school, which was a Church School, be taken over by the Board of Education, he subscribed heavily and worked indefatigably to raise sufficient money to retain it for the Church. It was a great grief to him some years later when the requirements of the Board proved too great for them to be met by public subscription, and the school had to be handed over.

He was the first chairman of Bramford Provident Club, which was formed to help Bramford men when ill or out of work and which, owing to the sound manner in which the funds were invested and distributed, was one of the most prosperous in Suffolk when the Sickness Insurance Scheme was instituted.

In 1922 he received his knighthood for services to politics and to the Borough of Ipswich.

After the First World War, Sir Edward was largely responsible for the building of the Bramford Memorial Hall, towards which he subscribed generously. For many years he was regarded as the 'Father of the Parish of Bramford'.

His son, Walter G.T. Packard (to whom we are indebted for much of this text about his father), believed that of all his interests, Edward derived the greatest pleasure from art and painting. He was encouraged in this by his wife Ellen and W.R. Symonds, a member of the Royal Academy of Art, who gave him some lessons when he first started sketching in his spare time.

When he was about 30, Edward was in a boat one summer's day on the River Gipping with the vicar of Bramford, Revd H.E.T. Cruso. Both were interested in painting and, as a result of their conversation, Edward became the prime mover in starting the Ipswich Fine Art Club in December 1873. Although the name has since changed, this club is still in existence in 2003.

A great deal of his spare time was spent producing watercolours of the peaceful meadows around his home in Bramford. In the spring he never failed to make one or two sketches of his beloved bluebell wood in the Grove. He was still painting at the age of 86.

Sir Edward was said to be always courteous in business, scrupulously honest and ever anxious for the welfare of his employees. He was much respected by those who worked under him in the Packard firm which, when he retired in 1929, had been established for 86 years.

Sir Edward died at Bramford on 11 April 1932 at the age of 89. On the day of his funeral St Mary's Church was full to the brim with residents. At the same time in Ipswich the church of St Mary le Tower was filled with the townsfolk of Ipswich who also wanted to pay their respects. Sir Edward Packard, together with members of his family, is at rest in St Mary's churchyard.

Sir Clavering Fison DL

Frank Guy Clavering Fison was born in Sproughton in Suffolk in 1892. He was educated at Charterhouse and Christ Church, Oxford, where he studied medicine. His university studies were cut short by the First World War, during which he saw service with the Suffolk Regiment in France and later with the newly-formed Royal Air Force.

After the war he joined the family business of Joseph Fison and Co. which operated from Bramford.

He was the second son of its chairman, James Lorimer Fison, and it was his elder brother, Lorimer, who was to have succeeded as chairman of the family business. Sadly Lorimer died from pneumonia resulting from gas poisoning and consequently Clavering joined the Board. Later he took the lead in negotiations resulting in the amalgamation of Fison, Packard and Prentice in 1929, and was appointed chairman of the newly-formed company.

In 1942, when Fison, Packard and Prentice decided to adopt a national sales policy for fertilizers, the company's name was changed to Fisons Ltd and Clavering became its first chairman. In 1957 he was knighted for his services to agriculture. Sir Clavering's roots in the family firm gave him a deep sense of commitment to the business and its employees, an attitude with which he inspired his juniors. Although he saw the need for diversification after the war his ventures into pharmaceuticals and scientific instruments only provided the foundations for later development. The major change from a fertilizer company to a pharmaceutical company would be carried out by others.

In 1962, after 33 years at the helm, he retired as chairman, becoming life president. He died in 1984 after a short illness, aged 92.

Sir George V.K. Burton CBE DL

George Burton was born in London in April 1916. He was educated at Charterhouse, and studied music at Weimar University in Germany. He joined Fison, Packard and Prentice Ltd as a management trainee in 1934. At this time George Burton was a tall, charming man, not yet 20 years old, who had a passing eye for attractive ladies, opera and fast cars. His close Dutch friend who resided in Sproughton, adjacent to the beet sugar factory, possessed a streamlined, silver, low road-holding motor car, which they both drove at quite a pace in the late 1930s.

The company employed other young management trainees during this period who worked their way

Left: *Peter Packard, Sir Edward's grandson, (right) congratulating Cecil Emmerson on 40 years' service with Fisons. Cecil began his working life with Prentice Brothers of Stowmarket. Both Sir Edward Packard and his son Walter, father of Peter and vice-chairman of Fisons, were involved in many activities long after reaching retirement age. Peter, after a successful* career with Fisons and at the time of writing in his late seventies, has followed their example. In 2002 he retired from running his own management training consultancy.

Above: *Sir Clavering Fison.*

through all aspects of business, from production, administration, sales and marketing. George had a cottage in Woodbridge and drove daily to Bramford in his Morgan three-wheeler that was prone to catching fire.

The Second World War brought an early termination to his management skills when he was called to the Colours and joined the Royal Artillery. He saw active service in North Africa, Sicily, Italy and Austria, before demobilisation as an Acting-Major, and the honour of an MBE.

He returned to Bramford as Fisons Works Manager and immediately formed a management team which, under his direction, established Fisons as a market leader and a household name. He continued his career in Ipswich, at the deep-water Cliff Quay Works where sulphuric acid, high-grade superphosphate and granular compound fertilizers were produced. He soon reached the head offices at Felixstowe, Ipswich and London.

Sir George Burton

In 1960 he became chairman of Fisons Horticulture, of which Bramford Works was a significant part. He also became Deputy Managing Director of the Fertilizer Division and six years later was appointed Chief Executive of the Fisons Group – a position he held for ten years. Upon the retirement of Lord Netherthorpe in 1973, George Burton took the chairmanship of the Fisons Group until he retired in May 1981. In 1977 he received a knighthood for 'Services to Export'.

In April 2003, Sir George (in his late eighties and residing with Lady Burton not many miles from Bramford) commented on his early days in Bramford Works:

After the war I was manager at Bramford Works which I remember with pleasure to this day. Of course I had no idea that I was going to work for Fisons for more than 50 years! What a tremendous company it was to work for.

Ex-employees say that George was much respected and affectionately known as Bunny. Employees at Bramford believe his affection for the company's oldest chemical works ensured that its horticultural products would remain a profitable and valued part of the Fisons Group throughout its lifetime.

Fisons Pensioners

Although Fisons ceased to operate as a company in 1995 the final pages of its history, including that of Bramford Works, have yet to be written. The genuine concern for the welfare of employees shown throughout the lifetime of Fisons continues in 2003 when just under 5,000 Fisons pensioners and dependents are in receipt of a company pension. Over 600 of these live in Suffolk. In due course a further 3,000 will receive one. It will be well into the third quarter of this century before the final pension payments are made.

A journalist arriving to visit Bramford in 1879 wrote:

Upon nearing Bramford Works along the straight road from Ipswich I was confronted with the picturesque sight of its seventeen mysterious leaden chambers, its eight Gay-Lussac towers and its great chimneys. (See photograph page 4.) No nauseous fumes from the manufacture of sulphuric acid were apparent to me. Mr. Edward Packard, who was accompanying me, and whose house was only half a mile away from the works, assured me that only when the wind was from the north did the irritant gases trouble them a little.

The following extract is from a Fison Packard and Prentice Ltd Works committee meeting held on 16 April 1930:

Mr Walter Packard told the committee that during the month of March from all works a total of 22,400 tons of fertilizer was despatched and that for fourteen consecutive days the daily total from all the works exceeded 1000 tons a day.

The following is from another committee meeting held on 30 April 1931:

The committee members reported they had enquired amongst the men as to what kind of meal they preferred at the Works Dinner and they were practically unanimous in that a good plain meal of a choice of beef or mutton with vegetables plus one sweet would be more appreciated than the more elaborate dinners that have been served during the last two years.

Fisons Works committee meeting minutes of February 1929 reported the following regarding quality control:

The Railway Boy had written saying that a truck load of fertilizer had been sent away from the Works which had averaged as much as 3lbs per bag overweight. Taking the number of bags of fertilizer leaving the Works per annum as 288,000, if each of these was 1lb overweight and the average cost of fertilizer £6 per ton,

Left: *Rushbrook's Mill, c.1920, formerly the paper-mill.*

Right: *Rushbrook's delivery lorry, c.1930*

Below: *Bramford Mill in Mill Lane, before the top three floors were destroyed by fire in 1917.*

Bramford Mill in the 1930s, after a fire had destroyed the top three floors.

this would mean we were giving away fertilizer to the value of £780 per year. While making it perfectly clear that on no account must bags go out short weight Mr Peter Chevallier asked the gang leaders to be as accurate as possible so that this money could be saved.

BRAMFORD MILLS

It is likely that the first mills along the River Gipping were built by the Anglo-Saxons, some time around the eighth century. The first documentary evidence is in the Domesday Survey of 1086, when two mills are mentioned. It is possible that part of the entry for Bramford actually refers to Sproughton, but there must have been at least one mill at that time.

The Bishop of Ely's survey of 1251 also mentions a mill. This was probably in the present Mill Lane, but there may have been another mill further along the river near Bramford Common. This second mill was mentioned in the survey of 1568, but the site is now lost.

By the sixteenth century there were two mills, one of which was a flour mill in Mill Lane, and the other a fulling mill. Fulling was a process in cloth making, originally performed manually, whereby the woven cloth was 'walked' or trampled in water to clean and thicken it. Water-power was used to beat it with large wooden hammers, after which it would be stretched out to dry.

By 1688 the mill had changed in use from cloth to paper. The parish registers record the death of a stranger who drowned in the millpond. At this time the cloth trade had fallen into decline, but the demand for paper was growing as it became possible to print books by machine instead of reproducing them by hand on parchment or vellum. The mill was sometimes referred to as 'Laxfield Mill' in documents.

In 1866 the mill was taken over by the Hurry family. Miss Edith Hurry recorded her childhood memories of her grandfather, father and uncles involved in paper making. The ingredients were rags, paper, flax, peat, chalk, soda, umber, blue crystals, and magenta dye. In the rag loft one man and two boys would sort and chop the rags, and five or six women would sort the paper. The rags would then go to the boiler house where they were boiled in water with soda until soft. In the engine-room two men turned the paper and rags into pulp, which was then passed down into the machine house, over wire gauze, then rolled between five hot cylinders to dry it. Once dry it was cut into sheets by two paper makers, then folded and pressed by two more. The two stokers used to work alternately, from 12a.m. on Monday morning to 8p.m. on Saturday.

Some of the names that Miss Hurry remembered were Holland and Randall, and two engine men were Bloomfield and Caley, with 'Old Giles' in the rag loft. The paper maker was Charlie Scrutton, and Jonah Pryke was responsible for keeping the sheets of paper in a tidy pile as they came out of the machine. The paper was folded by her Uncle Bob and Amos

Workers standing outside Bramford Mill in Mill Lane, before 1917. Names are unknown, but the man in front of the horse was probably called Hitchcock.

One steam barge towing another under the old wooden bridge; the chimney on the barge was hinged so it could be lowered. (SROI from Clarke's Grangerised History and Description of Ipswich, Vol. 3, p.355 Ref: S Ipswich 9)

Baskett, and her Uncle Will used to make paper bags. The cutting of the paper was dangerous and several men had nasty accidents with the mechanical cutter.

The wooden building was vulnerable and several disastrous fires took place there. One on 10 July 1869 totally destroyed the mill. It was a foggy morning and men from the village did not see the smoke, so very few people turned out to help. All that remained after the blaze was some of the machinery. A newspaper report stated that it was the fourth serious fire in the village that year.

At the end of the nineteenth century the demand for paper fell as cheap imports came in from abroad. Also the cost of providing fuel when the river level was low became more and more expensive. In 1912 the mill began producing animal feed, and at the time of writing it is used by the Rushbrook family to produce sports turf and associated products.

The flour mill in Mill Lane was always owned by the lord of the manor and everyone in the village had to grind their corn there. A fee would be charged by the manor, and payment in kind would have been taken by the miller. In 1498 it was let to Richard Brook who was given permission to build a house nearby, possibly the present Mill House.

In 1793 the Gipping Navigation Company made the river navigable for barges by removing difficult bends and installing lock gates. The plan for the work clearly shows the two mills.

For many centuries the mill was driven by an undershot wheel, but as there were times when the water-level was low, it was decided, probably in the nineteenth century, to introduce steam power. At this time the mill was one of the largest along the Gipping Valley, with 12 pairs of stones and a tall chimney which was visible from some distance away.

The last working mill was built in 1861 and stood five stories high, two of brick and three of wood. Bricks on the front of the building have the initials J.B.B. (possibly James Bowman the baker), and E.H. 1861, who was almost certainly Ebenezer Hitchcock, the miller at that time.

George Hardwicke started working at the mill in 1906. He worked for 11 hours a day at a starting wage of 2s.6d. (12p in modern money) a week, at the age of 16 his wages increased to 4s. (20p) a week, and at the age of 18 to 10s. (50p). He worked there for nine years.

In 1917 an overturned lamp caused a disastrous fire, which destroyed the top three wooden floors. After this the machinery was removed and the building continued to be used for storage and as a workshop. In the 1960s the river beside the mill was widened and the mill-stream was filled in. In 1980 it was purchased and converted into a private house.

THE RIVER

The River Gipping runs roughly north–south through the village. In past centuries it would have played a very important role in powering the mills in the parish.

Before the arrival of turnpike roads, the river would also have been the easiest way to transport heavy goods. It has been suggested that the stone used in the building of the Abbey in Bury St Edmunds was transported up the Gipping from the Continent, but in the following centuries much of the river has silted up.

In 1790 a group of local businessmen got together to have the Gipping Navigation Act passed, which enabled lock gates to be built at intervals and the worst bends straightened, making the river navigable for barges from Ipswich to Stowmarket. The work was not completed until 1793 but, after this, trade for the area was greatly improved.

At first the barges were pulled by horses; the tow-path still exists in the form of a footpath. Later the barges were driven by steam power with tall chimneys to keep the smoke away from the barges being towed behind. As many of the bridges were quite low, especially when the water-level was high, the funnels had to be set on hinges so that they could be lowered to pass under the bridges.

Some barge owners had an arrangement with local people who would leave food and drink to be collected at one bridge, with the dirty containers left at the next. There were two bridges in Bramford, one at the village centre where Ship Lane crosses the river,

Left: *A photograph taken from the church tower between 1904 and 1917, with Church Green in the foreground, the iron bridge on right, Bramford House on the left and the flour mill in the centre. The area behind this is now covered with houses.*

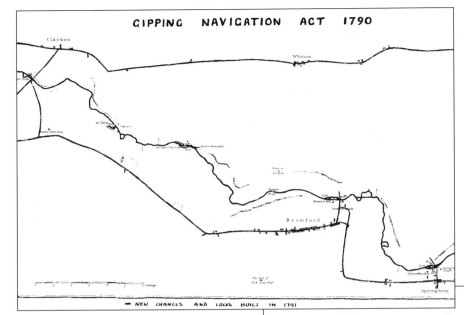

GIPPING NAVIGATION ACT 1790

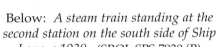

— NEW CHANELS AND LOCKS BUILT IN 1791

Left: *Plan of the River Gipping in 1790 showing the bends to be straightened and the locks to be built to make the river navigable for barges. Bushmans Bridge was then called Bishops Bridge. (SROI HD 25/1)*

Below: *The iron bridge built in 1904.*

Below: *A steam train standing at the second station on the south side of Ship Lane, c.1930. (SROI SPS 7930/B)*

and the other which, now as then, gave access to the water meadow, called Bushmans Bridge. In earlier times it was also known as Bishops Bridge and Black Bridge.

When the railways arrived in 1846, some of the river trade was lost. Eventually navigation rights were sold to the rail company and barges stopped going to Stowmarket, although they continued moving goods in and out of the fertilizer factories in Paper Mill Lane until the late 1920s.

In her will dated 1420, Margaret Weyland left a sum for the maintenance of Bramford Bridge. The earliest photograph we have is of a wooden bridge, which was replaced by an iron structure in 1904. During the 1930s there were some complaints that the bridge was not sound, and these were proved to be justified when in January 1939 a serious flood caused the bridge to collapse. A temporary bridge was erected, but because of the outbreak of war shortly after, it was nearly 20 years before the present bridge was built.

In the 1960s a sluice was installed at the lock near Ship Lane to help control the flow of water and prevent flooding. The old walls of the lock are still there, though the gates have long since disappeared. There is a chance that one day the locks will be restored and traffic will again navigate the river.

THE RAILWAY AND STATION

The railway through Bramford was constructed by the Ipswich and Bury Railway, for which Royal Assent had been obtained by an Act dated 21 July 1845, with initial capital of £400,000. The line between the two towns was opened for goods on 7 December 1846, and to passengers on 24 December 1846. The chief engineer was Joseph Locke, with Peter Bruff as resident engineer. The architect was Frederick Barnes and the line was built by the contractor Thomas Brassey.

From Ipswich, the double-track main line was laid approximately in a WNW direction, and then gradually curved to pass through the first station, Bramford, two-and-a-half miles from Ipswich in a NNW direction on an embankment.

There have been two stations at Bramford. The building and platforms of the first were constructed largely from timber. Since the promotion of the line was towards Bury St Edmunds, it appears from the few photographs available that the more substantial building was provided on the Bury line platform. The building housed the booking-office, waiting-rooms and storerooms. The station was sited on the Bury side of the Ipswich to Bramford road (B1067), adjacent to the bridge over the road. The platforms extended for a train's length in the Bury direction (north), and were backed by a wooden fence. There was a signal-box at the end of the 'down' platform. On a siding off the 'up' line, opposite the signal-box, were a timber-built goods shed and some coal pens. The station had canopies supported by wooden pillars let into the platforms. These were characteristic of this line, with similar structures at the next two stations, Claydon and Needham Market.

Since the railway passed through Bramford on an embankment, the station was above road level and access to the Bury platform was by a stairway. Another stairway led from road level to the opposite platform and building, which was little more than a canopy and a waiting-room. A driveway sloped up from the road to give access to the goods shed and coal siding.

On 28 February 1860, severe gales caused some parts of the station buildings to collapse, but workers were quickly despatched from Ipswich to clear the tracks, and there was little hold-up to rail traffic.

With most of the buildings being constructed from wood, it is hardly surprising that on a hot summers day, 1 August 1911, a spark from a passing

THE BOOK OF BRAMFORD

locomotive set fire to the station. The main building and platform on the Bury line were totally destroyed, and nearby cottages badly damaged, but the Ipswich-bound platform was virtually untouched. The Great Eastern Railway quickly erected makeshift platforms on the Ipswich side of the road bridge, with a board crossing over the two tracks for access.

On 10 February 1919, the goods shed was destroyed by fire; once again the cause was believed to be a spark from a locomotive.

On 7 November 1912, the GER Way and Works Committee approved a new station for Bramford at a cost of £4,410. The second station was then built on the other side of the road bridge, the Ipswich (south) side. This time a substantial brick building was erected on the embankment on the east of the line leading to Ipswich. The building housed the booking-office, waiting-room, toilets and a lamp store. The platform and buildings were reached by a covered stairway from a narrow lane, which ran from the main road. A GER canopy was supported on cast-iron columns and spandrels reached the length of the building at an elevated level on the long 'London' concrete platform standing on the steep embankment. On the opposite platform, a smaller brick building with its own canopy housed a waiting-room and gentlemen's toilet. A lattice structure footbridge provided access between the platforms. The goods siding off the 'up' line remained, with some pointwork alterations over the years. The exact date of the opening of the new station has not yet been discovered.

The first signal-box was sited alongside the Bury line, opposite the goods shed. After the 1911 fire, and the building of the second station to the south side of the road bridge, a new signal-box was provided, again alongside the Bury line, just off the end of the platform. This box was removed in the early 1950s.

Bramford Station was closed to passengers on 2 May 1955. The goods siding remained open for some time and it is believed that this closed in the mid-1960s.

Occasional attempts to reopen the station by local-interest groups failed and in 1965 it was demolished in the space of a few days.

BYPASS NURSERIES

Bypass Nurseries were founded by David Fenwick on land near the Colchester bypass. The Bramford site was taken over from Mr Clover in 1942 and Dick Pegg started work there in December of that year. During the Second World War, the nursery grew lettuces and tomatoes for food, but before and after they were grown for seed. Prior to 1939, most UK tomato seed came from abroad, but by 1943 stocks were low and for the next few years tomatoes were grown for seed. The most produced in one year was 1cwt (55 kilos).

The nurseries were bombed twice during the war, the first time little damage was caused, but the second time only 53 panes of glass remained intact and repairs took six months to complete. Most of the work was carried out by nursery

Daffodils being picked in the greenhouses, c.1940s, names not known.

52

Workers in 1988. Left to right: *Jane Bloomfield, Audrey Squirrell, Sheila Welsh, Dick Pegg, Linda Newell, Janet Crouch, Moira Burder.*

staff together with Sadlers, builders from Ipswich.

In the late 1940s and 1950s the soil in the glasshouses was sterilised by steam from a portable boiler.

From 1946 to 1972 the main winter crop was the forcing of daffodil bulbs, as well as tulips and freesias grown for local and London markets. At first most of the bulbs came from Holland but by the late 1950s the majority came from Norfolk and Lincolnshire.

In 1946 Simon Van Damm, a Dutchman who had been in the Free Dutch Army during the war, came to work at Bramford to teach the art of bulb forcing. That year just 2,000 tulips were forced but by the mid-1950s 250,000 tulips and 16 tons of daffodils were being forced.

From 1946 to 1972 the main indoor summer crops were cucumbers, tomatoes and melons, all grown for seed, but from 1972 these crops became unprofitable. As 12lbs of tomatoes produces 1oz of seed, approximately 9 tons are needed to make 1cwt of seed.

From 1972 until the mid-1990s the main crop was the cultivation of F1 primrose for seed. This was very labour-intensive as every single flower was hand pollinated, but the return was good – £6,000 to £7,000 per kilo. Each year about 50,000 pots of primroses were used to produce 6–8 kilos of seed.

During the late 1950s the land between the nurseries and Ship Lane had been allocated for allotments but not many were in use. The site was taken over and worked by the nursery for a few years until Cherryfields was built on the allotment site behind The Street. This caused the land off Ship Lane to be returned to allotments.

Between 1959 and 1989, the nursery recorded the earliest ground frost of the winter on 22 August and the latest on 11 June. The coldest was a night in 1963 when a temperature of 2 degrees fahrenheit was recorded at 3 feet above ground level, and that same year the soil was frozen 2–3 feet down.

Once again, by the mid-1990s, imports of primrose seeds made it unprofitable to continue growing them. The glasshouses, which were built between 1924 and 1937, were becoming uneconomical to repair, and the site was run down. The nursery was very badly damaged in the 1987 gales, and was closed soon after.

BLOMFIELD AND JACKSON

This firm of haulage contractors was founded by two brothers-in-law, Baron Jackson and Herbert Blomfield, who operated from a corrugated-iron garage next door to Suvla Cottages in what was then Mill Lane (now Ravens Lane).

B&J started trading on a shoe-string budget in the 1920s with second-hand lorries and very little money. Initially they were so short of cash that they would pull into a garage as they neared London, fill the lorry tank with petrol, and then tell the garage owner that they would pay him on the return journey after they had been paid for delivering their load. Obviously the garage was not very pleased with this arrangement but once they had honoured their promise a few times it became a regular arrangement.

After a time the firm was bought by Mr Charles Luke Hibbard who had been the owner of a coal delivery business which operated from the premises roughly opposite The Angel Inn. The coal business was subsequently taken over by the grocers, Henry Abbott, but Hibbard also retained a small coal business which only made deliveries on Saturdays. Hibbard's name appeared on the lorries in very small lettering and the firm continued to be known locally as Blomfield and Jackson for many years.

Until the mid-1930s they operated mainly AEC (Amalgamated Engineering Company) lorries which were considered to be more reliable than the more popular Leyland trucks, which were very similar in appearance. Financial constraints meant that these were bought second-hand and were rather clapped out when they arrived at Bramford.

Initially the AECs were equipped with oil-lamps which gave very little light and, as there were no windshields in the vehicles, there was always a possibility of driving into something hanging in the road on dark stormy nights. Later vehicles had the much more modern 'acetylene' gas-lamps. The gas was produced in the vehicle from carbide crystals in a cylinder housed in the driver's cab. The cylinder also contained water in a separate compartment. The water was drip fed onto the crystals in order to generate the gas which was then carried by tube to two front lamps and one rear lamp.

A fault in one of these gas generators caused a fire in the lorry driven by Nelson Bugg and resulted in two families being evacuated from their homes in Suvla Cottages. Fortunately, Nelson and his immediate neighbour, Arthur Bloomfield, who was also a driver for B&J, eventually extinguished the flames with the garage hose. They were later assisted by

Employees at Blomfield and Jackson with their fleet of lorries. Left to right: *Baron Jackson, ?, Les (Nobby) Cook, Frank Boggis, Nelson and John Bugg, 'Darkie' Fairweather, Bill Bloomfield, ?, Doug Moss, Arthur Bloomfield, Jack Dye, Charles Hibbard (son of Luke Hibbard).*

some of their colleagues who arrived on the scene.

At the end of the working day it was essential to make sure that the lorry parked in the front row was a good starter so that it could tow start the others if necessary. On cold mornings it was not unusual to see four or five vehicles being towed after their drivers had become exhausted, trying unsuccessfully to crank start them.

When Mr Hibbard died in the mid-1930s, his widow, Mrs E.A. Hibbard, inherited the business and her name was discreetly painted on the lorries. Her son, Mr Charles Ashby Hibbard, became manager, his sister Ruby already being the clerk. The office was in their mother's bungalow which was at the top end of what was later named Hillcrest Approach. This arrangement continued until the house and the office were destroyed when Bramford was bombed fairly early in the Second World War. The office was then transferred to the front room of one of Suvla Cottages for the duration. Suvla Cottages were owned by a relative of the Hibbard family and Mrs Hibbard collected the rents.

Under the management of Charles Hibbard, the firm eventually bought new lorries, the first of which was an American-made 'REO' (registration number ABJ 20). The arrival of this caused great excitement because it had electric lights which could be switched on by the driver from within his cab and it had an electric self-starter and side windows.

More REOs were added to the fleet, which numbered 12 by the outbreak of war in 1939. In order

to get a comparison of operating performance, Mr Hibbard also bought a Ford, a Morris Commercial and a Thorneycroft Sturdy, and later two Austin lorries. Drivers were not keen to drive the 'Thorny' because it was not equipped with an electric self-starter and had to be hand cranked – obviously a retrograde step.

In pre-war years the goods transported by B&J were mainly 'Bakers Sundries' (icing sugar, fondant, jam, etc.) manufactured by Burton, Son and Sanders of College Street, Ipswich, to bakeries in London. On the return journey they carried imported foods such as New Zealand butter, cheese, dates and figs, which were picked up from London docks.

Other transported commodities were soda from Imperial Chemical Industries of Silvertown, and preserving chemicals from Boake Roberts, the latter being used by Burtons to preserve fruit, especially apples, prior to use for jam making. It was rumoured that these chemicals were so strong that a man would be knocked out if he breathed over the barrels when they were opened.

B&J also delivered groceries for wholesale grocers such as H.W. Raffe of St Peters Street and Squirrel and Cleveland of Museum Street in Ipswich.

Another regular contract was transporting sacks of sugar (in 1cwt and 2cwt capacity sacks) from the Ipswich beet sugar factory to Burton's jam factory and warehouse in Ipswich. This frequently involved two or three lorries with up to three 7-ton loads per lorry, each making three trips per day.

Another firm that received regular substantial deliveries was Copeman's of Norwich. Usually this run was combined with deliveries to Burton's own warehouse in Norwich, as well as other smaller deliveries in that area.

Deliveries to destinations other than 'remote' places like London and Norwich, were loosely referred to as 'locals' and drivers on those runs would seldom do a London trip.

In the mid-1930s Weston Biscuits built a factory on the new Slough trading estate which became a regular delivery for B&J lorries. It was a favourite with the drivers because the company had a policy of providing a large bag of broken biscuits. It was a full load drop which meant that once the load had been discharged the driver could start collecting his return load earlier in the day than if he had to make perhaps 10 or 12 other small deliveries before doing so.

It is worth noting that the distance from Bramford to Slough was almost exactly 100 miles (as opposed to the shorter journey of 70 to London) and some of the drivers who did the Slough run initially felt that they had done something rather heroic.

Return loads would be picked up from a variety of places: London docks, ICI or the Tate & Lyle factory at Silvertown, as well as other less well-known customers.

Regular deliveries were made to Renshaw's of Mitcham and Hemmings bakeries, who sometimes took substantial loads of Burton's products.

Until the Blitz the London run was always a two-day trip and the lorries were garaged overnight at the Thorneycroft garage in Pimlico, which was also a stopover for the flour lorries of Bouys & Anger who were trading associates of Cranfield Bros of Ipswich. When the Blitz was at its worst, drivers would try to make the return journey from London in one day. If that was not possible they would drive out to Chadwell Heath where they had digs and then return to the city to complete their deliveries or collections the next morning.

Another delivery which resulted from the war was to Joseph Travers & Sons at Brantham who had moved out of London because of air raids; B&J transported spices to them from London.

A journey which took place approximately once a month was a delivery to the Lincoln, Grantham and Nottingham area. This was a three-day trip and was almost exclusively made by Herbert Blomfield because the other drivers were not keen to be away from home on two consecutive nights.

Lorry maintenance, including major engine repairs, was completed on site by Baron Jackson who also doubled as transport foreman until he left the firm and was succeeded by Nelson Bugg.

Before and immediately after the war, until the company was nationalised, old engine oil from the lorry servicing was saved in a 40 gallon drum and placed on the camping ground bonfire (where

Leggatt Drive is now). No matter how wet the bonfire material was, the fire was so fierce that the grass didn't re-grow from one year to the next.

The business was nationalised by the postwar Government and eventually the fleet, which by then comprised 13 lorries, was transferred to the BRS (British Road Services) depot at the junction of London Road and Hadleigh Road in Ipswich, situated roughly where the Sainsbury's store is now. The lorries all had to be repainted mid-green, which was somewhat less attractive than the maroon livery of the B&J fleet. Charles Hibbard joined Burton's as transport manager and some of the drivers also joined, but others stayed with BRS.

GODDARD'S TAR WORKS

In the small triangle of land formed between the White Elm public house and Fisons Works in Paper Mill Lane stood the tar works of Ebenezer Goddard. The materials stored on site were combustible, which meant that insurance was not possible.

One disastrous fire was reported in May 1868 when the sheds and vats were completely destroyed by a fire which started when a cask of naphtha burst into flames, and spread quickly to the other materials. A fire engine was called from Ipswich, but had to get to the site via Claydon as the lane was by that time impassable. Luckily, because of the proximity of the river, the fire was prevented from spreading to the neighbouring properties, even though the lane was completely blocked by burning fluid, which also spread along the tramway into the chalk-pits opposite. The estimated value of the loss was £300.

Production must have restarted, as eight years later another fire occurred which was due to an exploding boiler. Mr Packard raised the alarm by means of his private telegraph wire. Fire engines were sent for from the Fire Station in Waterworks Street, Ipswich, but as they had just returned from a fire in Mount Street, Ipswich, fresh horses had to be obtained from the Great White Horse Hotel. This meant there was a delay and by the time the engines reached the fire it was out of control and the smoke was visible for miles around. This drew a large crowd of onlookers, but also volunteers to help with the fire-fighting. The fire was prevented from spreading to the neighbouring White Elm. Luckily six of the fire engines from Fisons Works and one from Packards were able to prevent the fire from destroying the nearby acid tower. The exploding barrels shot flames and smoke high into the sky and a large crowd from Ipswich congregated to watch from the hill overlooking the works. The smoke could even be seen from as far away as Hadleigh, as a fire engine started from there thinking that the fire was close, only to turn back when they found out how far away it actually was. The only casualties of the fire were a horse and donkey which had been

Above: *Workers digging clay from the pits in Paper Mill Lane to make bricks, c.1930. Bert Keeble is standing at the front holding the shovel, the names of the other men are not known.*

Right: *Southgate Bros account, dated 1919.*

Left: *Bricks being laid out to dry in rows at Bramford Brickworks in Paper Mill Lane. Names are not known, c.1930.*

standing in the yard and were so badly burnt that they had to be destroyed.

The *East Anglian Daily Times* gave the following report:

The sight was magnificent, great bubbles and explosions of flame rising one after another into the air to a height of fifty feet, far above which was the towering column of smoke.

The fire-fighters were helped by the arrival of a detachment of 35 men of the Royal Artillery with their own fire engine, and eventually the fire was brought under control. But the works of Ebenezer Goddard were completely destroyed and never reopened. The estimated value of the loss on this occasion was between £2,000 and £3,000.

BRAMFORD BRICKWORKS

To the east of the River Gipping the soil changes from alluvial on the valley floor to a base of chalk overlaid by clay and sand deposited at different depths within a small area. It is this mixture which led to the establishment of two industries, lime burning and brick making.

Lime is made by burning limestone in chalk kilns, and had many uses in the past – as a fertilizer, disinfectant, mortar, render, cement and colourwash. The present large waste dump near the northern edge of the parish started as a modest chalk-pit in the eighteenth century, with another further to the south-east which also included a limekiln. This reflects the geology of the valley sides further to the north, with chalk-pits in both Claydon and Blakenham where, until the last decade of the twentieth century, the huge chimney of Blue Circle cement works dominated the skyline.

Whereas at the large chalk-pit, formerly known as Coe's, the chalk deposit was overlaid by a thin layer of clay and several different sands, just a quarter of a mile south, the geology varied in that a good 14 feet of clay lay just 16 feet below the surface under two layers of sand. As sand is a vital element in brick making, the easy accessibility of both these components must have been extremely useful in a pre-mechanised age.

It is not known when bricks were first made in Bramford, but it is very likely that the brickworks were in existence for several centuries. The clay was dug out of pits along Paper Mill Lane and was taken further down the lane to be moulded, dried and fired. The clay in the pit is red, so it is likely that the bricks were used in many local buildings. It is said that the lost farm buildings at Lovetofts were built with Bramford bricks. On the 1881 Census 12 men worked there.

During the Second World War the brickworks were not allowed to operate. The firing process took several days, during which the kiln would glow and could attract the attention of enemy aircraft at night.

Bramford Brickworks reopened briefly after the war but closed again after only a few years.

SOUTHGATE BROTHERS

The earliest mention of this name in the village appears in records of the marriage between Elizabeth Southgate and William Fox in 1630. The name occurred several times over the following centuries. In 1845 Robert Southgate was an agricultural labourer living in Grindle Lane and his son James was a carpenter. James had two sons, George and William, who started the business called Southgate Bros.

They were builders, carpenters and funeral directors and had premises behind The Street with access opposite Bramford Cock. During the 1920s the firm built many local houses, including most in Duckamere, the council-houses at the top of Fitzgerald Road, round into Loraine Way, and at Parish Pond. Other houses were built in the neighbouring villages of Claydon and Great and Little Blakenham. At this time they employed about 30–40 people, one of whom was Maurice Brown who worked at Southgate's in the 1930s for 10d. (4p) an hour, from 6a.m. to 6p.m., five-and-a-half days a week. Maurice Brown lived in a small cottage at Runcton with his wife and three children, plus his mother-in-law, father-in-law and two sisters.

The business closed during the war and when it reopened in 1945 there were only 12 employees, one being Mr Dodman who worked at Southgate's for about ten years. He was a driver and odd-job man for the firm. His starting wage was £8 a week and one of his tasks was sometimes to take a deceased person to Ipswich hospital for a post mortem, for which he was paid 6d. (2¹/₂p).

As the years went by there was not so much work locally, and the business eventually closed in 1957. Dicksons furniture makers then took over the site.

The hamlet of Runcton, between Bramford and Sproughton. The photograph includes three generations of the Brown family, baby Beatrice, her mother and grandmother, c.1922.

Above: *Young Wives pancake race in Ship Lane, 1979.* Left to right: *Janet Pipe, Helen Mayhew, Christine Gardiner, Sylvia Harvey, Betty Gissing.*

Below: *Young Wives float, Bramford Carnival, 1982.* Pictured are: *1 Jenny Bardwell, 2 Dianne Curran, 3 Margaret Southgate, 4 Sue Rhodes, 5 Terry (?) Day, 6 Barbara Scruby, 7 Margaret Mayhew, 8 Elizabeth Boyce, 9 Lyn Vinnicombe, 10 ?, 11 Doreen Golding, 12 Sylvia Harvey, 13 Val Ellis, 14 Helen Mayhew, 15 Bridget Harvey, 16 Trudie Harvey, 17 Sharon Ellis.*

FIVE

⚜

THE VILLAGE AT LEISURE

YOUNG WIVES

When the Mill Lane estate was built in 1963/4 a number of newly-weds and young families moved in. A group of young mums decided they would like to form a club and, with the help of the Revd Christian, the Young Wives was formed, being a younger version of the Mothers' Union. A constitution was written which stated that the committee should consist of eight members, half of whom should be confirmed members of the Church of England, the chairman being one of these. The office of chairman was to be held for one year at a time, and the vicar was to preside over the Annual Meeting. Subscription was 5s. per annum and meetings were held on the first Thursday of every month at 8p.m., there was a Pram Service at 2.30p.m. on the third Thursday and Corporate Communion on the second Thursday of every month at 9.15a.m. Refreshments of tea and biscuits were provided by committee members, for which a charge of 4d. was made. The preparation of the room and refreshments was undertaken by members on a rota system.

The first meeting was held in the Parish Room, Ravens Lane, at 8p.m. on Thursday 1 October 1964, and was attended by 35 members.

The first chairman was Pat Jarman and after introducing the committee, Mrs Stephens (secretary) and Janet Cunningham (treasurer), the constitution was read and the routine arrangements described. The programme for the next four meetings was given as follows: flower-arranging talk by Mrs Russell, an outing to the beet sugar factory at Sproughton, a children's party and a talk from Mr Bales the local butcher about cuts of meat (unfortunately on the day Mr Bales was unable to give the talk so a social was held instead).

On 19 November an experimental afternoon meeting was held when members were invited for a cup of tea and a gossip. This proved very popular, so future afternoon meetings were held at 2.30p.m. on the third Thursday of every month.

The first AGM was held on 4 February 1965 at the Parish Room and 35 members were present. Mrs Jarman briefly outlined the group's activities during the past four months and noted an increase in the number of members to 42. The new committee was elected: Mesdames Ball, Cunningham, Jarman, Laurence, Stevens, Downing, Taylor and Watson. At the first meeting of the new committee, which was held at the vicarage and presided over by the Revd Christian, Mrs Jarman was invited to continue as chairman, and Mrs Cunningham as treasurer but Mrs Stephens did not wish to continue as secretary so Mrs Ball was elected in her stead.

The club's success continued with make-up and beauty demonstrations, discussions on how best to bring up children, first aid in the home, Christian moral welfare, and talks by Woman Police Sergeant Copsey, Mr Bales on cuts of meat, Mr Thorne from Footmans on cheeses, and antique jewellery, among others. There were also outings to the theatre, the telephone exchange, the Fire Station, the *East Anglian Daily Times*, zoos, dinners at various venues and hostelries, garden parties, barbeques at Mather's Farm and children's parties.

The next significant date was the move from the Parish Room to St Mary's Schoolroom on 16 January 1969. A talk was given by the staff manageress of Marks and Spencers and 26 members attended.

Young Wives continued to flourish, membership increased and it became a very ecumenical club. Corporate communion fell by the wayside in the 1960s. Pram services continued for several years until of course there were no more members with babies in prams. The group continued to clean the church, and clean the church brasses one month a year.

Throughout the 1970s and '80s the Young Wives held a lively club meeting twice a month. For many years the older members of the community who belonged to the Silver Threads Club were provided with a Christmas party. Dances, darts matches, children's parties, quizzes, Mr and Mrs competitions, village football and cricket matches took place. There were outings to the seaside for the children when a bus loaded with Mums, children, babies, trippers, nappies and potties descended either on Clacton or Walton (not always in good weather). From 1972 to 1985 the Young Wives held an annual pancake race, a picture of which would appear in the *Evening Star*. The group also had a float in the four parades through the village for the annual fête, entitled 'Old methods of teaching are best' (a classroom), 1976 'Wimbledon' (a tennis court), 'A Hareem', and 'The Undercover Story' (underwear through the ages), which was the most popular!

At the AGM in January 1986 it was decided that the name of Young Wives was no longer applicable so, with the decrease in numbers and the sense that members were no longer young, something had to be done. It was decided to change the name to Bramford Ladies, and the remaining funds were disposed of by purchasing a brick for St Elizabeth Hospice for the sum of £10. Half of the remainder went to the Home School Association and the rest to St Mary's Church Roof Appeal.

Bramford Ladies carried on for nearly two years with little support, and on Thursday 8 December 1988 a party was held and the club disbanded, although there were a faithful few who still decided to meet once a month in the Parish Room for a friendly chat and a cup of tea, to enjoy a few games like Trivial Pursuit, or perhaps have a ramble. But by the end of the 1990s most members belonged to the Women's Institute and some were involved with carpet bowls, making it difficult to find an evening that suited everybody. The last meeting was held in February 1999.

THE WOMEN'S INSTITUTE

Bramford Women's Institute was formed in November 1918 but unfortunately no minutes were recorded until 1924. Apparently for the first six years it was run by Mrs Packard, assisted by Miss Nunn.

The first recorded minutes were in March 1924 when the meeting was held in the Parish Room and the subject of the lecture was 'The Noble Life of Elizabeth Fry'.

However, in April 1924 the minutes state that the meeting was held in the New Victory Hall when a 'papier maché' demonstration was held and new institute songs were practised as well as 'The King'. In May that year a maypole dance was held, when Rosie Boggis was crowned May Queen, and entertainment was provided by the Girls' Friendly Society.

During 1924 funds were raised for heating in the church, Bramford Nurses Association and Ipswich Shelter (5s.). An entry was exhibited at the Suffolk Agricultural Show at Bury St Edmunds, but the minutes do not say what it was. In November of the same year a group of ladies attended who were

Women's Institute committee in the 1950s or '60s. Left to right, back row: *Mrs Winkworth, Mrs Howlett, Mrs Drane;* front: *Mrs Dowsett, Mrs Jolly (president), Mrs Bray, Mrs Simpson.*

about to start their own WI group in Sproughton.

Throughout the old minutes it was recorded that eggs were collected and garments made for the Ipswich Hospital, as the institute had a Linen Guild.

Social time always played an important part in the programme, including pianoforte solos, recitations, gramophone selections, dancing, comical songs, violin solos, banjo, plays, duologues, fancy-dress parades and charades, the latter sometimes being given by Brownies or Guides.

Talks and demonstrations included: making raffia bags, caning and covering chairs, home remedies, making poultices and hot fermentations, how to change a sheet on an invalid's bed, helpful hints for the treatment of bed sores, poultry keeping, witches, 'Passe Partout' picture framing, dressing fowl, making soft slippers, making paper flowers, turning collars, making jam and jelly, life saving (of the 'apparently drowned'), darning socks, Hay Boxes and what to cook in them and a lantern lecture of the Prince of Wales in Canada.

In December 1925 membership stood at 68. A social was held that year when:

120 members and friends including children attended a programme of music and competitions, very pretty dancing, songs by Mrs Walter Packard, recitations by Miss Fiske, piano duets and solos by Miss King and Miss Southgate, a balloon race, sweet guessing and chalking the pigs eye.

In 1926 the first committee was recorded as follows: Miss K. Packard, Miss N. Packard (president), Mrs Jackson (vice-president), Miss Fiske, Mrs Eaborn, Mrs Voules, Mrs Hurry, Mrs Hazell, Mrs King, Mrs Sewell, Nurse Richardson, Mrs Giles, Mrs Rattle, Mrs Graves, Miss King and Mrs Lillie. At this meeting there was a demonstration of tailoring.

By 1927 membership had grown to 86, and Lady Packard, the first president of the Institute, died. An outing of 41 members went by charabanc to Yarmouth and arrived back at 11 o'clock. Members were concerned about the lack of a night-time telephone service and so 'a letter was sent to our member representing Bramford in Parliament, requesting him to lay before the house such needs.'

In 1928 a much larger committee was recorded. The president was Nina Packard who lived at The Grove, also H. Fiske (secretary), Mrs Hurry, Mrs Lacon, Mrs and Miss Lay, Mrs Boggis, Mrs C. Giles, Mrs Lockwood, Mrs and Miss Tuppen, Miss Fiske (national delegate), Mrs Keeble, N. Pryke and Mrs G. Pryke, Mrs Carr (vice-president), Mrs Eaborn, Mrs Quinton (county delegate) and N. Banyard.

In June 1937 five members won prizes outside the WI for the best decorated houses on Coronation Day and two for fancy dress. Miss Fiske invited all members to her garden for the twenty-first birthday celebrations of the WI to hear the radio broadcast of Lady Denman, founder of the WI college.

In 1938 Miss Tuppen gave a report on the annual meeting at the Albert Hall, London, telling members it was a wonderful experience and they should all try to go at some point. An outing took place to the Ovaltine factory, Kings Langley, Herts, by Morley's bus via Bury, Newmarket and St Albans, returning via Bishops Stortford, in all about 200 miles for a fare of 7s.6d. Another outing went to Carrow Works, Norwich, via Lowestoft and Great Yarmouth.

In 1939 a request was received for help towards the Victory Hall piano fund. But in September that year no meeting was held because of the outbreak of war and the evacuation of mothers and children. Over the winter months, meetings were held at 3p.m. instead of 7p.m. owing to the blackout. A working party was formed to knit comforts for local men who had joined the Forces and to sew and knit for the poor children of Suffolk. Patterns were sent by the Red Cross and the working party met once a week on a Thursday at 2.30p.m. in the evacuees clubroom at the vicarage.

In 1940 the January social was held at 7p.m. because of the moon being almost full.

In May a letter of thanks was received from the searchlight detachment for socks which they had received. The following month 12s. (60p) was collected at the door for comforts for Dunkirk men. In July a grant of 15cwt of sugar was received for making surplus fruit into jam. A collection for the WI ambulance raised 8s. (40p). In September the result of the jam making was 4,757lbs of jam from 23cwt of sugar and 25cwt of fruit.

WI tree planting. Left to right: *Pam Hulford, Rosemary Keeble, Margaret Gant, Annie Aitken;* kneeling: *Sylvia Harvey, Joan Mills, Judy Kemish.*

In May 1941 packets of vegetable seeds were received from America and it was later announced that propaganda films were available to view.

At the Annual Social in January 1942 the food was provided by members and it was wonderful to see so much all at once in wartime. There was enough left over to provide a tea for the evacuees the next day. In August the WI purchased a canning machine and in September the meetings were changed to the first Friday in the month as the hall was needed by the Home Guard on Thursdays.

On 1 September 1945 between 80 and 90 Bramford men and women aged 65 or over were invited to a Victory Tea. Jam making had made a profit of £25 which was divided amongst the Nursing Association, the Hospital Linen Guild and the Welcome Home Fund. In December Mr Wilfred Hurry gave an interesting talk on the beauties of the countryside, illustrating it with some excellent pictures he had painted himself.

In May 1946 the WI received 2lbs of jam from Queensland, Australia, and it was decided to use this for refreshments at the monthly meetings. In December Mrs Jackson offered to find out from the Food Office whether it would be possible for members to each exchange one of their ration points into bread units so that the meat received from Australia could be made into sandwiches.

Owing to the bread rationing in January 1947 it was not possible to have a full 'sit-down' tea as usual, but each member contributed two cakes. In March several members had to leave before the end of the meeting because of the floods, but even so some had to go through a lot of water to get home.

In October 1948 the talk was about 'Children's Awkward Questions', and the following month it was suggested that assistance should be given to help members who were unable to pay the extra 1s. (5p) increase in membership fee.

In April 1954 there were 50 members, and a talk on the 'Progress of Corseting' was given. In August of that year committee members and two others gave a demonstration of handicrafts as follows:

Miss Francis – machine knitting
Mrs Humphries – spinning wheel
Mrs Perfect – rug making
Mrs Pinkney – applique, quilting and embroidery
Mrs Rope – smocking
Mrs Hitchcock – sewing
Mrs Hopkins – lace making

Above: *WI Christmas party, 2002. Pictured are: 1 Ann Chappell, 2 Margaret Woollard, 3 Jean Parker, 4 Olive Godbold, 5 Valerie Ellis, 6 Ally Riley, 7 Mrs De'ath, 8 Maggie Razzell, 9 Margaret Fish, 10 Judith Partridge, 11 Margaret Gant, 12 Margaret Cook, 13 Margaret Southgate, 14 Pat Jarman, 15 Valerie Prentice, 16 Judy Kemish, 17 Joy Barrett, 18 Eileen Hurren, 19 Janet Hurren, 20 Pam Hulford, 21 Brenda Ransome, 22 Sue Maskell, 23 Sue Withell, 24 Mary Sago, 25 Dianne Curran, 26 Dianna Wolton, 27 Stella Alderton, 28 Pam Castleton, 29 Margaret Boag, 30 Maureen Woods, 31 Margaret Mayhew, 32 Lynn Banks, 33 Sylvia Harvey (president), 34 Ruby Parker, 35 Joan Mills (secretary), 36 Violet Lockwood, 37 Beryl Sims, 38 Janet Hewitt, 39 Margaret Welham.*

Mrs Howlett – lampshade making
Miss Tuppen – stool making

In October 1954 Mr Bumpstead gave a film show which ended with the Coronation procession of Queen Elizabeth II. In June 1955 the members were unable to go to the AGM because of a railway strike and in August a letter of protest was sent to Eastern Counties Omnibus Co. regarding the cancellation of buses. A representative talked to Mrs Howlett and Mrs Humphries and promised to do his best to restore the buses at 10a.m. and 2p.m.

In May 1956 a demonstration was given on the many uses of Jiffytex glue and in October the outing was to Reckitt and Coleman, Norwich. The 29-seater Bickers bus started from the village at 9.30a.m. and the cost was £7.10s. (£7.50).

Over the years, many members have attended the AGM, sometimes at the Albert Hall, or in recent years Birmingham, Cardiff or Brighton. Mrs Fish from the bakery often related the fact that the WI chartered a whole train which picked up at Bramford Station, presumably to attend the AGM at the Albert Hall, when a delegate from each institute would attend. It is wonderful to think that a representative attends from every corner of the British Isles; no other organisation could bring together such a diverse group of people from so many towns and villages. The WI is a worldwide organisation which began in Canada, but now has institutes in many countries. At the AGMs there are resolutions which are put to the vote, and if passed, are presented to the Government. These are usually things that the WI feel will make a difference to the world or improve quality of life. In turn the Government often consults the WI on important matters or law amendments.

In 1928 a beautiful tablecloth was embroidered by members, showing things to be seen around the village. Another was embroidered in 1953 to celebrate the Coronation of the Queen, and a third embroidered by every member with her own name in 1986.

WI members always like to be included in village events, with floats being entered in the processions around the village on fête days in the 1970s, and litter picking, friendly cricket matches, stalls at village events, arrangements at flower festivals and special fund-raising 'knit-ins' for charity.

In 1991 the WI planted two trees in the village and in 1995 a clock was presented to the Loraine Victory

Hall to commemorate the WI's eightieth birthday. There is also a carpet bowls and darts team, and the members enter regional quizzes and Suffolk Show competitions. Theatre visits, carol services, social nights, barbecues, rambles and bike rides are always part of the programme.

At the time of writing Bramford WI's membership numbers 46. The group meet on the second Monday of the month at 7.30p.m. in the Loraine Victory Hall. It is a friendly gathering, certainly not to be confused with the old 'Jam and Jerusalem' image. Yes, 'Jerusalem' is still sung, but the jam bit only lasted through the war years when the WI made a terrific effort to help the war campaign and made so much jam. But this image has unfortunately 'stuck'! The group are grateful to its ancestors who started the WI in Bramford in 1918

FOOTBALL

A football club was first started in Bramford in 1896, but very few records survive from that time. Most of the village boys would have played unofficially. Les Beckett used to play football with his neighbours at Runcton, Arthur and Alf Lloyd. They did not own a real football, but were able to stuff an old leather cover with newspapers, which made a passable (but heavy) ball, and they put their coats and hats down in the road (the B1113) as goalposts.

In the late 1920s Les used to accompany his brothers to watch the Bramford football team who played on the Broadwater ground near the chemical works in Works Lane (now Paper Mill Lane). Access was via the village paths, across Chapel Field (behind the Chapel) and down Pound Lane to Bushman's Bridge. The bridge was treacherous to cross because of its dilapidated state, with wide gaps between the wooden boards. Once onto the meadow, it was necessary to negotiate further

rotten footbridges to get to the Broadwater ground.

The Bramford team colours were blue and amber halves with white shorts. Jack Barrel in his bright-red jersey played in goal and other team members were: Jim and Ted Page, Sunny Rodwell, Bill and Charlie Cook, Jack Lambert, Albert Lillyman, Albert Garner, George Markham, Jack Francis, Lawrie Garnham (secretary) and Gilbert Lambert (linesman).

In 1928–29 the Bramford team were very successful. They were champions of the Ipswich Junior League and runners-up in the Suffolk Minor Cup. The final, which was played at the Portman Road Ground in Ipswich, was the only game lost that season. Many village lads played football for the local team at various times; some of the names were Jack and Bob Barfield, Cliff Francis, Frank Boggis, Ron Tibble and Charlie Stagg. Mr Hurry was the club president for many years and was seldom away from the touchline when there was a home match.

In 1973 Bramford re-entered Suffolk and Ipswich League, playing on the new playing-field at Acton Road. After a couple of years a reserve team was formed, then in the 1979–80 season a youth section was started.

Since 1973 Bramford United has progressed through the lower divisions and, at the time of writing, is playing as a senior club in the league. Over this period the club has won three league championships, reached two County Cup finals, won the Junior Cup in the 2000/01 season, won the Ross Taylor Cup three times, and the Saul Cup twice. In the 1996/97 season the team was awarded Suffolk Coaches Club of the Season award, and in the same year were presented with a plaque by the FA to celebrate its centenary.

The youth section has run continuously since 1979. The number of teams has varied each season, but at the time of writing there are five youth teams, ranging in age from under 8 years to under 18.

Left: *Bramford Football Club, 1950. Left to right, back row: Don Lockwood, Derek Clements, Brian Hill, Derek 'Fish' Whiting, 'Chutney' Payne, John Godfrey, Frank Hillman, Ronnie Brown; front: Derek Sillett, Robert Worledge, Russell Brown, Peter Page, ? Wolton.*

Above: *Bramford United Football Club, 1996–97. SIL Division 1 champions. Left to right, back row: T. Connell (coach), I. Crick (junr 1st team manager), S. Burman, S. Lee, A. Crown, S. Bunn, K. Baxter, C. Williams, W. Emerson, D. Woods, R. Stollery, S. Brown, A. Fowler (asst. reserves manager), I. Bragg (reserves manager); seated: S. Gray, G. Parker (junr 1st team manager), P. Connell, N. Tibble, R. Wakeling (secretary), A. Woods (chairman), M. McEreane (vice-chairman), S. Wakeling (treasurer), J. Gray, S. Girling, A. Rudge, P. Page; front: S. Crick and C. Crick. Trophies, left to right: Ross-Taylor Cup, Centenary Plaque, Division 1 Winners, Suffolk Coaches 'Club of the Year' Award, Saul Cup.*

Left: *Bramford Works Football Club fixture card.*

Bramford United Reserves, Ross-Taylor Cup winners, 1999–2000. Left to right, back row: Russell Armstrong, Matt Clarke, Martin Foster, Adam Steele, Bartley Kirby, Wayne Soza, Adie Fowler, Roger Norman, Mark Leeks (manager); front: Barry Lockwood, Ivan Butcher and son, Darren Kemp, Lloyd Clayton, Kieron Hetherington, Callum Powell, Gavin Hiskey.

Over the years the team has won many age league championships and club competitions, including the Suffolk County FA Minor Cup.

The facilities at Acton Road have improved vastly since the days of the wooden pavilion that was initially used for changing. However, due to changing and updating regulations the club is always having to improve even these facilities. Although stones caused problems in the early years, the playing surface is highly regarded, and the club stages many County Cup semi-finals and finals, as well as various League finals at youth and senior level.

Some notable servants of the club since the 1970s have been the late Eric Garnham, the late Brian Barfield, Bob and Susan Wakeling, Colin Sparrow, Adie Fowler, and many others who have made a great contribution. The club is also indebted to various village-based firms and individuals for their support, without whom it could not have survived.

1ST BRAMFORD SCOUT GROUP

Scouting existed in Bramford over at least two separate periods prior to 1971 but few details are available. The first Wolf Cub pack was formed in 1929 by Miss May King and her cousin Agnes, and the boys met weekly, round the wolf-headed totem pole, in the Parish Room. Some members attended a jamboree in Chantry Park, Ipswich, in 1932 when the Chief Scout visited. A Scout troop was formed about the same time under the leadership of Archie Smith (Skip), one of their main fund-raising events being their Annual Scout Concert which was held in the Victory Hall.

It is not known how long these units lasted, but another Scout troop was started by Bill Pulfer in 1947 and again met in the Parish Room. Cliff Whiteman, Norman Sewell and Derek Pulfer helped to run the small troop of two patrols which ran until at least 1951.

The most recent Scout Group was registered on 27 October 1971 when a few enterprising parents, who had sons belonging to Ipswich groups, could see the growing need for Scouting in Bramford. After meetings with the district commissioner, a group was formed under the leadership of Bill Roberts (Group Scout Leader – GSL) who had previous experience in Scouting. There was a Cub pack for boys aged 8–11, led by Mrs Baxter (CSL), and a Scout troop for boys aged 11–16, led by Les Knight (SL). Linda Game and Chick Mayhew helped to look after 25 to 35 boys in the respective sections.

It soon became obvious that to cater for this number of boys, equipment would have to be purchased and a Parents and Supporters Committee was formed to raise funds. The first officers to be elected were Clive Powell (chairman), Daphne Bloomfield (secretary) and John Robertson (treasurer). The

committee worked hard and within two years had raised enough money to purchase three patrol tents, a large gear tent and several items of camping equipment.

Initially, the Cub and Scout Sections met in the Old School building but when that fell into disrepair they moved to St Mary's Schoolroom. All sections met here until 1983, when the new Guide and Scout HQ opened in the converted school buildings in Ship Lane, except for a short period when the second Cub pack met in the Coach House on Church Green.

The equipment was stored in a shed next to the Parish Room (where the bottle bank is now) but this was destroyed by fire early in 1973. All the new tents were lost but when they were replaced following an insurance claim, they were stored in the loft of the Victory Hall.

In 1975 a steering committee was formed to look into the possibility of building a HQ in conjunction with the Guide Company. Soon after, the committee started fund-raising as initial enquiries had shown that a new HQ was viable, but costly. Early events included jumble sales, dances and 'garden days' at Lord Blakenham's estate, including strawberry-and-cream teas, but the main fund-raiser over the next ten years was the popular Friday-night disco.

The Parish Council, early in 1978, asked the Guides and Scouts if they would like to use the Old School for a nominal rent, provided they refurbish it. This building was obviously the cheapest route to a new HQ so the offer was accepted, but, although the building was due to have the roof and floor replaced throughout and the walls were solid, it was in a derelict state inside and needed a tremendous amount of work.

The work was started in 1981 by a dedicated team of volunteer parents and friends, helped by young people from the Manpower Services Commission. The refurbished Guide and Scout HQ was officially opened in March 1983. The main people involved in the work and fund-raising were Stephanie Thomas (chairman), Brian Conen (treasurer), Joy Barrett (secretary), Janet Cunningham/Edmundson and Don Golding (Guide and Scout representatives), David Day (electrician) and Eric Wolton (Clerk of Works).

The Scout Movement is an International Youth Organisation, set up in 1907 for training young people in the principles of good citizenship. The aim is to help young people to develop physically, mentally and spiritually so that they will be better prepared to accept adult responsibilities. This is achieved through the provision of a balanced programme of meetings, activities, events, competitions and camps. The activities offered to members have always depended on the section but remained very similar to Baden Powell's 'Scouting for Boys' until the first major review in 1966. The Cubs and Scouts had progressive training schemes which allowed members to work towards an award for each level achieved.

Canoeing on the River Gipping by Bramford Bridge, 1986. Left to right: *Ian Golding, David Ward, Chris Pipe, Roger Hatton, Ray Ransome, Robert Collins.*

Boys could also gain any number of proficiency badges for a sport, interest or hobby.

The programmes offered to Cubs reflect their age and are based around games and learning by doing, with outings to places of interest and minimal adventurous activities (camping), concentrating, whenever possible, on 'outdoor' activities in the spring and summer months. In their meetings, Cubs are formed into small groups called 'sixes', which are known by a colour, and many of the Cub Leaders have a jungle name (such as Akela) based on characters from the Jungle Book.

Ready for camping in Scotland with the new minibus, 1996. Left to right, back row: *Leon Studd, Jonathan Gildersleeves, James Stewart, Daniel Cooper, Ryan Studd, John Tunaley, Andrew Beckinsale, Wayne Gardiner;* front: *Neil Potter, Phillip Foulger, Neil Foulger, David Ward, Tyree McKinney, Nick Cooper, Jamie Connor.*

The badge scheme continued in the Scouts but greater emphasis was placed on adventure activities, including hillwalking, rock climbing and camping. Boys were grouped in Patrols which were named after African animals.

Although the 1966 review made provision for Venture Scouts, older members between 16 and 20 years, there were no Ventures in Bramford until 1981 when the Gipping Valley Venture Unit was formed. This unit has proved to be very successful both in the programme it has offered to the young people and the way it has fed the group with young leaders (roughly half of our leaders have been Venture Scouts). The programme and events were decided by the members and included more adventurous activities. To a large extent, the unit has been self-governing and by the mid-1980s they had voted to make the unit mixed.

About the same time that mixed Venture Scouting came to Bramford, a new section for 6–8-year-olds called Beaver Scouts was introduced to the Scout movement. A Colony was not formed in Bramford until 1990. The boys were formed into Lodges and the leaders were given names associated with the Beaver world but their programme was based on 'Fun and Friends', with no training scheme or badges initially. At about this time all Scout Groups in the UK were allowed to become mixed, but in view of the strong Guiding influence in the village a decision was made to stay single sex (except for the Venture Unit) and it has remained so to the time of writing.

The seventy-fifth anniversary of the Cub Scouts, 1991.
Village residents over the age of 75 were invited.

In 2002 a new structure was introduced which changed the age ranges of the older sections and provided new programmes for all sections, designed to modernise the movement and make it 'relevant and attractive for the twenty-first century'. The new programme, in all sections, has a greater emphasis on outdoor activities and adventurous opportunities. The five sections are, Beavers 6–8 years, Cubs 8–10, Scouts 10–14, Explorer Scouts 14–18 and Network Scouts 18–25. The Fellowship still exists for members over 25 but does not have any programme material. All sections offer a progressive training scheme with associated activities and awards, the highest award being the Queens Scout Award and, for the first time, links for members with the Duke of Edinburgh's Award scheme. Several members have gained their Queens Scout Award since the 1980s, namely John Wolton, David Ward, Andrew Renton, Caroline Wolton, Sue Ward, Jo Rhodes and Peter Sago.

Throughout all the changes since 1907 the movement has kept its Law and Promise and the motto, 'Be Prepared', is now encompassed in the new logo.

In the 1970s, as the group was establishing itself, activities were limited to weekend camps for Cubs at Hallowtree, Ipswich, and the annual summer camp for Scouts, over a week, further afield. The group was involved in the village fête by providing a float in the procession and running stalls and sideshows. Barn and Valentine dances were also popular fund-raising events.

One activity that was started in 1983 was a regular father and son camp at Hallowtree campsite on the shores of the Orwell at Nacton. These annual camps proved to be very popular, giving fathers a chance to spend some 'quality time' camping with their son whilst taking part in various out-door/adventurous activities. In the early 1990s it was changed to a family camp; the last one was held in 1996 to celebrate 25 years of Scouting in Bramford.

In the spring of 1986, links were formed with a Belgian Scout Group, 156 De Havik, from Ghent, when they held a week-long camp based at Bramford

HQ and several joint activities were arranged. The following year a party of Guides, Scouts and Venture Scouts from Bramford travelled to Belgium for a joint adventure camp with the Havik group and many long-term friendships were forged. Bramford returned to Belgium in 1993 and the Belgians reciprocated in 1994 with a joint camp in London, followed by home hospitality in Bramford.

Bramford and Claydon Scouts competed in activities such as raft racing, archery and pioneering for the Claydon and Bramford Troop Challenge Trophy in the late 1980s. In sport the Scouts won the district five-a-side football competition each year between 1999 and 2002.

Cubs held successful weekend pack camps at least once a year from the 1980s onwards and took part in many district camps as well, including the seventy-fifth anniversary camp in 1991. Bramford Cubs also held a seventy-fifth birthday party in the HQ to which all Bramford residents over 75 were invited. Cubs and Beavers have also attended Cub and Beaver activity days at Gilwell Park campsite – the Scout HQ campsite and training ground in Epping Forest.

On two occasions the group has won the Ipswich South District Challenge Trophy – in 1998 all sections competed in different activities to win over-all and in 2000 the trophy was awarded to Bramford for best interpretation of the Scouting concept and administration.

Early in 2003, an assistant Cub Leader, Claire Self, attended the World Jamboree in Thailand as a Group Leader and, with the others in the East Anglian contingent of 30 or more members, had the experience of a lifetime.

Tenth birthday party of Cubs and Scouts, October 1981.
Left to right, back row: *Maureen Renton, John Risbridger, Jeremy Conen, Jonathan Davis, Iain Renton, Don Golding SL, David Ward, Andrew Renton, Betty Game CSL, John Wolton, Carol Scurrell ACSL;* third row: *Steven Hunt, Tim Hewitt, Nicholas Moss, Glenn Risbridger, Michael Hoggarth, Michael Atkins;* second row: *Neil Dadswell, Alan Rudge, Chris Wright, Nicholas Ashford, Robert Scruby;* front: *John Pearson, Andrew Laws, Keith Thomas, Robert Collins.*

Left: *The Guides at Bramford Hall, c.1920. The lady in the centre is probably Miss Isaura Loraine.*

Below: *Guides laying a wreath at the grave of their founder Isaura Loraine on their fiftieth anniversary, 1968. Left to right: Cheryl Lay, Louie Garner, Jenny Ford, Kitty Garnham, ?, Elizabeth Pegg, Sandra Cunningham, Anne Bumstead and Mary Christian.*

Ipswich and District Girl Guides' Local Association.

PROFICIENCY BADGE CERTIFICATE.

I hereby certify that *Louisa Metcalfe* has passed the required tests for the *Cyclist* Badge, and I recommend that the Badge be awarded.

Signed *Marjorie Noble* Examiner.

Date *May 22* 1926.

Ethel H. Fiske Secretary.

Isaura Loraine Commissioner.

93 %

Left: *Copy of proficiency badge certificate awarded to Louisa Metcalfe, signed by Miss Fiske and Miss Loraine.*

Bramford Guides, 1950s. Left to right, back row: Mr Hardwick, June Mee, Mrs Hardwick, Jean Pryke, June Upton, Jackie Steel, ?, Janet Francis, Pam Brown, ?, Revd Harford, Dot Bradford, ?, Stella Wolton, ?, Cora Francis, Mrs Steel, Mr Steel; middle: Daphne Goodway, Ann Beckett, Judith ?, Ann Taylor, Gillian Steel, Cora Garnham, ?, ?, Margaret Lay; front: Connie Parker, Ann Pulfer, Barbara Chaplin, ?, ?, ?, ?.

The fund-raising group (Scout Executive Committee) have raised money in many different ways over the years, but one of the most successful has been the bi-annual Grand Auction that was started in 1993. This event depended on the generosity of Bramford villagers who donated items for sale (surf boards, cement mixers, bikes, lawn mowers, etc.) and then spent an enjoyable summer afternoon watching people bid for them! Other events have included stalls at the village fête, craft fairs, dances, jumble sales, car-boot and table-top sales, car washes and barbeques. From the 1970s to the early 1990s members (mainly Cubs) took part in the annual Bob-a-job Week or Scout Job Week to raise funds for the group, but this activity was stopped for safety reasons.

Fund-raising for charities also featured in the activities of the Scout Group. Cubs and Scouts have swum on many occasions for the British Heart Foundation Swimathon and for several years Scouts and Venture Scouts walked either 12 or 25 miles in the Orwell 25 sponsored walk. Venture Scouts, Leaders and Fellowship members have walked the Lyke Wake Walk in Yorkshire (2000) and competed the Three Peaks Challenge (2002), raising over £4,200 for various charities.

The Scouts main links with the Guide Sections have come about since the idea of a joint HQ was first mooted in 1975. In 1977 a Gang Show was produced to raise funds for the HQ and, although it was a success, it was not repeated until 1986 since when it has been a regular, bi-annual event, most of the shows being produced by the Guide Leader, Bridget Harvey. These shows, besides raising cash, have proved great fun with a variety of song and dance routines and comedy sketches, when many Venture Scouts and leaders have shown their talents as 'panto dames' or similar!

The Scout uniform was changed in 1969 from the old 'shorts, with long socks and garter tabs and shirts with epaulettes' to mushroom-coloured shirts and long trousers. Cubs stayed in green but modern fabrics were used to give relief from the 'itchy woollen jumpers'. In 2001 the uniform was changed again to bring it up to date and modern fleeces replaced heavy, impractical felt uniform jackets, 'activity' trousers became the norm and baseball caps replaced caps and berets. The colours changed to blue trousers and different coloured tops for each section.

The first change in leaders/Scouters came towards the end of 1973 when Bill Roberts moved from the area and Mrs Baxter decided to retire. Les Knight became GSL, Don Golding took his place as SL and Linda Game became CSL. Betty Game and Carol Lay soon joined Linda in the Cubs and then in 1978, when several new leaders joined, a second Cub pack was formed with Betty Game as leader, the first pack being led by Carol Scurrell. Leaders have come and gone since 1978 but the main ones have been:

Beavers – *Pat Wright, Roger Teague, Duncan Chenery, Michael Keegan and Jo Rhodes.*
Cubs – *Maureen Renton, Betty Game, Caroline Wolton, Maureen Dell, Keith Sparrow, Peter Sago, Matt Deal, Maureen Dell and Lorraine Williams.*
Scouts – *Don Golding, Ed Christian, Dave Bloomfield, John Risbridger, Dave Crown, Roger Hatton, Dave Ward, Mark Cooper, Sue Ward and Roland Dakin.*
Venture Scouts – *Tim Game, Nick Bestow, Janet Thomas, Andrew Renton, Adrian Bacon, Jenny Norris, Nick Day, Tony Whitmore, Rhonda Pipe and Claire Self.*

The group has survived, not only due to the hard work of leaders, but also the support of the Group Executive or Fund-Raising Committee. This team have raised many thousands of pounds over the years to buy camping and adventurous activities equipment and also buy and maintain a minibus, which has proved a very useful asset. Officers of the committee since 1971 have included George and Joan Mills, Doug Lainchbury, Janet Hewitt, Diana Wolton, Delia Ward, Doreen Golding, Brenda Ransome, Jan Valentine, Wendy Wellum, Ed Gildersleeves, Chris Wrigley and Ann Russ.

BRAMFORD GUIDES

The 1st Bramford Guide Company was founded in 1918 under the patronage of Miss Isaura Loraine from Bramford Hall. Other Guide Leaders since then have been Miss Francis, Mrs Webb, Mrs Willis, Mrs Janet Read and, in 2003, Bridget Jackaman (née Harvey).

The original meeting-room was in the old Coach House on Church Green, but by 1945 the Company had outgrown it. So the group split into two and all the Guides on the village side of the river stayed in the 1st Company, while those on the east side of the river formed the 2nd. Their captains were Miss Upton and Miss Lingley.

A very sad event took place in 1921 when one of the Guides, Mildred Hill, died in hospital from meningitis, aged 13. Her funeral in Bramford Church was accompanied by full Guide honours.

One of the group's most enjoyable activities was camping. One memorable year they went to Scotland, travelling by train via Liverpool Street Station, London, carrying all their camping gear. Other holidays have included travelling to Switzerland to stay in the Guides chalet and a narrow-boat camping trip to Warwickshire. Most of the travelling was on the back of an open lorry, which of course would not be allowed today.

In 1921 the Guides started fund-raising to provide a bed in Ipswich Hospital, Anglesea Road. It took them 19 years to raise the necessary £1,000. Together with the Rangers, they also raised money to provide two chairs for the church in Ypres, France, which were dedicated on Armistice Day 1928.

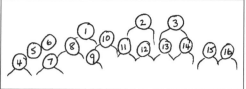

Left: *First Bramford Brownies planting a tree on the village green, 1984.* Leaders: *1 Margaret Dakin, 2 Jane Steward, 3 Rosemary Steward;* Brownies: *4 Jo Rhodes, 5 Alison Gardiner, 6 Jenny Page, 7 Rhonda Pipe, 8 Chloe Peck, 9 Katie Alderton, 10 Shona Lee, 11 Clare Hall, 12 Jodie Cook, 13 Alison ?, 14 Clare Hunwicks, 15 Rachel Davis, 16 Victoria ?.*

In 1968 a Golden Jubilee service was held in the church, followed by tea in the Loraine Victory Hall. A wreath was laid on the grave of the troop founder, Miss Isaura Loraine.

The Coach House in Church Green was purchased from the Loraine family, but it was not until 1972 that sufficient funds were raised to replace the old barn door with a more suitable one.

One of the Bramford Guides, Mrs Anne Smith (née Pulfer), later became Mayor of Ipswich. The newly converted Guide and Scout HQ in Ship Lane was opened by her father, Mr Pulfer, and Mrs Janet Cunningham in 1983.

Margaret Warton, who died in 2002, was the first Queen's Guide in Suffolk.

FIRST BRAMFORD BROWNIES

The first Company was formed in 1918 and registered in 1922. The first meeting place was in the Parish Room. Later, like the Guides, they transferred to the junior school, and then in 1983 to the newly-refurbished Guide and Scout HQ in the old school.

Brown Owls were Mrs Dowsett, Mrs Pegg, Mrs

Brownies in their new uniform, 1990s. Left to right: *Sophie Parsons, Holly ?, ?, Emily Beckinsale, Amy Parsons, Jo Rutter, Lauren Ross (kneeling), Rachel Main, Joy and Jackie ? (twins), Katherine Watts.*

Janet Read (Cunningham), Mrs Knight, Mrs Sandra Abbs (née Cunningham), Mrs Rosemary Steward and Mrs Margaret Dakin.

When Mrs Knight, the policeman's wife, left the village in 1973, Margaret Dakin and Sandra Cunningham took over and, when Sandra left to get married, her place as Tawny Owl was taken by Rosemary Steward, who carried on until she retired in 2000. After this they were joined by Pauline Mayhew and Elizabeth Stow.

There have been many young leaders, a few of whom were: Jane Steward, Karen Chappell, Susan Algar, Sarah Bickers, Helen Golding, Rhonda Pipe, Bridget Harvey, Clare Rutter and Lucy Mann.

Over the years the uniform has changed considerably, becoming much less formal. It is due to change again in 2003. The pack has enjoyed many activities over the decades and hopefully this will continue into the future.

SECOND BRAMFORD BROWNIES

In the late 1960s when, due to the increasing number of young families in the village, the First Bramford Brownie pack had a large waiting list of girls wanting to join, it was decided there was a need for a second pack. So three friends from Bramford, Jenny Ford, Cheryl Lay and Wendy Earthy, agreed to set it up.

The pack was officially registered on 19 May 1967 with Jenny as Brown Owl. Cheryl and Wendy were her assistants until 1969 when they were then old enough to become warranted Guiders.

Meetings were held in the small building on Church Green where there was not much room for boisterous games, except in summer when the girls could play outside. They transferred to the new Guide and Scout HQ in the Old School when it opened in March 1983, which gave them a much warmer and roomier environment.

Jenny married in April 1973 and moved away from the village, so Wendy took over the role of Brown Owl, and Cheryl as Tawny Owl. The

Second Bramford Brownies, winners of the Bosmere and Bramford Sports Cup, 1986. Left to right, leaders: Cheryl Hollins, Wendy McGinty, Libby Lamming; Brownies: Charlotte Collins, Rebecca Ransome, Janine Hall, Annette Lait, Clare Smith, Karen Ratcliffe, Samantha Eve, Flora Heathcote, Helen Palmer, Kerrie Gardiner, Saffron Turnell, Suzanne Espener, Genna Hollins.

Brownies formed a Guard of Honour at Jenny's wedding and again the following year at Cheryl's, both of which were at Bramford Church.

Libby Lamming then came to help as young leader and stayed to become a Guider. In the summer of 1984 she represented Suffolk at an International Camp in Japan and the Brownies made pressed-flower bookmarks for her to take as gifts. On her return she brought Japanese sweets, food and tales of her travels to share with the Brownies.

Dressed in an old-style uniform, Libby also took part in a procession through Ipswich town on 26 June 1985 to celebrate 75 years of Guiding, which ended in a flame ceremony outside the Town Hall on Corn Hill.

The Brownies formed another Guard of Honour, this time at Sproughton Church, when Libby married in November 1988.

A party was held to celebrate the eighteenth birthday of the pack in 1985, when Blue Owl, Mrs S. Gayfer, the district commissioner for Bosmere and Bramford, was invited along to cut the cake.

In June 1986 the Chief Commissioner for Anglia, Mrs M. Johnson, presented Cheryl and Wendy with their 15-year long service awards at the AGM of Suffolk Girl Guides, held at Farlingaye School, Woodbridge.

Over the years the pack raised money for a variety of charities and causes, from children's charities to bone-marrow appeals, collecting silver foil for Guide Dogs for the Blind, and used postage stamps for the RNLI. They have also sent pens to Poland and toys to Tanzania.

One year the pack was the winner and holder of the Revels Cup, an annual competition between the Brownie packs of the district. In July 1986 they were the winners of the Annual Sports Cup.

Unfortunately, although the pack had been running successfully for 22 years, the number of girls gradually dwindled and there no longer seemed to be a need for a second pack, so it held its last meeting at Christmas 1989.

BRAMFORD TENNIS CLUB

In 1977, on a rough patch of grass behind the Victory Hall, a few village inhabitants got together to try to create a tennis court. From these few founder members the idea of a village tennis club took hold. A committee was formed and a lot of hard work began in order to raise the funds necessary to build some hard courts for year-round play, as the high maintenance and limited playing potential of grass was realised. Various fund-raising activities were employed, a 100 Club was formed with monthly cash prizes, and car-boot sales, stalls at village fêtes and dances were held, until a couple of years later, with the help of sports grant aid, two courts were opened at the playing-field. This, together with the entering of teams into the Ipswich tennis leagues, meant that the village had a new sports facility for both serious and casual tennis players.

As more teams were entered into the various leagues, it was becoming obvious that the club was hampered by the lack of a third court, particularly in the summer leagues where teams consisted of three pairs. With this in mind further fund-raising took place, until in 1984 a third court was opened, again with the help of sports grant aid.

Throughout the intervening years Bramford Tennis Club has regularly entered teams in men's, ladies' and mixed summer leagues. The hardy (or

Ann and Mick Russ, winners of the mixed doubles, 1985.

Bramford Ladies, 1998. Left to right, standing: Pat Jarman, Libby Lapworth, Ann Russ; seated: Sally Wilkinson, Lorna Jones, Corinne Butler, Betsy Butler.

should that be foolhardy?) among the team also play in club sides in the winter floodlit and winter Sunday-morning leagues, as well as running junior coaching sessions in the summer for children aged 7–14 years.

Although Bramford Tennis Club is small, it holds club tournaments during the season, and there are regular club sessions on Sunday mornings and Tuesday evenings during the summer. After 26 years most of those early enthusiasts have ceased to be club members, indeed only Pat Jarman and Bob Carter remain. Others, like June and Brian Flint, have moved, and some early stalwarts such as Wally Betts

and Roger Teague have hung up their racquets. In order to continue the tradition of a tennis club in Bramford, and to help ensure its future, any new and prospective members are welcomed, whatever their standard!

STEEL QUOITS

This used to be a popular village game but it died out in the 1930s. Bramford Angel and Bramford Cock both had teams, and there was a Samford League comprising of Holbrook, Claydon, Barham and Somersham. They used to play '61 UP' with teams of six players, three standing at each end, and changing ends when the first team scored 31. When Ron Earthy was a boy he used to score for the Legion, which had three beds behind the premises in The Street. Before that they played in Vicarage Meadow near the churchyard. He began to play at Parish Pond in 1932 on a three-cornered piece of land, near where the gas station is now. He was in a team that used to play against the farmhands of Jackson, the farmer. They had a set of beds up at Copenhagen, a cart track off Tye Lane.

Also in Ron Earthy's team were Brooky Lay, Rusty Lay, Ted Lay and Nobby Welham. In Jackson's team were Job Laffling, Charlie Coleman and Shrimp Coleman, among others. He played in the Bramford Cock team in the early 1930s with Walter Diaper, John Versey, Harry Scopes, Harry Reeve, Bert Sage,

Bramford Works Quoits Club, winners of the league, 1935. Left to right, standing: Bert Keeble, Ron Earthy, ?, ?, 'Hay' Plummer; seated: ?, father of Dennis Hayes, ?.

Carpet Bowls Team, 1990s. Left to right: *Peter and Jill Castle, Eric Wolton, Margaret Southgate, Gwen and Stan Boston, John Alderton, June Laws, Jim Southgate, Diana Wolton, Stella Alderton;* front: *Albert Last and John Austin.*

Stan Seadon and Walter Lay. Early in 1938 he played at the Waveney Hotel with E. Earthy, Cheffie Page, Shuddy Rattle, John Versey, Walet Lay, Monty Keeble and Frank Hewitt. They were in the Ipswich league then, with such pubs as Handford Cottage, Whitton Maypole, Westerfield Swan and, in Ipswich, Gainsborough Labour, Rosary, Westgate Ward, Bridge Ward, California and Newton Road. However, the start of the Second World War called a halt to the game.

In 1946 Ron Earthy started playing again at the White Elm in Paper Mill Lane, when some of the other players were: Dodd Rose, Ronnie Rose, Shuddy Rattle, Frank Hewitt, Jim Lingley, Jack Lambert, Sixer Lay, Harry Marsh and Jack Herring. After a few years the team broke up and Ron Earthy didn't play again until 1969 when he played for the Rosary. When the bowls ground was built on, the team moved to Castle Hill Sports Centre, but that ground was also subsequently built on, forcing a move back to Whitton Maypole. Some of the last games were played on the King George Playing-Field, and the last team was Harry Ward, Fred Beares, Nelson Plummer, Scotchmere and Wooby. The team also travelled to Butley, Hesset, Drinkstone, Hadleigh and Stoke by Nayland. From the point when they started playing independently they managed to win 13 cups out of 15, such as the singles, pairs and team in 1980.

Ron Earthy was one of the few players left, and he played until his late sixties. He passed away in 1996.

BRAMFORD CARPET BOWLS CLUB

The club was founded by Wally Betts of Leggatt Drive in December 1986 and the first AGM was held on 29 January 1987. In 2002 the officers were June Laws (chairman), Margaret Southgate (captain), Gwen and Stan Boston (secretary and treasurer), Stella Alderton, Diane Curran and Gill and Peter Castle (committee members).

The club is a member of the Suffolk Carpet Bowls Association and, in 2002, Margaret Southgate was vice-chairman of the association. She has also been chairman. The club play against other village teams in the winter league matches in the first division of the East Suffolk League. They also play in the summer league and sometimes against teams in the West Suffolk League.

There are three divisions in the East Suffolk League and Bramford won promotion to the first division in the 1999/2000 winter season. The team also takes part in the Joe Rice Cup and the Chairman's Plate each year and has reached the final.

The home matches, inter-club competitions and club practice evenings are held in the Loraine Victory Hall on Wednesdays. The away fixture matches are held in community centres and village halls.

In 2002 Margaret and Jim Southgate, who live in the village, were selected to play for the Suffolk County Team against county teams throughout England. There are also charity matches arranged by

Winners of the Suffolk Guild Striking Competition, 1969. Left to right: Cheryl Lay, Sandra Cunningham, Susan Abbott, Christine Leech, William Whittell (known as Keith), Brian 'Buster' Crouch, Alan Bridges.

Gipping Valley Ringers, December 1995. Left to right: Janet Algar, Sandra Abbs, Doreen Golding, Kelvin Dakin, Margaret Dakin, Susan Algar, Paul Abbs.

Right: *Bramford Bowls Club members, 1980s.* 1 Malcolm Parsley, 2 Hugh Lyons, 3 Roy Spratt, 4 Bob Hetherington, 5 Frank Illman, 6 Jim Thompson, 7 Basil Farrow*, 8 Ginger Challis*, 9 Gerry Mason, 10 John Godfrey, 11 ?, 12 Richard Gee*, 13 ?, 14 Norman Kearney, 15 Ivan Jordan, 16 Mark Compton, 17 Ralph Ballentine, 18 Stan Scrivener, 19 Bernie Page, 20 Doug Welham*, 21 Arthur Lockwood, 22 Alan Manthorpe, 23 Peter Smith, 24 Peter Sutton, 25 Andy Farrell, 26 Fred Woolnough, 27 Brian Barfield, 28 George Cunningham. (* Non-members)

various clubs to which Bramford are invited to enter teams. These matches are usually an all-day Sunday affair, the proceeds from which are donated to various charities.

The club holds an annual dinner, when winners of the inter-club competitions are presented with their trophies, which in 2002 was held at the Bramford Cock.

BRAMFORD BOWLS CLUB

The bowls club was opened on the Queen's Silver Jubilee, 7 June 1977, by the Bramford Carnival Queen, Nicola Billingham. The Silver Jubilee of the club was celebrated on the same day as the Queen's Golden Jubilee and the RAF kindly put on a fly-past, including the Red Arrows and Concorde! John Godfrey, Norman Kearney, Peter Laughlin, Gerry Mason, Roy Spratt and Peter Smith (the groundsman at the time of writing) are the only remaining players of the 24 founder members.

Despite being a relatively new club, the bowls team have achieved success both financially and competitively. The club started with nothing, yet the driving force of Brian Barfield, Cyril Bird's unfailing support and the voluntary work of so many people, have led to Bramford having one of the best greens and members' facilities in the county.

In 1998 the bowls team were the first club to win both the Suffolk Senior Cup and Suffolk Junior Cup trophies in the same year.

BELL-RINGERS AND RINGING

Not surprisingly, nothing is known of the bell-ringers who rang on the old five bells of St Mary's Church before augmentation in 1805. What can be said

about these men, is that they were obviously very competent change ringers. This can be surmised with some certainty because soon after the augmentation they were ringing a peal in seven different methods on the six bells that they now had to practice on. This peal occurred on 1 January 1817. If 12 years appears a long time to us now, it must be realised that the amount of free time those men had to practice and learn all the new methods of change ringing was very limited. To do this and score the peal is a remarkable achievement by any measure. The ringers involved in this peal were: T.C. Chamberlain, W. Pearce, W. Watson, G. Wood, S. Allen and J. Lewes, the whole peal taking 3 hours and 15 minutes. The peal was regarded as notable enough to be mentioned in what is regarded as the definitive book on bell-ringing, *The History and Art of Change Ringing* by Ernest Morris.

After the ringing of the extraordinary peal in 1817, the record of ringing in Bramford fades somewhat, although we can assume that the bells were still rung by the same men for a long time after that.

Bramford ringers first appear in the reports published by the Norwich Diocesan Association in 1885 with the three names of A.A. Pryke, W. Read and C. Smith being mentioned.

In 1922 another notable event occurred at Bramford. The ringers at that time had obviously been practising hard and scored a peal of Plain Bob Minor, the first by a band of local ringers for over 100 years. The ringers in this peal, rung on 25 November 1922 in 2 hours and 46 minutes were P. Southgate, Archie Bowman, Walter Brown, Arthur Rodwell, Frederick Kinsey and Edgar Rivers, who conducted the peal.

The first report of the Suffolk Guild of Ringers in 1923 records six Bramford men: Archie Bowman,

PEALS ON BRAMFORD BELLS

Date		Conductor
1 Jan. 1817	Minor 7 methods	S. Allen
11 April 1885	Minor 7 methods	J. Motts
1 Dec. 1900	Minor 7 methods	E. Rivers
23 Oct. 1909	Minor 4 methods	E. Rivers
26 June 1921	Minor 6 methods	E. Rivers
25 Nov. 1922	Plain Bob Minor	E. Rivers
10 Jan. 1926	Minor 5 methods	E. Rivers
19 Dec. 1934	Minor 7 methods	G. Blaxcell
16 Jan. 1935	Minor 4 methods	E. Rivers
30 Nov. 1935	Minor 4 methods	W. Brown
2 June 1937	Minor 7 methods	W. Brown
1 Nov. 1937	Minor 4 methods	V. Wildney
29 Nov. 1937	Minor 7 methods	A. Andrews
24 Dec. 1937	Cambridge S Minor	G. Fleming
31 Dec. 1937	Minor 4 methods	E. Rivers
18 Feb. 1938	Plain Bob Minor	V. Wildney
25 April 1938	Minor 2 methods	V. Wildney
20 June 1938	Minor 7 methods	V. Wildney
29 Aug. 1938	Minor 4 methods	S. Bowyer
9 Nov. 1953	Minor 7 methods	J. Blythe
7 Sept. 1954	Minor 8 methods	J. Blythe
28 Dec. 1964	Doubles 4 methods	N. Whittell
21 April 1966	Doubles 12 methods	N. Whittell
11 July 1966	Minor 5 methods	N. Whittell
11 Aug. 1966	Minor 8 methods	N. Whittell
22 Aug. 1966	Minor 9 methods	N. Whittell
9 Sept. 1967	Minor 7 methods	D. Derrick
31 Dec. 1967	Minor 7 methods	N. Whittell
16 Aug. 1968	Minor 7 methods	C. Groome
3 May 1969	Minor 7 methods	A. Andrews
31 May 1969	Minor 7 methods	L. Pizzey
3 Jan. 1970	Minor 3 methods	L. Pizzey
28 Sept. 1970	Minor 7 methods	J. Whittell
12 July 1971	Minor 7 methods	R. Whittell
9 Oct. 1971	Minor 5 methods	H. Egglestone
2 Jan. 1972	Minor 7 methods	N. Whittell
12 March 1972	Minor 7 methods	A. Andrews
25 May 1975	Minor 7 methods	R. Whittell
15 June 1975	Minor 7 methods	S. Pettman
16 Nov. 1975	Minor 7 methods	R. Whittell
28 Dec. 1975	Minor 7 methods	R. Whittell
13 Sept. 1976	Cambridge S Minor	R. Whittell
7 June 1977	Minor 6 methods	R. Whittell
31 July 1977	Minor 4 methods	R. Whittell
28 Jan. 1979	Doubles 4 methods	P. Archer
13 April 1980	Doubles 9 methods	A. Mayle
21 Sept. 1980	Minor 7 methods	R. Whittell
5 July 1981	Minor 4 methods	C. Pegg
29 July 1981	Minor 5 methods	R. Whittell
4 April 1982	Doubles 42 methods	T. Bailey
26 Sept. 1982	Doubles 42 methods	P. Archer
22 April 1983	Plain Bob Minor	S. Pettman
21 Aug. 1983	Minor 5 methods	A. Mayle
31 Dec. 1983	Minor 7 methods	C. Pegg
14 July 1984	Doubles 8 methods	P. Archer
3 Aug. 1984	Minor 16 methods	S. Pettman
19 Feb. 1985	Doubles 42 methods	T. Bailey
27 Sept. 1986	Minor 6 methods	D. Salter
22 March 1987	Minor 10 methods	D. Salter
22 Dec. 1990	Surprise Minor 7 methods	S. Pettman
3 Aug. 1993	Minor 3 methods	G. Pipe
17 April 1995	Minor 7 methods	D. Salter
29 May 1995	Minor 6 methods	S. Pettman
28 May 2000	Minor 6 methods	S. Pettman
27 April 2001	Surprise Minor 7 methods	P. Waterfield

Walter Brown, Arthur Rodwell, Percy Southgate, A.E. Sewell and Albert Gynn. A snapshot of ringers at Bramford up to the outbreak of the Second World War shows the same ringers as in 1923 with the addition of E.E. Grimes. In 1939 they had reduced to just two ringers: the Revd Dr A.W. Evans and E.E. Grimes. The first report after the war records Ernest Grimes as the only remaining ringer in Bramford.

When the wartime ban on ringing was lifted in 1943, and due to the enthusiasm of Mr J. Burch, a teacher at Bramford School, some young members of the church were taught to ring by Mr J. Jennings of Rushmere. From 1945 until the early '50s, with help from other ringers, the bells were rung on most Sundays and Thursday evenings, as well as for the funeral of Mr Harry Fiske and the Coronation of Queen Elizabeth II.

Revd Ronald Christian arrived in Bramford in 1956 and set about getting the bells ringing once more. Young people were trained by the few locals with ringing skills and they all rang together for a few years until ringing faded at Bramford again.

In the early 1960s the Master of the South East District of the Suffolk Guild, Howard Egglestone, began teaching a band of ringers at Henley and encouraged Neville and Roger Whittell to restart a band at Bramford. The report for 1964 shows ten names in the village: M. Howes, R. Southgate, A.R. Walters, M.H. Whittell, N. Whittell, S. Christian, M. Kinsey, M. Hore and R. Lockwood.

Ringing at Bramford at that time rapidly assumed the dimensions and activities of the village youth club. Within four years of the start of the new band, 26 names were listed under Bramford in the Suffolk Guild report.

In 1966, Neville Whittell, who with his brother Roger had been instrumental in starting the new band, signalled his intention to stand down. Neville and Roger thought that Robert Southgate was the right person for the job, and he became the captain.

As the experience and confidence of the ringers at Bramford blossomed, it was decided to begin entering a team, or teams, for the Suffolk Guild Striking Competition. The band had at this time incorporated the then assistant curate, the Revd Lawrence Pizzey, an experienced and highly competent ringer. At Ashbocking in 1968 a Bramford team won the competition for the first time, ringing 240 changes against 11 other teams. The Bramford team comprised: Robert Southgate, Martin Whittell, Lawrence Pizzey, Neville Whittell, Roger Whittell and Simon Christian.

As a lighter relief from ringing the bells in the tower at Bramford, tune ringing on handbells was started. This was generally held after ringing for evensong on Sundays, and had the advantage that it could be carried out in the warmth of the home of one or other of the ringers.

After much fund-raising, inspired and organised by Robert Southgate, enough money was raised to purchase a set of 13 handbells, made by Mears and Co. of London. These were used regularly, especially at Christmas when the ringers would tour the village ringing carols and collecting for a charity. All the pubs were visited and it became a tradition to ring at the Cock, and then move on to the church to ring for the midnight service. The Gipping Valley Ringers group in 2003 is the direct descendent from the tune-ringing activities that began in the 1960s at Bramford, using loaned handbells initially and later the 13 bells purchased with the funds.

Peals, the ringing of bells lasting about three hours, are generally regarded as a measure of the competence and prowess of the ringers taking part. The ringers at Bramford became competent enough to ring peals together either at Bramford or occasionally at other towers. The first peal on six bells by the new ringers at Bramford was rung at Hintlesham on 2 October 1965. Because of the absence for repair of the tenor at Bramford, this was considered to be the best option, as the weight of the tenor at Hintlesham is similar to Bramford. The ringers on this occasion were Simon Christian, Alan Walters, Roy Lockwood, Roger Whittell, Robert Southgate, and Neville Whittell. Rung in 2 hours and 45 minutes, this was the first peal rung by Simon, Alan, Roy and Robert who had begun training on the re-forming of the band in 1963. A peal was completed in 1967 to commemorate the 150th anniversary of the first recorded peal on the Bramford bells. It was a significant achievement because the peal was rung using the same methods as in 1817, including some unusual techniques that are no longer in use.

The vicar, Ronald Christian, was the instigator of the resurgence of bell-ringing in Bramford, and it is of interest to note that during his incumbency all the members of his family were taught to ring, and all completed at least one quarter peal containing 1,260 changes. The vicar tried once himself but decided that all this rope waving was not for him. A total of 65 peals have been rung on the bells in Bramford.

Not every fact regarding the bells and ringers of Bramford has been recorded and not every person given as much credit as perhaps is due. Tower captains continued to be elected and approved by the vicar, thus ensuring that the tuition of ringing has also continued. Thus the bells have rung out over Bramford for more than 40 years, and hopefully will ring out to celebrate the centenary of the rehanging in 2006.

Tower Captains since 1963
Neville Whittell, Robert Southgate, Roy Lockwood, Kelvin Dakin, Stephen Christian, Roger Whittell, David Blomfield, Roger Whittell and Stanley Harris.

BRAMFORD LOCAL HISTORY GROUP

The group was started in 1994 as a result of the interest of two local historians, Beryl Sims and Terry Mayes, who became secretary and chairman respectively. Other founding members were: Bernard Purbrick (treasurer), Wendy Hall, Bernard Petch, Jill Mullins and George Dedman.

The first meetings were held in the Parish Room, but by the end of the second year numbers had grown substantially, so the group moved across the car park to St Mary's Church Room, which holds up to 60 people, and have remained there ever since, as it is also possible to offer refreshments at this venue.

Membership in 2003 stands at more than 50 and is growing steadily each year. Not all members live in Bramford, several live in surrounding villages, and others travel from Ipswich and Felixstowe.

There is a varied programme of talks, from archaeology to automobiles, and each season one or two visits are made to places of local historical interest. The group has also published several small booklets, a calendar, postcards and tea towels, all of which have boosted solvency and been enthusiastically received.

The officers at the time of writing are: Brian Blomfield (chairman), Les Beckett (vice-chairman), Beryl Sims (secretary) and Bernard Purbrick (treasurer). This book is the Local History Group's most ambitious project yet.

BALLROOM DANCING

Pat Lait first started her classes for ballroom and Latin dancing in the Loraine Victory Hall in the early 1970s. Classes are held every Tuesday, with children at 5.30p.m. followed by adults. Over the years her pupils have won many trophies.

TREFOIL GUILD

The Trefoil Guild was started in 1943 for ex-Guiders. Membership in 2003 stands at 21.

BRAMFORD ART CLUB

The art club was started in the early 1980s by Alec Pryke, one-time chairman of the Parish Council, who died in 1986. Several people interested in painting and drawing used to meet in a room at the Methodist chapel. Stan Howard and Paul Pinkney, both men no longer with us, were two of the original members. Gradually the numbers grew and in 1989 the club moved to the Parish Room, where they still meet every Wednesday morning.

Several exhibitions have been held by the club. These took place in the church, in the school, at the Robert Cross Hall in Ipswich and in the Parish Room. A lot of paintings have been sold, with local subjects being the most popular.

The club does not have a tutor, but the members help and advise one another. Membership in 2003 stands at 14.

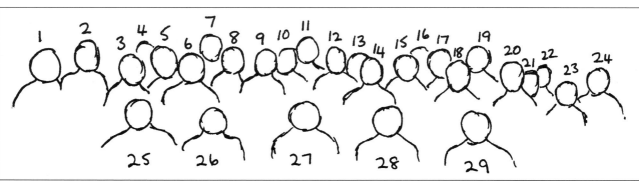

Members of Bramford History Group at the Christmas Social, December 2002. Included in the picture are:
1 Maureen Blomfield, 2 Dick Pegg, 3 Sylvia Harvey, 4 Hazel Mayhew, 5 Dianne Curran, 6 Val Ellis, 7 Derek Mayhew, 8 Jean Austin, 9 Sue Maskell, 10 Caleta Thomas, 11 Barry Earthy, 12 Denis Knott, 13 Don Mayes, 14 Arthur Taber, 15 Janet Jackaman, 16 Yvonne Earthy, 17 Ray Child, 18 Peter Jackaman, 19 Michael Earthy, 20 Derek Porter, 21 Sheila Heath, 22 Carol Kerridge, 23 Jean Clarke, 24 Peter Clarke, 25 Brian Ward, 26 Mary Ward, 27 Brian Blomfield (chairman), 28 Beryl Sims (secretary), 29 Les Beckett (vice-chairman).

SIX

FOR KING (OR QUEEN) AND COUNTRY

LIEUTENANT FRANK B. HENDERSON, RN, DSO

During the late-nineteenth and early-twentieth centuries the Henderson family lived at Riverhill on the Bramford Road. *White's Directory* of 1892 names the occupier as Mrs Henderson and in *Kelly's Directory* of 1896 Henry Henderson, Inspector of Schools, is named. He was one of the first members of Bramford Parish Council. The Misses Henderson lived at Riverhill until the 1920s.

Lt Henderson served in the Army on several campaigns in Africa. An article in *The Idler* in 1898 described his experiences as a travelling commissioner in the Gold Coast Hinterland. He departed from Accra in November 1896 and travelled inland on a goodwill trip with his companion, Mr George Ferguson, a column of hussars and native carriers.

Having travelled for some time through forests, they emerged on to the plain where they stayed for a few days with the King of Nkoranza, before crossing the River Volta, which took five hours. Inland trouble was brewing between the local tribes and 'Sofas' – a term used to describe marauding horsemen. Many derelict villages were seen on the way to visit the King of Wa who was grateful to have the support of the British Empire. En route the men suffered from dysentery, risked being shot with poisoned arrows and were attacked by about 1,000 Sofas which led to Mr Ferguson being injured. It was estimated that at least 400 of the enemy were killed, as well as two of Henderson's own men. Following a 'palaver', or talk, between the rival factions, Henderson was briefly taken prisoner, though Ferguson was not so lucky, having been decapitated. Having experienced terrible deprivation and shocking sights, Henderson finally made it to the coast on 14 June 1897. He wrote his report about the trip on 1 October 1897 whilst staying in Bramford.

WILLIAM HARDWICK

William was born in Bramford in 1872; his parents were Joseph (Parish Clerk and church sexton) and Maria who lived in Church Green. He sent a letter to his parents just before the Relief of Ladysmith in 1900, during the second Boer War.

Dear Mother and Father,
Just a few lines hoping you all are well. I am quite well, and I wish Lizzie luck and happiness. We have a hard

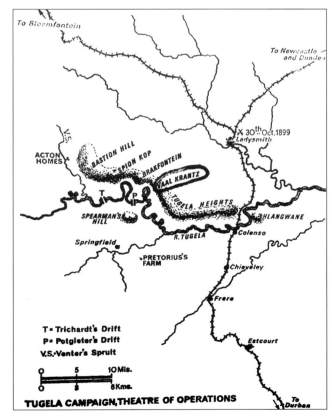

Map of the area where William Hardwick was fighting the Boers.

Killed in action (First World War):

Staff: Col. H.N. Packard   S. Gooding
      Lt H. Row   I.E. Row

Men: H. Driver   M. Emsden

G. Goodall	A. Hogger	A. Keeble
H.G. Keeble	H.W. Keeble	W. Lay
E. Lewis	H. Lockwood	W. Miller
B. Moates	F. Scrivener	W. Scrivener
T. Spurling	C. Turner	F. Versey

Rolls of Service:

Staff: C. Barfoot   A. Cherry

W. Diaper	W. Hitchcock	C. Lease
C. Ling	C.T. Packard	W. Pike
F. Shepherd	D. Sizer	W. Taylor

Men: J. Arnold   A. Benstead

F. Benstead	H. Bloomfield	A. Boon
W. Bumpstead	A. Chaplin	R. Church
A. Cocker	J. Cutter	A. Driver
F. Emsden	T. Finter	F. Folly
A. Francis	J. Francis	H. Garnham
J. Garrod	F. Giles	G. Giles
W. Giles	W. Goodall	A. Gynn
C. Gynn	J. Hardwick	J. Hardwick
F. Hill	A. Keeble	C. Keeble
J. Keeble	W. Keeble	W. Keeble
A. Keen	P. Keen	S. Keen
F. Kinsey	W. Lambert	G. Lay
W. Lay	A. Leeks	H. Lewis
R. Lewis	M. Lloyd	F. Lockwood
H. Lockwood	W. Lockwood	F. Mahoney
R. Mann	C. Miller	E. Minns
W. Minns	E. Moore	W. Munnings
B. Page	C. Page	A. Parker
C. Parker	C. Payne	D. Pilbrough
J. Porter	A. Pryke	C. Pryke
C. Rattle	A. Rodwell	W. Rowland

B. Ruffles
C. Ruffles
T. Scopes
F. Scott
A. Snowling
S. Snowling
J. Slapp
T. Spurling
W. Stone
J. Stowe
E. Taylor
W. Taylor
A. Thain
W. Thain
F. Tricker
G. Wallace
B. Whight
H. Whight
W. Worledge

The memorial to members of Packard's workforce.

Above: The memorial to those who died in the Second World War. It can be seen on the south wall of Bramford Church.

Below: The names on the Second World War memorial. The three men marked * are noted on the plaque below the memorial in the photograph (left).

BARFIELD	Jack*	Pte Suffolk Regt
GIRLING	Lancelot	Gunner R.A.
GREEN	Clifford	Pte Cambs Regt
HAMMOND	Neville	RFN Rifle BDE
HAYES	William	LAC RAF
JENNINGS	Ernest	AB Royal Navy
KEEBLE	John*	Pte Suffolk Regt
LAUGHLIN	William	AB Sgt RAF
LAY	Arthur	Pte RAMC
LUCAS	Donald	Pte RAMC
MITCHELL	Charles	AB Royal Navy
MOSS	Olaf	Pte Suffolk Regt
RUFFLES	Frank*	Spr. RE
SADD	George	Tpr 11th Hussars
SEELEY	Edgar	Pte Cambs Regt
SMITH	Frank	ARP
WORLEDGE	Frederick	Sgt RAF

battle to fight in a day or two, we are going through to Ladysmith no matter what the cost – we are anxious for it to be over, there will be a lot fall, but I hope we shall succeed to relieve those poor fellows shut up there, we are face to face with our enemy, and we mean to do our duty, to a man, we can see the Boers from here and they are in a very strong position. Don't worry for me, I feel if I get through this it will be a good step toward the return to Old England. God Bless You All and my poor wife, if I fall try and comfort her, we must do our duty and fight like British soldiers as our country has a lot at stake, and we have an artful and deceitful enemy to cope with, but beat them we must and will. We hear there are nearly 50,000 to fight here, they are stronger than us. The paper came in handy I had none, we have never received anything from England yet, only a small piece of pudding, but we are not near the railway now, so its hard to get things to us, but its worse for the poor fellows in Ladysmith.

Walter is sending a letter as well and he is all right, and sends his best respects to you all. Give my love to all the girls, and tell them to accept this as a letter to all, I was pleased with yours today, the heat is 114 in the shade today.

Goodbye this time from your affectionate son William Hardwick x x x x x x x x x
Tell Joe to be a good boy.

William did not return. He was killed in action at Spion Kopp, South Africa, on 5 February 1900.

The memorial to those who died in the First World War. It can be seen on the south wall of Bramford Church.

WAR MEMORIALS

Bramford has three memorials to men of the village who have served in the Forces during the twentieth century. Two of these are on the south wall in the church and were erected in honour of those who gave their lives in the First and Second World Wars. The third is in the offices of Scott's Fertilizers in Paper Mill Lane and records the names of the men from the factory, which was then Packards, who joined the Armed Forces.

The first memorial is inscribed with the 54 names of those who perished in the First World War:

CAMERON	Peter	Capt. M.C. R.G.A
CHAPLIN	George	Sergt. 1st Suffolk
COBBOLD	Rowland	Lieut. R.F.A.
COOK	Thomas	Pte 10th Royal Fusiliers
DRIVER	Harry	Pte Royal West Kent
ELMER	T. Ebiner	Pte Suffolk
EMSDEN	Maurice	Pte 9th Suffolk
GARROD	Arthur	Pte 1st Suffolk
GARROD	William	Pte 1st Suffolk
GARROD	Roger	Cpl 2nd Suffolk
GASKIN	James	Pte 1st Suffolk
GOODALL	George	Pte Royal Fusiliers
HARDWICK	William	Pte Royal West Kent
HART	Frank	Pte 7th Suffolk
HART	Frederick	Pte 17th Australian I.F.
HAYES	Dennis	Pte R.A.M.C.
HAYES	William	Pte 2nd Suffolk
HOGGER	Albert	Pte 2nd Lincoln
HOOD	Malcolm	Pte 2nd Suffolk
HUGHES	Alex. A.	Capt. S. Wales Bdrs
KEEBLE	Alfred	Pte 9th Royal Fusiliers
KEEBLE	Robert	Pte Queens West Surrey
KEEBLE	Frederick	Pte 11th Canadian Inf.
KEEBLE	Harry	Pte 13th Royal Fusiliers
LAWES	Alfred	Pte 9th East Surrey
LAY	James	Pte 11th Suffolk
LAY	Joseph	Pte 2nd North Hants
LAY	Frederick	Pte 9th Suffolk
LAY	William	Pte 1/24th London (Queens)
LAY	Oliver	Pte 1st Suffolk
LEACH	James	Pte 1st Suffolk
LEWIS	Edward	Pte Royal West Kent
LOCKWOOD	Harry	Pte 12th East Yorks

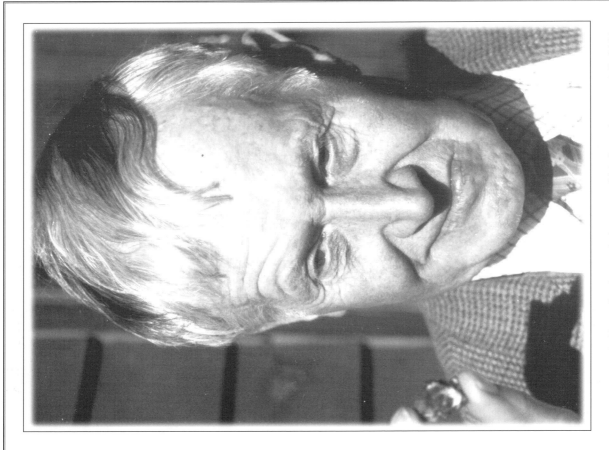

Dennis Page holding the shrapnel that pierced his lung (see page 84), 2003.

Bert Keeble in his Home Guard uniform, c.1940.

The ARP Wardens, Second World War. Left to right, back row: ?, ?, ?, Dolly Keeble, Margaret Hurry, Winney Lingley, ?, Arthur 'Puddy' Allum; middle: ?, Ruby Hibbard, Mabel Bales, Peggy Coupland, Cora Francis, Nelly Banyard, Muriel Hurry; front: ?, ?, ?.

MATHER	William	Pte 4th Suffolk
MILLER	William	Pte 1st Suffolk
MOORE	Alan	Pte 7th S. Staffordsh.
MOORE	Frederick	L/Cpl 7th Suffolk
MURRELL	Alfred	Gunner R.G.A.
PRYKE	Arthur	Pte 11th Lincoln
PRYKE	Ernest	Pte 2nd Suffolk
PRYKE	Frederick	Cpl 2nd Suffolk
PRYKE	William	Pte 2nd Suffolk
PRYKE	Victor	Pte R.A.S.C.
READ	Bertie	Pte 6th Essex
ROWLAND	Charles	Pte Australian I.F.
RUFFLES	Ernest	Cpl 2nd Suffolk
SANDERSON	Richard	1st C Petty Officer R.N.R.
SEAGER	Charles	Sergt. 2nd Lincoln
SHEPPARD	Gerald	Pte 4th Grenadier Guards
SHEPPARD	Stanley	Pte 3rd Grenadier Guards
STEWARD	Percy	Pte 1st Suffolk
SPURLING	Thomas	Pte Kings L'pool Rifles
SQUIRRELL	Hanshard	Gunner R.G.A.
VERSEY	Francis	Pte 23rd Middlesex

The second memorial is inscribed with the names of 17 men who died during the Second World War *(see page 80)*. The names on these memorials are read out each year on Remembrance Sunday.

The third memorial was designed by Miss Packard and is painted in the form of a triptych with doors that close to protect the painting. There are portraits of some of the 21 men who died and on the inside of the left-hand door is a soldier in uniform, while on the inside of the right-hand door is a knight in shining armour. The names can be seen on page 80.

Little is known about many of the men on the memorials. However, some information can be gleaned about others:

George Rivers Chaplin was born in Bramford, son of Fred and Alice who lived in The Street. He was killed in action in 1917, aged 23.

Harry Driver was born in Bramford, son of Mrs Ada Driver of Papermill Cottage; he was killed in action in 1916, aged 20.

Maurice William Emsden attended Bramford School; he was killed in action in 1916.

Arthur James Garrod (Chum) was also born in Bramford, son of Mr W. and Mrs M. Garrod who lived opposite the butcher's shop (now the chemist) in The Street. He was killed in action in 1915, aged 18.

William Garrod (Willie) was the brother of Arthur; he was killed in action in 1915, aged 23. William and Arthur both worked for the railway, and their names are on a plaque at Liverpool Street Station in London.

William Hardwick was the fifth child of John and Emily (née Hood) at Runcton in 1882. He was killed in action in 1918, aged 35.

William Ernest Hayes was born in Bramford. He died of his wounds in 1916.

Albert Frederick Hogger was born in Sproughton, but worked at Bramford factory. He was killed in action in 1917, aged 32.

Malcolm Hood was the son of Charles and Sarah Hood who died of his wounds in 1916, aged 20. He is commemorated on his parents' gravestone in Bramford churchyard.

Alfred Keeble was the son of Alfred and Mary Ann Keeble and died of his wounds in 1916, aged 35.

Robert Keeble, brother of Alfred, was killed in action in 1917, aged 37.

Harry Keeble was born in Bramford and worked at Bramford factory. He was killed in action in 1918.

James Ernest Lay was born in Bramford; he died of his wounds in 1917.

Joseph Lay was born in Bramford and was killed in action in 1918.

William Lay was born in Bramford, son of Mr and Mrs Fred Lay of Parish Pond. He was killed in action in 1916, aged 29.

Oliver Lay was the son of Ambrose Lay and was born in Bramford. He was killed in action in 1915, aged 19.

Edward Golly Lewis was the son of Mr and Mrs G. Lewis of Rose Cottage, Bullen Lane, Bramford. He worked at Bramford factory. He died of his wounds in 1916, aged 33.

Harry (Henry) Lockwood was born in Bramford, worked at Bramford factory, and was killed in action in 1917.

Allan Moore was not born in the village, but he lived in Bramford before the war. He was killed in action in 1917.

Frederick Moore was a pupil at Bramford School. He died of his wounds in 1915.

Alfred Murrell was born in Bramford; he died in 1916.

Arthur Edward Pryke was born in Bramford and was killed in action in 1918.

Frederick Pryke was born in Bramford and was killed in action in 1915.

William Edward Pryke was born in Bramford and was killed in action in 1916.

Victor Reginald Pryke was the son of William and Alice Pryke of Works Lane. He died in 1917, aged 18.

Bertie Read was the son of Charles and Rosa Read, he died in 1918, aged 42.

Ernest James Ruffles was born in Bramford and died of his wounds in 1915.

Percy William Steward was born in Bramford and was killed in action in 1916, aged 23.

Francis Joseph Versey was born in Bramford, the son of Henry and Susannah of Suvla Cottages in Ravens Lane. He was killed in action in 1918, aged 19.

There is a single memorial in the church to Edward Turner Packard who died in South Nigeria in 1910, aged 42, having previously served in Pagets Horse in the South African War from 1899 to 1900, and then becoming Solicitor and Attorney General in Sierra Leone from 1902 to 1908. Another memorial is dedicated to:

Alfred Farrar who was lost at sea Nov. 28th 1917 through enemy action on his way home from West Africa where for many years he faithfully served God, his King and his Country.

Ernest John Jennings was the son of Effie Jennings who lived in The Street. He served on HMS *Achates* and died in December 1942, aged 19, when the ship was attacked and sunk.

Dennis Page served with the First Battalion Black Watch during the Korean War (1950–53). In November 1952 Dennis' company was notified that a fellow company needed extra support having become surrounded by the Koreans at The Hook, a key ridge overlooking the Samichon Valley some 30 miles north of Seoul. On their way to mount a rescue the company came under very heavy mortar fire. Dennis and two colleagues immediately dived for the ground where a shell exploded beside them. Dennis was seriously injured. A piece of shrapnel tore a 6-inch hole in his back and pierced his left lung. He was given immediate first aid and was then transferred to a nearby American MASH Unit (Mobile Army Surgical Hospital). Dennis believes that here the Americans saved his life. He finally ended up in the general hospital in Kure in Japan before returning to the UK to the Queen's Barracks of the Black Watch in Perth. Here he served the rest of his time. On leaving the Army, Dennis volunteered for another four years in the Army Emergency Reserve.

In 1993 Dennis was employed as a gardening instructor with the occupational therapy unit at St Clement's Hospital, Ipswich, where he was working with disabled and handicapped people. On 1 March Dennis woke up to find he was bringing up blood at various intervals, and so he was rushed off to hospital. The cause? That same piece of shrapnel which had pierced his back and his left lung nearly 41 years earlier. The wound had not become gangrenous because the white-hot metal of the shrapnel was sterile. It was removed and Dennis, still resident in Bramford, remains fit and well at the time of writing. His piece of shrapnel will always be a reminder of his service with the Black Watch in Korea.

SEVEN

❧⊙❧

FOR THE GOOD OF THE COMMUNITY

EASTERN STAR

Residents of Bramford will probably have heard of the Eastern Star and might have wondered what it was all about. It was in fact a Friendly Society named Eastern Star Provident Association.

Friendly societies came into being around 1830 and met secretively in a similar manner to Masonic lodges, which were formed earlier. The purpose of the societies was to help members financially in times of sickness, distress and death, and to pay doctors and undertakers for their services. In the event of misfortune, benefits also supplemented decreased earnings. During the nineteenth century many destitute people were, at death, buried in a pauper's grave.

In 1875, 22 members formed a new branch, registered as the Star of Bramford. In the early days meetings were held at the White Elm in Paper Mill Lane. Isaac Meakings, who lived at Claydon, was elected its first secretary.

In its first year the Star of Bramford had an income from members of £19.8s.2d. Expenditure was £8.4s.4d., which included a 3s.8d. levy paid towards the chief district secretary's salary of £19.12s.3d. In Bramford the treasurer held £7.18s.7d., and the bank balance was £3.5s.3d.

In 1879, William Diaper, who lived in The Street,

Eastern Star Provident Association in the garden of the Cock, c.1928. Left to right: ?, ?, ?, Frank Moss, George Beckett (holding banner), J. Pilbro (chairman), Robert Francis (branch secretary), W. Leveritt (association secretary), 'Cabby' Scopes (holding banner), Robert Clover.

85

Eastern Star Provident Association members. Left to right, standing: *Harold Double, ? Kinsey, R. Kinsey, H. 'Bert' Frost, ?, ?, ?, Brother H. Fenn, Alan Day (secretary);* seated: *Alf Gooch MM, Dennis Ford Br 29, William Taylor, Alec Pryke, Les Beckett (chairman), Brother Jennings IFSC, S. Pryke.*

Presentation by Eastern Star Provident Association of a seat along the river bank in Fraser Road, 1980s.
Left to right: *Tim Curran, Roy Scruby, Graham Jones, Maureen Renton (Parish Council Clerk), Alec Pryke, Ivy Beckett, Allistair Renton (chairman of Parish Council), Les Beckett, Harry Double.*

became secretary, and it was probably at this time that the meetings moved to the Cock Inn. The branch now had funds of almost £20. Rituals, such as secret handshakes, recognition door knocks and doorway peep-holes would have been used before entry to meetings was granted. White and black balls placed in a box were used for voting purposes, hence the term 'being black balled'. Coloured sashes and collars were also part of the meeting routine.

The Eastern Star Provident Association was founded in 1857 and first met in Great Yarmouth where the annual district meeting of all branches was held. By 1896 the meeting of delegates had transferred to the Rose and Crown on Norwich Road, Ipswich, and W.V. Leverett was elected as chief secretary. William Diaper attended as the Bramford representative.

In 1915, 36 years later, Bill Diaper was still the Bramford secretary, but his address in the annual accounts read 'near the Cock Inn'. The annual report on the Star of Bramford was very impressive; Mr Diaper had paid £95.10s.10d. in sickness benefits to 59 members and was also delving into mortgages. He had £1,125 on loan and £92 in the bank. Brother Diaper was elected to the chief committee of the association, a position of some esteem.

In the years following the First World War numerous returning soldiers joined the benevolence of the Star of Bramford branch. Membership, including a juvenile class, became very popular and, by the mid-1920s, annual church parades took place on hospital days. Forming up in the yard of the Cock Inn, where Mr and Mrs Tom Lloyd were landlords, members, families and children walked behind a huge blue and yellow ritual banner, carried by six members wearing regalia. Some of the members were: J. Pilbro (chairman), Godfrey Francis (secretary), Robert Clover, George Beckett, Frank Moss and Cabby Scopes (standard-bearers). Alf Gooch, Bert Frost and others also attended, as did the chief secretary W. Leverett.

Each summer an annual tea party for juveniles was provided on the meadow at the foot of Vicarage Lane. By the 1930s children were taken instead to Felixstowe by double-decker bus where they would spend two hours of Saturday afternoon before being gathered for tea and cakes on the first-floor flat roof of Trents Café. In around 1935 Tom Lloyd moved to become publican at the Half Moon in Walton and so, before reaching Felixstowe, the committee had an excuse to call and see him for a top-up.

Members of the branch who were sick and had called on the club with a doctor's certificate would have to be in their homes by 6.30p.m. Anybody seen outside by Billy Moss after that hour would be docked part of their sickness benefit. There were no female members of the branch at this time.

By the 1950s younger members were encouraged to take part in the branch management and Alf Gooch MC, Bill Taylor, Alec Pryke and Bert Frost were still playing an active role. Dennis Ford, who had returned from the Forces, joined the management committee, which still met quarterly at the Cock where Fred Page was the host. Having joined as a juvenile in 1930, Les Beckett was the next to be invited to join the management team where he was greeted by Harold Double. By the late 1970s the older members had departed and, when Alec Pryke stepped down, Les moved to the chair in order to keep the branch active. However, membership could not be maintained.

There were five other active branches at this time: Butley, Hintlesham, Ipswich, Somersham and Tunstall. After much persuasion these groups were coerced into becoming a single branch. Soon after, meetings took place in the Loraine Victory Hall to merge with the Friendly Foresters. Later an official and rather unique ceremony, chaired by Brother Beckett, was held in the packed Methodist chapel when, after discussion between the Foresters High Chief Ranger and his officials, Norman Sewell and members of the Parish Council, the Bramford branch was accepted into the Ancient Order of Foresters.

BRAMFORD CHARITIES

In the days before State benefits it was generally the responsibility of the wealthy members of society to help those in need. The first evidence of this in Bramford is the will of William Acton of 1705 in which he left £200 for the purchase of land. With this money a small farm was purchased at Mill Street, Stowupland, and the profits from the rent used to help the poor and needy of Bramford.

Francis Brooke left £5 a year for the poor of the parish and, in the will of Miss Penelope Leggatt of Bramford House, who died in 1902, a bequest of £200 was left in trust, with the income to be used for the poor widows of the village at Christmas. She also left £200 in trust with income to the church expenses fund, £50 to Bramford Coal Club and £50 to Bramford Clothing Club.

A letter from the vicar, Revd Payne, to Sir Lambton Loraine at Christmas 1905 stated that all applicants for the charity had received 4s. each from the Leggatt bequest and a share of about 80lbs of beef supplied from the Vicarage. Some of the poorest had also received ¼ton of coal, a gift first started by General Russell, tenant of Bramford Hall. Also Mr Packard gave 1s. to every widow who called at Grove House.

The Eustace Broke Loraine Charity was founded by Sir Percy Loraine in 1935 in memory of his brother Eustace. It helps with the purchase of text books for children of Bramford who have been educated at the village school and who wish to go on to further education.

In 1953 the Bramford Charity Trustees arranged an outing for the pensioners in the village to celebrate the Coronation. This proved so popular

BRAMFORD

Dear Sir or Madam

The time has arrived when the question. "Is a memorial Hall needed in Bramford"? has to be definitely settled.

A PUBLIC MEETING will be held at the SCHOOL on MONDAY next May 17th at 8.0P.M. to consider the financial position, and determine what further steps shall be taken

In the meantime, will you be good enough to use every endeavour to insure that the meeting will be well attended, so that the fullest opinion may be obtained?

Yours faithfully

SIGNED —

H. FISKE }
W. HURRY } Hon. Secs

MAY 12th 1920.

A letter sent to parishioners in 1920.

The Victory Hall, c.1930. (From the Gillson Collection, SROI JI6/42)

that a small committee was formed to raise funds for it to become an annual event. In 1959 the Old People's Outing and Comfort Fund was started to provide help and entertainment for retired people in the village. Money was raised in various ways, mainly through the flower and vegetable show held each summer and jumble sales. The money was spent on an outing followed by tea in the Loraine Victory Hall. By the end of the twentieth century, State care for retired people had become more readily available and fewer residents needed to take advantage of the charity.

In 1963 the inaugural meeting of the Silver Threads Club took place and was attended by 49 men and women. By 1977 the number had grown to 63 and meetings were held on the first and third Wednesdays of each month. Jumble sales and Christmas bazaars were organised to raise money, and proved successful both financially and socially. The secretary was Mrs Kinsey. The Silver Threads Club ceased in the 1980s.

Due to recent improvements in the care and help provided for the elderly, at the time of writing discussions are under way regarding the possibility of amalgamating all of Bramford's charities for the benefit of the young people of the village.

LORAINE VICTORY HALL

In May 1920 a letter was circulated in the village by Harry Fiske and Wilfred Hurry announcing a public meeting to be held at the school in consideration of the provision of a Memorial Hall.

Following fund-raising in the parish, the organisers approached the Loraine family with regard to the siting of the hall. By 1923 the village had raised funds of £826.3s.4d. and in August that year Dame Frederica Loraine and her son Percy gave the land in Ship Lane on which the hall was built. The Bramford men who signed the contract were Albert Firman, Harry Fiske, Robert Francis, Harold Garnham, Wilfred Hurry, Willie Mills and Charles Packard. The new building was called the Victory Hall and was officially opened on 7 March 1924.

Some 12 years later Sir Percy Loraine and his sister Isaura gave land adjoining the hall for a term of 99 years at a peppercorn rent. Just before his death in 1961, Sir Percy Loraine arranged to grant the freehold of the property to the village with the Parish Council as custodian trustees.

By the late 1960s it became evident that the hall needed to be refurbished and, following more fund-raising, a new extended hall was opened in 1974.

Over the decades the hall has been used for almost every social occasion: dances, parties, weddings, meetings, exhibitions, shows and even a funeral. As we enter the twenty-first century, talks are again under way regarding the refurbishment, or possible replacement, of the hall to cater for new leisure activities.

LOCAL GOVERNMENT

During the Anglo-Saxon era, the control of the village was probably in the hands of a local chief, but by the time of the Norman Conquest all land was considered to belong to the King. He granted small units to faithful friends or followers, usually in the form of a manor, and in return his subjects had to provide the finance for a fully-equipped knight to help fight wars.

The lord of the manor had almost total control over the people on the manor, holding regular courts at which complaints would be heard and wrong-doers punished. More serious crimes, that carried greater punishments, would have been heard by Hundred Courts.

Following the Black Death in the mid-fourteenth century and the Peasants' Revolt of 1381, the manorial system started to break down. Although manorial courts continued for many decades, they were used less to control behaviour and more as a record of land sales and exchanges.

Opening of the Bramford War Memorial

"VICTORY HALL,"

On FRIDAY, MARCH 7th, 1924,

At 7.30 p.m.

Hymn—"O God, our help."

Prayer - - - By the VICAR.

Address - - - By the CHAIRMAN.

Financial Report - By the Hon. Treasurer of the Fund, A. TOWNSHEND COBBOLD, Esq.

Vote of thanks to the Hon. Treasurer and Hon. Sec. - - By H. FISKE, Esq.

Song - - - Mr. ALIX CLAXTON, A.R.C.M.

"The Opening" By the HIGH SHERIFF OF SUFFOLK.

Vote of thanks to the High Sheriff General READE, C.B., C.M.G. Capt. C. T. PACKARD, M.C. Mr. R. FRANCIS, J.P.

Song - - - Mr. ALIX CLAXTON, A.R.C.M.

Vote of thanks to the Chairman - Capt. CLAVERING FISON. Miss LORAINE. Mr. E. A. GOOCH.

Vote of thanks to the Building Committee and their Adviser, Mr. W. G. Mills Rev. W. H. LILLIE. Mr. W. WOLTON.

NATIONAL ANTHEM.

Programme for the opening of the new hall.

Above: *The opening of the newly refurbished and enlarged Loraine Victory Hall, 1974. Alec and Vera Pryke are front left with Canon Christian standing behind them. George Mills is second from the right in the front row and Joyce Manning and Allistair Renton are in the background. The names of the others are not known.*

Left: *The first accounts for the hall.*

Below: *The first council-houses in Acton Road.*
(SROI K/PF/063)

Much of the everyday running of the parish often fell to the Church and its churchwardens and, in 1572, a new officer was established known as the overseer of the poor. Because of the continuing problem of wandering vagabonds during the sixteenth century, much of the control passed into the hands of national rather than regional government. Also responsible for the enforcement of law and order were Justices of the Peace (JPs) who became increasingly powerful during the eighteenth century. In national elections most of the parishioners would have voted to support the candidate of the lord of the manor and in 1705 the parish had a majority of Tory voters. In 1710 Bramford had 29 electors eligible to vote but by 1790 this had been reduced to nine.

Following considerable reorganisation of local government during the Victorian era, a Local Government Act was passed in 1888 which placed much of the administration of county matters into the hands of the newly-formed County Council or, in the case of Suffolk, the newly-formed East and West Suffolk County Councils. This council had charge of surveying, road building and bridges, weights and measures, finance, and later health, education, policing, archives and libraries.

In 1894 further legislation created District and Parish Councils. The District Council, at first known as Gipping Rural DC and later Mid Suffolk DC, took over responsibility for planning, care of the elderly, recreation and tourism, environmental health (including refuse collection), and local housing, etc. They were responsible for building some of the first council-owned houses in the area in Acton Road, Bramford, in the 1930s.

At first the Parish Council only met once or twice a year, the main concerns being public health and footpaths. The average expenditure for the first decade was £35 per annum, but most of this was spent on hiring a room for meetings.

Public health was a major concern, but although some parts of the parish had a fresh water-supply by 1914, many houses, especially those away from the village centre, were still not connected until the late-twentieth century. The dumping of rubbish was a continuous health hazard, but it was not until after the Second World War that a regular collection began. Although most areas of the village were connected to main sewers by the early 1950s the scheme was not completed until 1963, but even then some outlying houses were without flushing toilets.

Following several disastrous fires in the village, including the station and the mill, a fire appliance was purchased in 1914. Various residents, including Charlie Giles, manned the appliance over the years.

Following the First World War the Parish Council assumed many more responsibilities, such as allotments, street lights, traffic, transport, in fact anything which affected the daily lives of parishioners. The council also had charge of the Parish House, which was used to house tenants but needed constant repair and updating. It was eventually sold to the British Legion in 1959.

Having lost one obligation, others came along to replace it, as villagers now wanted a playing-field, improvements at the village hall, street lights, sewers (instead of the horse-drawn cart which came around once a week to empty the buckets of night soil) and a new cemetery, although not all of these were supplied at this time. As a result of these demands, expenditure increased dramatically to over £500 per annum by the 1950s, and even more when the new cemetery was opened in 1959.

Following the installation of street lights in the 1970s, expenditure increased to about £5,600 per annum. At the time of writing, because of ever-increasing demands on local services, the annual expenditure for the council is in the region of £60,000.

For the first four decades the Parish Council was composed of male councillors, and it was not until after the Second World War that ladies were elected, but it was another 50 years before the council chose their first female chairman. Similarly, the post of Parish Clerk was filled by a male until 1977; since then the post has been occupied by women.

Ongoing discussions regarding the increase in traffic in Bramford have taken place. Improvements have been made and the provision of parking modified, and several old properties

Left: *Runcton hamlet, between Ipswich and Sproughton. This road is now the lay-by outside Runcton Cottage. The houses on the left were demolished to widen the road in the 1960s.*

have been demolished in order to widen roads and improve safety, especially cottages at Runcton, Parish Pond and on the corner of Paper Mill Lane.

At the time of writing the Parish Council meets monthly in the Parish Room, and there is also an annual meeting in the Loraine Victory Hall. The councillors discuss planning applications, street-lights, allotments, the cemetery, footpaths, transport, environmental issues and tree maintenance, as well as many other items. Councillors receive no reward for their services which are undertaken to enhance the community.

Chairmen and Clerks to the Parish Council

Chairmen:

1894 Mr H.P. Henderson	1967 Mr S. Wade
1896 Revd R.V. Barker	1968 Mr Sewell
1904 Mr George Fiske	1970 Mr Alec Pryke
1910 Mr C. Packard	1981 Mr Allistair
1913 Mr Harry Fiske	Renton
1938 Mr George P. Jackson	1994 Mrs Beryl Sims
1946 Mr Wilfred Hurry	2001 Mr Graham
1949 Mr George Vinnicombe	Jones
1956 Mr S. Wade	2002 Mr David
1965 Mr Alec Pryke	Bailey

Clerks from 1894 at various times were:

Mr D. Long	Mr F.W. Long	Mr Hurry
Mr Rumsey	Mr G. Jackson	Mr Parker

Clerks from 1927 onwards were:

1927 Mr Edgar Eaborn	1973 Mr F.M. Ellis
1950 Mr Wightman	1977 Mrs M.A.
1951 Mr G. Ruffles	Renton
1954 Mr S.E. Keyte	1987 Mrs C. Butler
1965 Mr F. Pryke	1994 Mrs J.
1966 Mr C.M.	Edmundson (later
Lapworth	Read)

Councillors are due for re-election in May 2003, but members at the time of writing are: David Bailey, Amanda Brand, Ronald Cousins, Barry Earthy, John Gardiner, Doreen Golding, Mandy Goodchild, Veronica Hall, Peter Hodgkins, Graham Jones, Brian Kidby, Allistair Renton, Beryl Sims and Janet Read (Clerk). The County Councillor is John Field and the District Councillors Terry Green and Roger Saunders.

BRAMFORD COMMUNITY COUNCIL

Bramford Community Council was constituted in February 1969 as a means of providing a playing-field and other recreational facilities. Membership was purely voluntary and an executive committee was elected annually. Regular fund-raising events were organised, such as an annual flower show and fête and a weekly draw prize based on subscriptions of 3p per week.

The new council also raised funds for the provision of a playing-field and was responsible for

Parish Pond, before road widening, where The Street meets the old Roman road (now the B1113) and crosses to go on to Somersham, c.1910.

Parish Council, 1995. Left to right, standing: Roy Scruby, Terry Mayes, Bernard Purbrick, John Wilding, Tim Curran, John Hulford, Graham Jones; seated: Janet Edmundson (Clerk), Allistair Renton, Betty Burton, Beryl Sims (chairman), Joyce Manning, Stan Briggs (vice-chairman), Joy Barrett. Julie Ager and Charles Clarke are missing from the picture.

obtaining the old school premises and converting them into a community centre, namely a meeting-room for the Guides, Scouts and other uniformed groups, plus a Parish Room used primarily by the Parish Council, but also other leisure activities such as the history group, art group and marquetry group.

THE PLAYING-FIELD

During the 1960s and 1970s it became evident that with the expansion of the village, a playing-field was a priority for local children and adults alike. Publicity was gained in various ways, including a skipping marathon and a six-mile walk by local children to Needham Market Council offices. The preferred site for the playing-field was the area where St Mary's Close now stands but this was rejected by the landowners who, in 1970, suggested a seven-acre site at the northern end of the village, with access from Acton Road.

Bramford Community Council took over the work initially started by the Playing-Field Committee and, having received grants from Fisons and local government agencies, set to work on the project. By the time the work began, the cost had risen from an estimated £6,930 to £8,750. The total of grants was £5,746, leaving about £3,000 to be raised in the village. This sum was achieved thanks to the hard work of fund-raisers, and some of the cost was saved by using voluntary labour.

The original pavilion was purchased from an Orfordness building site and a toilet and kitchen block was added to it. The large site of the playing-field included a car park, football pitch, practice or hockey pitch, cricket pitch, a bowls green (constructed by members of the British Legion) and a children's play area.

The playing-field was officially opened in May 1976. A larger pavilion was erected in the 1980s at a cost of £45,000, with changing rooms and a leisure area. The keys were officially handed over by the contractor, Brian Barfield, to Roy Scruby, the secretary of the Management Committee, in 1987. In the

Miss Bramford, Margaret Brown, and her attendants, Sandra Cunningham (left) *and Susan Abbott* (right) *at the opening of the playing-field, May 1976.*

A British Legion parade on the dedication of the memorial to those who died in the Second World War, starting outside the Methodist chapel.

The Royal British Legion's parade on Remembrance Sunday 1997, led by Sue Withell and Michael Kinsey.

Early days of St John Ambulance. Mrs Peck (centre) *with cadets, August 1946.*

The Princess Royal inspecting cadets at the opening of the new St John Ambulance headquarters in the refurbished ambulance station, July 2000.

1990s a larger car park was added on land between the pavilion and the river, with access from Fraser Road. The pavilion is well used by all groups at the playing-field and there are plans in hand to provide additional capacity for changing rooms.

THE ROYAL BRITISH LEGION

The red poppy of the Flanders battlefields became the emblem of the British Legion on Poppy Day, when the millions of soldiers who lost their lives fighting in France and Belgium are remembered. The first Poppy Day was held in Britain on 11 November 1921 to commemorate those who died in the First World War, not only in France and Belgium, but also the sailors and airmen who lost their lives at the Battle of Jutland, at Gallipoli, the Dardenelles, Mesopotamia and in Egypt. The same year the British Legion, now the Royal British Legion, was formed to give practical help and companionship to ex-servicemen and women and their dependants.

Major George Howson, an infantry officer decorated for bravery, was deeply moved by the plight of ex-servicemen in peacetime. As a result he formed the Disabled Society, believing that the making of artificial poppies, wreaths and other such items associated with the poppy appeal would provide opportunities for its members. And so the British Legion poppy factory was established.

The Bramford branch of the British Legion was formed in 1922 and three years later moved to its present premises in The Street. It took over the former Parish House, owned by the Parish Council, at a rent of £25 per annum. The legion made several alterations to the building, including a .22-inch rifle range in the attic.

At the Annual Parish Meeting in 1957 approval was given for the building to be sold to the British Legion, and the sale went through in 1959 for the sum of £700. Included in the purchase was the old lock-up alongside, which has now been included in the building, though the front remains unchanged.

Each year on Remembrance Sunday a parade marches to St Mary's Church for the remembrance service, when the names of those villagers who died during twentieth-century conflicts are read out. The old standards are now housed in St Mary's Church.

Present club membership stands at 530 and the Bramford branch covers the welfare of Bramford, Sproughton and the surrounding area.

ST JOHN AMBULANCE

In June 1942 a visit by Miss M. Botwood, Lady County Cadet Officer, resulted in the formation of a first aid class, which was supervised by Mrs Gooderham and Mrs Peck from Ipswich. Later that year the group tied for first place at the County Cadet Sports held at Portman Road in Ipswich.

All 12 candidates passed an examination in September 1942 and were enrolled the following month in a ceremony held in the Victory Hall. In November that year the Bramford Cadet Nursing Division was officially registered, and at the end of the year had a financial balance of £2.1s.9d.

The following year Mrs Peck was officially appointed as Lady Cadet Divisional Superintendent. The Victory Hall was full for their first social in April, which brought in a further £8.13s.6d. Miss Loraine was appointed vice-president.

Some of the other superintendents were Mrs Beal, wife of the vicar, Miss Runnacles, a teacher at Bramford School, and Mrs Gedge (née Kemp).

Over the next few years the cadets attended cookery classes, training lectures and parades all over Suffolk, as well as holding social events, although German bombing sometimes disrupted proceedings. In 1944 they were inspected by Lady Louis Mountbatten at County Hall in Ipswich, with refreshments provided by the Earl of Cranbrook

The group continued after the end of the Second World War and, when the ambulance station in Duckamere was closed in the 1990s, it was taken over as a training centre for St John Ambulance. It was officially opened by the Princess Royal in 2000.

CHERRYFIELDS

In the mid-1980s Mid Suffolk District Council built a complex of assorted flats and bungalows as sheltered accommodation for the elderly. The building was given the name Cherryfields because on the 1846 Tithe Map this area was recorded as 'Cherry Ground Field'.

There are 20 flats in the complex and 12 bed-sitting rooms. There were originally six bungalows with one bedroom each, although more were later built across the road. Residents have access to medical and social services, along with leisure activities, laundry facilities and regular visits from staff. There is also a day-care centre where elderly people who are non-resident can benefit from a break away from home in a caring environment once or twice a week.

EIGHT

FARMS AND FARMERS

East Anglia is an ideal area for agriculture, in particular for growing wheat, barley and sugar beet, due largely to its low rainfall, chalky soil and rich boulder clays. The land in and around Bramford is no exception and during the past two centuries, local farmers have been engaged in constructing drainage systems to remove the water from the fields and divert it via ditches to the River Gipping running through the village.

From the nineteenth century onwards, Bramford farmers saw many changes in farming methods with the introduction of the steam age. Ploughing with two horses and a single-furrow wooden-framed plough, a man had to walk 11 miles in order to plough just an acre, a task which usually took all day. The introduction of the iron-framed plough in 1843 improved the durability of the implement but it was the development of the steam traction-engine around 1860 that was the catalyst for the drastic improvement in farming methods. A pair of traction-engines standing at each end of a field could pull a multi-furrowed reversible plough by cable backwards and forwards, ploughing at the rate of an acre every hour.

The invention by the Ipswich firm, Ransomes Sims & Head, of the threshing machine which could be towed around the local countryside and powered by the new traction-engines, revolutionised the way in

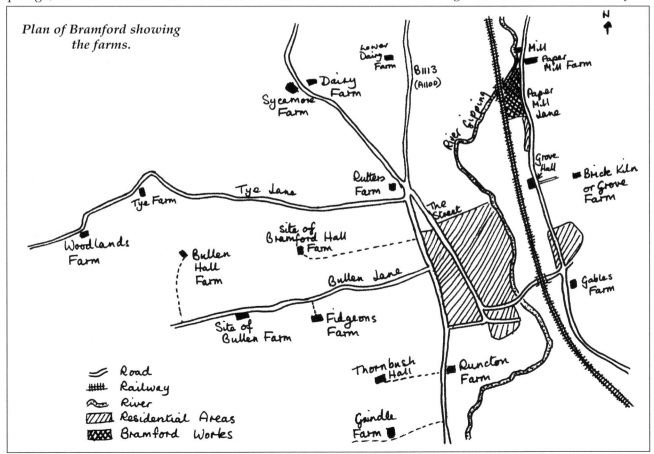

Plan of Bramford showing the farms.

Left: *Ploughing match in progress. Although this is a later photograph the scene would have been very similar at the 1905 event.*

Below: *Bullen Hall Farm, c.1993.*

SUMMARY OF LOTS

Lot	Colour on plan	Description	Tenant	Acreage	Total Acreage	Rent
1	Red	Site of Bramford Hall and Cottage and Drive	In-hand	13·61		—
		West Wing	J. G. Sillett	·36		245
		Arable Land	E. J. W. Fiske	3·29	17·26	20
2	Yellow	Bramford Park Woodland	In-hand	3·31		—
		Arable	E. J. W. Fiske	58·20	61·51	405
3	Blue	Woodland	In-hand	1·61		—
		Arable land	E. J. W. Fiske	68·21	69·82	475
4	Red	Keepers Cottage	P. Mayhew	·38		75
		Spinney	In-hand	1·46	1·84	—
5	Green	Arable land and Rose Cottage	E. J. W. Fiske	29·17		227
		Allotments	Various tenants	2·71	31·88	—
6	Blue	Runcton Farmhouse, Premises & Pasture	E. J. W. Fiske		70·16	800
7	Red	Church Green Cottages	E. J. W. Fiske		·12	100
8	Yellow	River Meadow	E. J. W. Fiske		1·28	6
9	Red	Arable land	E. J. W. Fiske	34·80		245
		Arable land	R. H. I. Jackson	13·13		105
		Allotments	Various Tenants	2·36	50·29	—
10	Yellow	No. 1 The Row	E. J. W. Fiske			50
		Nos. 2 & 4 The Row	R. H. I. Jackson	·54		104
		Nos. 3 & 5 The Row	J. R. Watkins		·54	80
11	Green	Low Meadows	W. Clowes		20·61	127
12	Blue	Low Meadow	W. Clowes		1·23	8
			TOTAL		326·54	£3,072

Analysis

Woodlands and other in-hand land.	19·99
Land let on agricultural tenancies.	301·12
Other let properties.	5·43

Robert Saddington Jolly

Right: *William and Louisa Jolly, c.1920s.*

Left: *Summary of Lots from the Sale by Tender document detailing the sale of 'The Major. Part of the Remaining Portion of the Bramford Estate', sold by Strutt and Parker, 12 March 1974.*

which the harvest was dealt with. These machines, owned by contractors, visited a farm and threshed the entire contents of the stack-yard to remove the grain before moving on to the next farm.

Development continued with the evolution of petrol and, later, diesel tractors. The power and complexity of these has continued to improve to the present day. Bramford farmers have always been at the forefront of agricultural methods and equipment and today the latest in sophisticated machinery can be seen operating in the fields around the village.

The interwoven manors in existence during the Middle Ages evolved into the large estates of the eighteenth and nineteenth centuries. Most of the Bramford farms that existed in the nineteenth century were part of the Bramford Hall estate owned by the Loraine family and let out to tenants for an annual rent. During the second half of the twentieth century these farms were sold off from the estate. Many are now in private hands and are farmed over a larger scale. Many of the traditional farm buildings have been restored and converted into attractive dwellings, as in the case of those at Tye Farm.

The farms that existed in 1861 (taken from the Census of that year) were as follows:

Brick Kiln Farm
Bullen Farm (90 acres employing 4 men and 3 boys)
Bullen Hall Farm
Dairy Farm
Lower Dairy Farm
Fidgeons Farm
Grindle Farm (28 acres employing 1 man and 1 boy)
Grove Hall Farm (581 acres with 30 men and 12 boys)
Paper Mill Farm

Runcton Farm (250 acres employing 7 men and 4 boys)
Rutters Farm
Sycamore Farm (400 acres employing 12 men and 3 boys)
Thornbush Farm (280 acres with 8 men and 4 boys)
Tye Farm (200 acres employing 4 men and 1 boy)
Woodlands Farm

In addition to these farms some inhabitants of Bramford in 1861 were listed as having land that they farmed, including Henry Palmer, the landlord of The Angel, who is recorded as farming 30 acres with staff of two men and two boys.

Bramford farmers and their workers organised an annual ploughing match, instigated in 1892, by means of grants from the Royal Agricultural Society and from East Suffolk County Council. There were four classes open to men working in the 25 parishes

Emma Jolly (née Norfolk)

within a radius of five miles of Bramford and also a class for young men 18 years and under. The organising committee included the following Bramford farmers: Harry Fiske from Runcton Farm, Isaac Jackson and his son Orlando from Sycamore Farm, William Jolly from Bullen Hall Farm, Robert Watkins from Tye Farm and Amos Rumsey from Fidgeons Farm. The event was held on Whit Monday and in 1905 attracted a record of 47 entries. As no grants were received that year the event was supported by subscriptions from manufacturers trading in the district.

BULLEN LANE FARMS

There were three major farms along Bullen Lane during the nineteenth century: Fidgeons, Bullen Hall and Bullen Farm, also known as Bullen Wood Farm.

In the 1840s, and for the next 20 years, **Fidgeons Farm** was farmed by John Morgan. It comprised 115 acres and employed four men and one boy. In 2003 the farm buildings form the core of an agricultural equipment hiring business.

Bullen Farm consisted of approximately 40 acres and was positioned at the top end of the lane surrounded by woodland. The Button family farmed it until the 1840s, followed by Joseph Lewis. Robert Saddington Jolly from Chattisham and his wife, Emma, moved to the farm in the late 1860s, where they raised 12 children. Robert died in 1908 at the age of 68 and his wife Emma continued to run the farm for another 23 years until her death in 1931, aged 80. Robert and Emma are buried in Bramford churchyard. Bullen Farm was demolished in the mid-1970s and the electricity distribution equipment for the National Grid now occupies the area.

Bullen Hall Farm, situated in the valley between Bullen Lane and Tye Lane, consisted of about 190

Bullen Farm, Bullen Lane, c.1910.

Above: *An aerial view of Tye Farm, 1972.*

Above: *Robert Watkins with his pony and trap in which he was apprehended for speeding in Princes Street, Ipswich. He was fined 10s. (50p). His son Bob is holding the horse.*

Left and above: *Cliff and Percy Watkins in the bean field, 1926.*

acres of arable and pasture land. The farmhouse, dating from the sixteenth century, is of a traditional Suffolk timber-framed and plastered construction. The Census of 1851 lists the tenant as David Narey and, in 1861, William Green, who employed four men and three boys on the farm. In 1881 and 1891 Henry Bumstead was the tenant, the acreage having risen to 220.

In 1869, William Jolly, the younger brother of Robert Saddington Jolly, married Louisa Pallant, whose family ran the butcher's shop in Bramford village. They moved to Bullen Hall Farm from Laffitts Hall, Pettaugh, in 1894. Farm workers usually moved at Michaelmas (11 October) and it is likely that this was the case with William and Louisa as Bramford school records show the first appearance of two of their children in January 1895.

Robert Watkins in 1915, aged 72.

Like many families of the day they lived through personal tragedies. Three of their daughters died under the age of three and their third son, Thomas Markwell Jolly (named after his grandfather), was killed in an accident at nearby Hintlesham in 1900 at the age of 25. He was driving a horse-drawn tumbrill carrying pigs when the horse faltered and the cart mounted the bank and overturned. Thomas fell through the shafts and sustained a serious head injury from which he died three days later.

During the latter part of the twentieth century Peter and Shirley Mayhew farmed at Bullen Hall from where they also tended the land of Tye Farm. They later purchased Tye farmhouse and its buildings, leaving their son Richard at Bullen Hall to run the farm.

TYE LANE FARMS

Tye Farm dates back to the sixteenth century and the house is another traditional Suffolk timber-framed construction that may have originally been thatched; it now has a peg and tile roof. There have certainly been people living on the site for at least 750 years, as in the Bishop of Ely's Survey of 1251 the name of Juliana of the Tye is listed.

Both the 1841 and 1851 Census list John Daines from Occold farming at Tye Farm, managing 200 acres and employing three labourers. It then changed hands several times as the following listings reveal: 1861 John Mudd from Cretingham, 1881 William Larking, 1891 Robert Sweetlove, and in 1901 Robert Watkins from Claydon.

Born in 1843, Robert Watkins started as a building contractor and was involved with supplying bricks and other materials for the building of the railway viaduct in Spring Road, Ipswich. He later moved to Gate Farm, Flowton, leaving the youngest of his 13 children, John Robert Watkins (Bob), to continue at Tye Farm in 1908 as a tenant of Sir Percy Loraine, who owned much of the land around Bramford. Bob, as well as being a farmer, was reckoned to be an astute general dealer. During a particularly difficult negotiation over an increase in rent, when he accused the landowner of trying to 'bally break me' (an old Suffolk expression not often heard nowadays), he eventually agreed an increase to £8 an acre, but only after insisting that it should be fixed for the duration of his life at the farm. His relatives are convinced that this is one of the factors that kept him alive to the age of 93! Bob, born in 1886, ran the farm for 71 years with the help of Mick Allum, until his death in 1981. He was also assisted by his nephew Cliff Watkins and Cliff's wife, Pauline.

The row of tied cottages, provided for the employees of Tye Farm, were situated at the north end of Bramford Street opposite what is now the cemetery, while employees from Bullen Farm were housed in the three brick cottages directly opposite Tye Farm.

Tye Farm consisted mainly of livestock, with cattle being moved down Tye Lane to the parkland behind Bramford Hall for summer grazing.

During the First World War, meadows in and around Tye Farm were used for collecting and rearing horses for military purposes. These were then led by road to the docks at Ipswich for shipping to the Western Front.

The parkland that existed between Bramford Hall and Tye Lane was also used during the Second World War for marshalling men and equipment prior to D-day. George Dunnet, who lived at Flowton, noted that on his way home from school the parkland was so full of military equipment there was not room for a bicycle. However, the next morning

Tye Farmhouse in 2003 showing what was originally the front of the building.

Left: Left to right, back: *Fred Jolly, Walter Jolly*; front: *Louisa Gladwell (née Jolly), Eva Gladwell, Charles Gladwell, Edith Jolly. This photograph was taken after the Jollys had left Woodlands Farm, c.1920.*

Left: *Planting potatoes at Rutters Farm.*

Above: *Frederick William Jolly junr, known as Willie to differentiate him from his father and grandfather.*

Highway Rate Book, 1896.

Alice Jackson (née Ranson), late 1800s.

Woodlands Farmhouse, 2002.

there was no trace – it had all been moved overnight.

Peter and Shirley Mayhew, having moved to Tye Farm in 1981, lived there until 1994 when they moved to an adjacent barn which they had converted to living accommodation.

In 1868, Robert Saddington Jolly from Chattisham, recently married to Emma (née Norfolk), moved into **Woodlands Farm**, standing almost on the western boundary of the parish in Tye Lane. They were followed by Samuel Robinson with his wife Sarah and their four children who moved from nearby Sproughton in the late 1870s. They farmed 59 acres and provided employment for two men and two boys. By the time of the 1901 Census, John Richardson from Bentley had taken over the tenancy and at Michaelmas 1908, Frederick William Jolly, his wife Edith (née Kitson) and their family moved into Woodlands. Frederick was the eldest son of William and Louisa Jolly of Bullen Hall Farm.

SOMERSHAM ROAD

Sycamore Farm was probably first established by John Sicklemore who was involved in the Peasants' Revolt of 1381. For over a century it has been presided over by five generations of the Jackson family, starting with Isaac who moved from Hitcham in the late 1870s with his wife Alice (née Ranson). Next came Orlando, George Percy, Raymond, Clifford and Michael.

Isaac Jackson, as well as being a farmer, was appointed Surveyor of Highways for the parish of Bramford. This entailed collecting the rate levied for the provision of road maintenance from all house occupants in the parish. The Highway Rate Book for 1896 makes interesting reading with the names of occupiers, owners and a description of properties, along with the rateable value. The rate levied for 1896 was 3d. in the pound, and the total rate raised from the parish that year was £83.8s.6d.

During the Second World War a fire in the adjacent stack-yard threatened to consume the whole of Sycamore Farm. The entire contents of the farm pond were used in order to save the fine fifteenth-century farmhouse, but the original barns and farm buildings were totally destroyed. They have since been replaced by modern buildings.

During the latter part of the twentieth century Sycamore Farm, while keeping pigs, dairy animals and chickens, was primarily involved in the growing of arable and potato crops. The potato crop provided the foundation for R. Jackson (Ipswich) Ltd., a group formed for the wholesale distribution of potatoes, fruit and vegetables.

Rutters Farm in Somersham Road was called Ruthouse Farm on old maps. The farm bailiff in 1851 was William Amos Sawyer aged 33 from Waldringfield, followed by John Fenn from Somersham by 1871, and Walter Baker of Finborough by 1891.

Michael Jackson farmed at Rutters from 1959 but in the early 1970s he moved into Sycamore Farm. During this period the farm buildings were improved and extended with the emphasis on providing housing for the rearing of pigs.

The farmhouse is now a private dwelling. A company specialising in contract fencing occupies the farm buildings and the land has been absorbed into larger farms.

OTHER LOCAL FARMS

Unusually, despite the 1950s and '60s revolution in agriculture, **Grindle Farm** has not been absorbed into any of the much larger farms and, apart from the loss of one field, has the same boundaries as those shown on eighteenth-century maps. The 'grindle', a gravel-floored stream, forms the southern boundary of the farm. It also denotes the parish boundary between Bramford and Sproughton and the ancient boundary between Bosmere and Samford Hundreds.

George Percy Jackson

Above: *Mr Isaac Jackson with his daughters (left to right) Winifred, Marjorie and Hilda.*

Left: *Aerial view of Rutters Farm, c.1980.*

Harvesting a field which is now St Mary's Close, c.1960.

Grindle Farm, 2003.

Above: *William Brown, cowman for Harry Fiske, at Grove Farm.*

Left: *Michael Jackson with Patch, 2003.*

Brick Kiln Farm, also known as Grove Farm, c.1920s. The Brown family (left to right) *Olive (later Page), Lilian, and parents Willam and Mary.*

Above: *Threshing at Thornbush Hall Farm, late 1800s.*

Right: *Harriet Fiske (née Wainwright), c.1880.*

Above: *Manasseh Beckett, coachman and gardener at Thornbush, waits by the front door of the hall for the family to climb aboard.*

Right: *Some of the fine thatched cart lodges at Thornbush, early 1900s.*

Above: *Harvest gang at Thornbush, 1927.* Left to right, standing: *Sam Leech (head horseman), 'Bunny' Lambert (warrener and stack thatcher), Albert Songer (shepherd); seated: Jim Hardwick, Billy 'Crippen' Hardwick, Frank Moss (eating bread and cheese), Ernie Leech (stockman), Herbert 'Hubby' Keeble (with cigarette). The child and adult* (behind) *are unknown.*

Left: *George Fiske, c.1880.*

Early photograph of workers at Thornbush, c.1880.

Left: *Highland cattle at Thornbush Hall, c.1880.*

The farmyard and buildings still exist but are no longer part of a working farm. Although they are generally in a state of disrepair, one can see that they were once part of an important and prestigious complex.

Thornbush Hall commands a panoramic view over the surrounding countryside and was one of three manor-houses in the parish of Bramford. It has long been important for its progressive agriculture, and the Census of 1851 describes land of some 260 acres, farmed by George Morgan and his wife Charlotte, employing ten labourers. In 1861 the Census returns gave Charlotte as a widow of 74 years and the household included George Fisk [sic], aged 24, described as a 'servant'. By the time of the 1871 Census, George Fiske (aged 33) and his wife Harriet occupied Thornbush Hall. The size of the farm had doubled to 530 acres. George Fiske became a leading East Anglian farmer and by 1881 had increased his farmland to 1,500 acres.

During an interview for an article in the *Cable and Agricultural World* in 1900 he described how he kept cattle and sheep for breeding and grazing, and also kept pigs. He said that he owned about 40 horses for working on the farm and grew various crops such as wheat, barley, oats, beans, peas, mangolds, swedes, kohlrabi, cabbage and turnips, grown both for human consumption and for feeding animals.

The farm is still being run as a thriving business by Herbert Godbold and now occupies most of the land between the B1113 in the east, the parish boundary with Burstall in the west, Bullen Lane on the north and Burstall Lane in Sproughton on the south.

Brick Kiln Farm, **Paper Mill Farm**, **Gables Farm**, **Street Barn Farm**, **Runcton Farm** and **Dairy Farm** are no longer working farms. The houses are private and the land has been absorbed by other farms.

Unlike most farms in the parish, Grindle Farm has always been independent of the Bramford Hall estate and indeed any other estate. A map of 1771 shows the farm retaining its separate identity, with the barn as it is today, under the ownership of a Mr Grimwade. The Tithe Map of 1846 indicates that it was owned by Stephen Haward and farmed by Henry Haward. The Tithe Field Book describes the farmhouse as being occupied by 'John Crickman and others' which indicates that the house had already been subdivided. This was commonly the case at the time due to a rapidly expanding population and a crushing agricultural depression.

By 1922 John Brooks occupied that land and eventually bought it. It was used for market gardening and his horses were a familiar sight around the estates of Ipswich, pulling carts loaded with produce.

Almost all the trees and hedgerows around the farm were cut down for firewood, the garden became a potato field and the house lost its last vestiges of its original doors and windows. The family was barely able to make a living but it was still not broken up. It was sold in its entirety in 1970. The owners at the time of writing still produce hay and keep horses.

During the mid-1800s, the farm associated with The Grove, **Grove Hall Farm**, was the largest in the parish with 600 acres of land and employing 30 labourers and 13 boys. It is possible that the original farmhouse was Brick Kiln Farm which lies on the eastern side of the lane, but by the late-nineteenth century it had been taken over by The Grove. Before the arrival of the railway in 1846, Paper Mill Lane ran to the west of The Grove. The road was then diverted to run behind the house, between it and the farm buildings. In the 1846 Tithe Book most of the surrounding land was owned by Robert Mumford of Ipswich.

In the early decades of the twentieth century the land was owned by Sir Edward Packard and was rented from him by George and Harry Fiske.

Thornbush Hall, 2002, showing the oldest part at the rear and the twentieth-century extension on the right.

NINE

∾⊙⟿

VILLAGE PEOPLE

The Census of 1881 recorded a population at Bramford of 1,336, but this included some residents of Bramford Road and Whitton, which are now within the Ipswich boundary. It is interesting to see the different occupations in the village at that time.

There were 165 men and 1 woman employed in agriculture, mostly farm workers, but including four thatchers, and there were 133 men employed in industry, mostly chemical and factory workers in the Paper Mill Lane area, but there were also 18 men working on the railway, 12 at the brickworks, 8 men and 1 woman at the paper-mill and 7 men working with lime.

A total of 90 men and 8 women were employed in 'trade'. These were grocers, general shop assistants and beer sellers, and also 3 blacksmiths, 7 saddle or harness makers, 5 shoemakers, 9 millers, plus several others in general building trades and 1 'lump sugar chopper'. Sugar in those days was purchased in large blocks which were then cut into smaller blocks and finally into cubes.

Perhaps the group in which there has been the largest change was that including those employed in domestic service. There were 105 women employed as house servants, cooks, nursemaids, laundresses and dressmakers, with 29 men employed as grooms, gardeners or coachmen.

There were very few 'clerical' occupations, just 6 clerks, 6 schoolteachers, 2 solicitors, 15 people of independent means, and a few others, 36 in total.

It is interesting that out of a total of 564 occupations given in the Census, approximately one quarter were employed on the land and almost none had clerical jobs. A comparison with present occupations would no doubt reveal the opposite.

The largest household listed in the Census was The Grove in Paper Mill Lane, where Edward Packard lived with his wife, nine children and five servants. The second largest was the Fiske family of Thornbush Hall, with George Fiske, his wife, seven children and four servants. Two houses had 12 residents each, one was Bramford Hall with Lt-Col

Frank Scott and his family, but the other was a cottage in Paper Mill Lane, where Walter Parker lived with his wife, nine children and one servant – quite a contrast in house size!

The place of birth was also given in the Census returns and it is interesting that 45 per cent of people living in Bramford were actually born in the parish. A further 19 per cent were born in adjoining parishes, 26 per cent in the rest of Suffolk and only 10 per cent born outside Suffolk.

In 1881 41 per cent of residents were under the age of 15 years, 25 per cent were between the ages of 16 and 30, 15 per cent between 31 and 45, 12 per cent between 46 and 60 and only 7 per cent over the age of 61.

NICKNAMES

In the days when the custom was to name babies after their parents, grandparents and other members of the family, life could be confusing in small communities where three or four people might share the same name. Consequently, nicknames became very popular. The word nickname is derived from the fifteenth-century 'nekename', mistakenly derived from 'ekename', 'eke' meaning addition.

Les Beckett recalled the following from his childhood in Bramford in the 1930s:

There are many names of village and local people, characters in their own right, whom I have not mentioned in my memoirs. Nonetheless, as the years rolled by, they became household names known to many of us, and I think it would be correct to record, with every respect to their relatives, friends and colleagues, the 'nick' names by which they were known.

Puddy Allum	*Skinny Allum*
Buskins Beckett	*Boofer Bloomfield*
Okepokey Bloomfield	*Dutchy Brooks*
Tubby Brown	*Tortoise Burch*
Tags Capon	*Hoppy Clark*

Above: *The Hayes family behind 2 Fitzgerald Road.*

Left: *Harry Fiske of Thornbush with his dog, c.1930.*

Below: *Amos and Emily Rumsy and children.*

Cully Coleman	Wibble Coleman
Bodger Cook	Nunky Cook
Tank Dale	Dodger Drane
Sheddy Driver	Dubba Farnish
Frip Ford	Hoppy Francis
Rooky Francis	Buster Garnham
Carrots Garrod	Tudie Gooding
Jerrie Hardwick	Crippen Hardwick
Brassy Hill	Wiggle Hogger
Cut-a-customer Holder	Porky Hood
Shoddy Hood	Wag Hood
Grumpy Jackson	Jummy Johns
Ha'penny Keeble	Hubby Keeble
Milco Keeble	Pongo Keeble
Moses Keeble	Cogan Keeble
Wiggle Keeble	Poke Laffling
Bunny Lambert	Arty Lay
Babe Lay	Butcher Lay
Lush Lay	Rusty Lay
Sixer Lay	Wag Lay
Nelson Lewis	Pen Lockwood
Chong Lloyd	Gun Lloyd
Titty Mee	Dordie Moss
Dummy Metcalf	Tubby Norman
Cast Iron Oldring	Ribby Page
Slop Parker	Tiger Pipe
Pip Pipe	Chaddy Pryke
Jointer Pryke	Muddick Pryke
Sharper Pryke	Sunny Pryke
Chuddy Rattle	Shrimp Rodwell
Sunny Rodwell	Ginger Rosier
Boney Rowland	Darda Ruffles
Happy Ruffles	Spud Ruffles
Cabby Scopes	Steel Scrivener
Nimmy Sewell	Stump Shepherd
Blin Smith	Spudger Sparrow
Wooppy Steward	Danky Taylor
Ike Taylor	Woolley Woolnough
Puppy Worledge	

And nicknames remembered by other residents:

Dood Driver	Chopper Harrison	Silver Lay
Girlie Frost	Maury Hood	Whoop Lockwood
Titch Garrod	Butner Lay	Wiggle Lockwood
Tooty Giles	Noller Lay	Dod Rose

THE ACTON, BROKE AND LORAINE FAMILIES

The Acton family came to Bramford having acquired their wealth as clothiers in Ipswich. A memorial to William Acton and his wife and children is in the north wall of the chancel of St Mary Elms Church; he was the first of that name to buy land in Bramford.

In his will dated 1616 he left money to the bailiffs of Ipswich for them to loan indefinitely to poor clothiers without interest for a term of four years each. He left £100 to his wife Juliana, all his property in Ipswich, Bramford and elsewhere to his son John, various bequests to members of his family, individual bequests to three preachers in Ipswich, and £10 for the purchase of books for the newly-erected Ipswich Library.

It was probably his son John who built the first hall in Bramford in the seventeenth century.

The estate passed through four more generations of the family until 1836 when Nathaniel Lee Acton died without a male heir and the estate passed to his niece, Sarah Middleton, and then by her marriage to Sir Philip Broke of Nacton. Because of their other estates, they had very little interest in Bramford so the hall was let to tenants. At the time of the Tithe Commutation in 1846, Sir Philip Broke, son of the above, owned 1,890 acres out of a total of 2,600 in the parish.

Sir Philip died without children so the estate passed to his brother Sir George Broke who in 1860 gave land in Ship Lane for a school to be built. He died from a seizure whilst out skating on the ice in January 1887 and as he too died without a male heir, his estate was divided between his nieces.

The Bramford estate went to Frederica who was married to Sir Lambton Loraine the 11th Earl of Kirkharle, Northumberland. The couple had four children: Eustace, Percy, Jacqueline and Isaura. Sir Lambton was described by William Smith (a stable lad at the hall), as being tall, white-haired and white-bearded.

Sir Lambton was a rear-admiral with a distinguished Naval record. As commander of HMS Niobe in 1873, he prevented the crew of an American

Portrait of Nathaniel Acton born in Bramford in 1684.
(From a private collection)

The funeral of Captain Loraine. A procession of Grenadier Guards passing the Cock Inn.

The Loraine family at the graveside, Percy, Isaura and Sir Lambton Loraine, 1912.

Above: *The funeral of Captain Eustace Broke Loraine in 1912. The photograph shows Church Green with the mill in the background.*

Left: *Isaura Loraine, c.1940.*

ship, *Virginius*, from being executed by the Spanish for transporting arms to Cuba during the uprising against Spanish rule. The Cuban Navy presented a plaque in memory of this event, which was placed at Sir Lambton's grave in Bramford churchyard on 29 May 1937.

However, Sir Lambton had very set ideas about the conduct of the people of Bramford. The village school had been built on land given by the Broke family and in 1908 he wrote to the school board:

I... regret not to understand what is meant by 'woodwork'. Personally I think that village children along with reading, writing, geography, etc., ought to be taught strictly with a view to what their prospects are likely to be amid our huge population. For example, girls cannot all rise to a superior position and play violin profitably; but housework of all kinds, in addition to cooking and laundry work, would not be thrown away if taught to all. The demand for well-taught self-respecting maids for house service does not decrease in Great Britain, while it is vastly increasing in our Colonies. As to boys, I hope they may learn outdoor Country work as much as possible. It is painful to think that there are Societies in existence for the sole purpose of keeping from starvation lads who desert the country thinking they must prosper in a town. Farming is the mainstay of every community, and schools should not work for its decline.

Captain Eustace Broke Loraine, c.1910.

In 1910, following recommendations from the East Suffolk Education Committee, the vicar, Revd Butler, wrote from the vicarage to ask if the school managers could move the toilets to the south of the playground. Sir Lambton replied:

I am afraid I consider the Ipswich people less qualified than ourselves to decide Village matters. The School's Closets are in the best position possible as regards the School, the Village, and the Church and Churchyard. They have been in use half a century, while the health of the school has never suffered from them, and I can see no more reason for moving them than for moving every Closet in the village to another place, nor any reason for placing them under public gaze.
P.S. Some years ago a certain friend and neighbour of mine when in Herefordshire, was maintaining a school (built by his family) in a way much superior to the ordinary school of later days. When the school committees were appointed and tried to dictate to him, he refused their dictation; but when they insisted on having their own way, he closed the school and they pulled the whole down.

Sir Lambton's elder son, Eustace Broke Loraine, was born in 1879 and was educated at Eton and Sandhurst. He was commissioned into the Grenadier Guards in 1899 and served with the 2nd Battalion in the South Africa War of 1899–1902, for which he was awarded the Queen's Medal with three clasps and the King's Medal with two clasps. For two years his commanding officer was Lt-Col Trenchard and the two men became good friends.

By 1911 Captain Loraine had become fascinated by the newly-invented flying machines. He learned to fly and gained his Royal Aero Club Certificate in November that year. He became a test pilot for the Royal Flying Corps, later to become the Royal Air Force. In his last letter to his friend Trenchard he wrote 'You don't know what you're missing. Come and see men crawling like ants.' As a result, Trenchard learned to fly and later became known as 'The Father of the RAF'.

In 1912 Capt Loraine was based at Larkhill near Stonehenge, test-flying newly-built aeroplanes. On Friday 5 July he took off with a military engineer in a Nieuport plane on a test flight, but as the plane began to misfire, he landed to make further adjustments. He took off again with Staff-Sergeant Wilson, but soon after take-off the plane went into a dive and fell to the ground, killing Wilson instantly. Capt. Loraine was rushed to Bulford Hospital in a horse-drawn ambulance, but died soon after his arrival. He was 33 years old.

His body was escorted from Bulford Camp with full military honours and brought to Bramford by train via London. A gun carriage was brought from Colchester, which was escorted from the hall to the church by over 120 officers and men of the Grenadier Guards, Royal Flying Corps and the Royal Bucks Hussars. The gun carriage was drawn by six black horses, followed by the representative of His Majesty the King and many hundreds of mourners, including his close family.

Capt. Loraine and Staff-Sergeant Wilson are commemorated by a memorial on Salisbury Plain near Stonehenge.

Following the death of Sir Lambton Loraine in 1917, the estate passed to the younger son Percy. He was an ambassador for the British Government and spent much of his time abroad in Tehran, Athens, Cairo, Ankara and Rome. In December 1946 he presented a tea urn to the Bramford Victory Hall Management Committee. Sir Percy was the 12th and last baronet.

His sister Jacqueline was apparently injured in a riding accident and was never seen in the village.

The other sister, Isaura, was by far the most popular member of the family. Born in November 1883, she lived most of her life in the village and played an active role in the community. During the First World War she worked in a munitions factory. She started the Girl Guides in 1918 and often had parties in the grounds for local children.

In 1937, after the death of her mother, she moved to Bramford Lodge while the hall was being renovated with a view to finding new tenants. However, during the Second World War the hall was used to house officers in the Army. She was godmother to several children in the village and several times housed families whose homes had been damaged in the bombing.

After the war Miss Loraine became a Parish Councillor but unfortunately she died four years later in July 1949 and was buried in the churchyard near her parents and brother.

Sir Percy Loraine died in 1961 and was buried with the other members of his family in Bramford churchyard to the north of the church. There are tablets in their memory at the west end of the south aisle.

THE PEOPLE OF BRAMFORD

Memories of Henry Arthur Palmer, who lived at The Angel, written in 1969:

My grandfather, Henry Palmer, was born in 1823, the seventh child of James and Sarah Palmer who kept the village shop at Barham Green, and were also cattle and horse dealers.

Henry entered the service of the Buxton family of Shadwell Court near Thetford (later the residence of Duleep Singh). In about 1845 he married Elizabeth Gill, the daughter of an ironmonger and builder's merchant in Thetford, and who at the time was a ladies maid in the Buxton household. Soon after the marriage they became licensees of Bramford Angel.

This house with its 45 acres of farmland belonged to the Shrubland Estate as did Bramford Hall.

Not only did grandfather become an innkeeper, but entered whole-heartedly into farming, and also developed a substantial business as hay, straw and corn merchant and maltster.

There was also a Job Masters Yard, specialising in the letting of pony traps for the use of commercial travellers doing business with farmers and shopkeepers in the surrounding villages. These travellers often stayed at The Angel for several nights at a time.

There were also carriages for the use of weddings and funerals, brakes and a waggonette for party and family outings.

Grandfather's speciality was dealing in carriage horses for London nobility and gentry. This entailed frequent and regular visits to the London horse sales at Aldridges, Tattersalls and Barbican. In the report of his

death in The Times, *it was stated that he was as well known and respected in the London horse world as in his own Suffolk village. Because of his highly dignified appearance, personality and devotion to the service of the church, he was affectionately referred to as the 'Bishop of Bramford'. He suffered severely in the great agricultural depression of 1880 and died a poor man of a broken heart.*

He had three children, my father Henry born 1855, Elizabeth and Frank, known as Dick.

My father rode daily by pony to Mr Buckingham's private school at 56 Berners Street, Ipswich, where he was educated.

All three children were trained in horsemanship which later qualified Father and Uncle Dick to serve in the Suffolk Yeomanry (the Duke of York's Loyal Suffolk Hussars) at a time when only sons of yeoman farmers were admitted to its ranks.

Uncle Dick married Ellen King, daughter of the village wheelwright and postmaster, and they moved to a farm at Somersham.

On the death of my grandfather, my father took over the whole concern at Bramford. He married Ellen Ward who had been living and working at The Angel for 14 years. Soon after, his health began to fail and my mother had to take on the responsibility for everything, besides producing a family of four children, of which I was the only one to survive.

Mother's education consisted of attendance at what today would be called a Dame School held in the village reading room by a Mrs Lewis, who I can just remember as a very old lady.

Mother was a very good writer and developed into a shrewd business woman. She was renowned for her kindness and generosity. After only six years of a very happy married life my father died when I was just four years old and he was 39.

What a challenge for mother – a busy public house open all day from 6a.m. to 10p.m., a farm, the posting business, and hay, straw, corn, etc. She did it for four years with the help of Geo Riches who had been engaged the previous year by my father to look after the outdoor work, carriages, horses and all cellar work. He was classified as an ostler. Ephram Keeble, horseman on the farm, was made responsible for all the farm work. Mr George Fiske of Thornbush Hall kept an eye on mother's acres and advised her.

One of the outstanding events during the four years when mother was on her own, was that Major General Russell (Equerry to the Prince of Wales) along with his lady wife and seven adult daughters, lived at The Angel for six months while the hall was being restored and prepared for their occupation. True – they brought their own cook (Mutford), butler (Percy Drake), ladies maid (Mrs P. Drake) and nanny (Eliza Dench), but the overall responsibility was taken by mother. However she always felt her great reward was the appreciation shown to her by all this family and their relatives. Even other members of the Russell family came and stayed

Staff at The Angel in 1897. Left to right, standing: Jimmy Keeble, Mildred Sheppard, George Pryke;
seated: Lizzie Mutimer, George Riches, Polly Woods, Ephram Keeble, Lizzie Keeble.

Bertie and Lily Frost with their children who were all baptised on the same day in 1938. The children are, left to right: Dorothy (Girlie), Charlie, baby John, Muriel, Ena; front: Mary and Betty.

The family of Harry Bloomfield. His wife Ada, his mother and children, Arthur and Lily (standing), and Daisy and Bill. Five more children were born after this photograph was taken: Harry, Ben, Albert, Sam and Jack.

Harry Bloomfield in the uniform of the Royal Fusiliers, c.1900. He served in the Boer War and the First World War. He died in the early 1970s, aged 92, and left 123 descendants, children, grandchildren and great-grandchildren.

with us for long periods over the following two years, so they could visit the hall without actually staying there.

After four hard but successful years on her own, Mother was faced with the problem of whether her health and strength would stand up to the continuous strain. When Harry Godding, a master plumber, house decorator and contractor from Stowmarket started visiting The Angel fairly frequently, and finally offered marriage, she accepted, sold up at Bramford, and moved with me to Stowmarket in 1897.

Mr and Mrs Charles Frost

A newspaper cutting of 28 December 1913 recorded the celebration of the golden wedding anniversary of Charles Frost and his wife of Railway Cottage, and gave a little of their history.

Mr Frost started work at Gables Farm at the age of seven for 1s. a week and by the time of the interview he had worked there for almost 70 years, 50 of which were as head horseman under Mr George Fiske. He was presented with a long-service award of £2 at the Suffolk Agricultural Show in Stowmarket in 1903. When he started work the farm had 21 horses and 12 ploughs. He remembered the stage-coach travelling through the village from Ipswich, stopping to change horses at The Angel, which was a bustling inn.

Mrs Frost was also still working at the time of the newspaper article. She was a trained midwife and helped to deliver many babies in the village. Her daughter died young leaving six children, one of which was still a baby. Mrs Frost took over the care of the children, and could often be seen walking to surrounding villages to deliver a baby carrying her youngest grandchild. She was also the 'knocker-upper' for the village, that is to say she would go round to people's houses early in the morning to wake them in time to get to work.

In 1913 they had 12 children, 25 grandchildren, and seven great-grandchildren.

Their son Bertie and his wife Lily had seven children and lived in a three-bedroomed house opposite the end of what is now Leggatt Drive. In

Mr and Mrs Charles Frost. She was the midwife.

Ha'penny Keeble and his milk cart, c.1931.

1938 after the birth of the seventh child, John, they decided to have the children, together with several cousins, all baptised in one mammoth session.

Bertie Frost's daughters remember a prank from their childhood whereby they used to tie the back doorknob of Cut-a-customer's house to the front one, then knock on the door and run away!

Ha'penny Keeble's Milk Delivery Round

John 'Ha'penny' Keeble (1890–1969) was married to Dorothy Topple (1892–1968). He left school at 14, like most children in those days, and went to work on the land for George Fiske. Ha'penny must have been a very responsible worker because before he was much older he was offered the job of delivering milk around the village by horse and cart. The milk was carried in churns and dispensed at the house door by an oval milk pail and ladled by half or one pint measures into the housewife's milk jug.

Runcton, Street Barn and Grove farms all sustained a herd of cows which grazed the Gipping meadows stretching from Runcton to the fertilizer works. At each farm, Mr Fiske employed cowmen to take care of the cows and milk them.

Government departments and inspectors were becoming sensitive to the quality and the dispensation of milk, particularly direct from farms to the public. Spot checks were made in dairies and on delivery floats, samples of milk being taken away for analysis after similar samples were handed to the farmer or employee. By 1928 relations with the Ministry were so strained that Mr Harry Fiske decided to pull dairy farming out of his business and handed the milk round to Ha'penny. It was a very generous offer which Ha'penny was pleased to accept, knowing the agreement included the pony Diamond and the milk float which were stabled at Grove Farm. However, it was not long before the Milk Marketing Board came into being and with it the order that all milk must be delivered in capped bottles. At considerable capital outlay Ha'penny installed a sterilising and bottling unit, and the whole family at some time or another gave a helping hand within the business.

Lindley (Moses), the eldest son, worked full time helping his father, but as the Second World War approached, he had to spend his regulation military service in the Army. Sydney, who was a shift worker in Ipswich, also assisted in the family business in his spare time, while not on military service in the RAF.

John (Cogan) was employed at the Fison, Packard and Prentice Fertliizer and Chemical Works and he too, when required, helped in the dairy. In the early days of the war, John was called to the colours in the Suffolk Regiment and, after training, he sailed for the Far East along with many of his friends. Thousands of lads from Suffolk and Norfolk were taken as prisoners of war by the Japanese. John, with great courage, endured the hardship, sickness and privation for many months, but like many of his friends he died – on 2 September 1943 at the age of 25.

Joyce, his sister, worked in the business on the milk-bottling and capping unit, bottle washing and the delivery round. But she too was called to the Colours and served in the Army until 1946. Again she joined Lindley and her father to expand the milk delivery service into Claydon, Sproughton and Ipswich. The horse and milk float were now something of the past and motor vehicles were the mode of delivery for a number of years.

Pansy, the baby of the family, was a good athlete in her younger days and this was perhaps her way of evading the family business.

In later years pasteurised milk became the vogue, both in bottles and cartons, but the installation of a pasteurising unit would not have enhanced the prof-itability of the business and so other arrangements were made to survive. The need to provide small milk bottles and drinking straws for schoolchildren was another development within the milk industry, and one not always appreciated by many youngsters. Much of the leftover milk from schools was fed to the pigs, which were housed beyond the dairy.

By the time Lindley retired he had lost the top of a finger with the compliments of a bull terrier. On another occasion he became very dejected and upset, because while delivering milk in Bullen Lane with Joyce one morning, their brand-new vehicle was ploughed into from the rear causing a lot of damage and inconvenience. Lindley was hardly a 'Moses' at the time, but which commandment tablet was shattered is difficult to tell.

Alec Pryke

Alec Pryke was born in Bramford and was a strong supporter of the Methodist chapel. He served on the Parish Council for 40 years, as chairman from 1965 to 1967, and again from 1970 to 1981. He was fiercely proud of his village and fought the expansion of

Alec Pryke, chairman of the Parish Council for many years, strong supporter of the Methodist chapel and a firm advocate for the village identity.

Ipswich to prevent Bramford from being absorbed into the town. He also opposed the boundary changes which would have moved Bramford into Ipswich. On both these occasions he won, but he was not so lucky when he fought the closure of the railway station in the 1950s. There were very few community activities in which he did not become involved, from school governor, to the village hall and local charities. He was the unofficial local historian who progressed to becoming local history recorder and gave talks to the schoolchildren.

Edith Stritch

Edith lived in Bramford all her life. She attended the school in Ship Lane and met her future husband Tony when he was billeted at Bramford Hall during the Second World War. He was originally from Ireland. After the war they settled in Ship Lane, and this was when she stopped working on the machines at Cranes in Ipswich and became the village post-woman, a position she held for 34 years. She not only delivered the post, but also other necessary items to people who were housebound. On her retirement the *East Anglian Daily Times* coined the pun which described her as a 'tough femail'. In retirement she could not sit still and she started delivering meals on wheels with her husband. Unfortunately illness marred her final years. Since she delivered mail in all weathers, it was considered only fair that it should be wet for the people who came to say goodbye to her at the funeral.

The Earthy Family Memories

Ron Earthy recorded these recollections in 1984. (Please note that all spellings of names have been left unchanged and may not necessarily be correct.)

My mother used to work for Lady Loraine at Bramford Hall. When my mother married she lived in a little place called the Round House (which stood at the entrance to the long driveway of the Hall). I was born there on December 9th 1918. The new road cut across the driveway, the house has since been demolished and a bungalow stands in its grounds. The bottom end of the driveway has been closed for several years as Bullen Close was built over it, but the top end still leads to Bramford Hall.

Miss Isaura Loraine was my godmother, and I shall never forget the time when she took me to see the Empire Exhibition at Earls Court in London. I was taken from Bramford Hall to Ipswich Station by coach and horses, driven by Mr Marshal who was the coachman. We stayed at Montague Square, and while in London I saw Don Bradman the cricketer, and the speedboat called Bluebird.

Edith Stritch, village postlady.

I left school in 1932, and my first job was at Bramford garage near the station, at that time owned by Mr Smith but now Keeble's Garage. My wages were 10s. (50p) a week. In 1934 I moved to the Co-op Dairy in Ipswich at 14s.6d. a week. I retired after 50 years, having cycled to work every day.

I can name almost everyone who lived in The Street when I was a boy. Starting at the Bullen Lane corner where the old people's flats are now:

Mr and Mrs Fred Sutherwood, Mrs Smith, Mr Green, Mr Moss, Mrs Garrod and Mr Holder the barber. Then came The Angel, where Mr Smith was the landlord. Mrs Jolly lived next door in what is now the British Legion. Next door to that was a gaol, the door of which is still there. Next to that was the Alms Houses for old people, then the nurse, and then a village shop run by Mr Hibbard where we used to buy a 1d. bag of coconut ice. Next to that was Ruffles sweet shop which has now been taken over by Spar [later West End Carpets]. The people who lived in the next houses were Taylor, Francis, Smith, Goddall, Horrex, and Cook – who was a harness maker. Where the electrical and fish shops are now used to be houses lived in by Colemen, Worlledge, Scopes and Mr Mee the shoemaker. Where the telephone box is now on the corner of Gipping Stone Road, the Salvation Army used to play, also selling War Cry at the pubs. Next came Worlledge, Metcalfe, Dedman, Hayes, Church, Brevington,

Taylor, Ford and Gooch. Next was Bales the butcher, where Mr Barfield's yard is now (later the Chemist shop). Then came Diaper, Root, Frost, Parker and Tricker. The landlord of Bramford Cock was Mr Lloyd. That was the west side of The Street.

On the other side, starting opposite the Cock:

King, Palmer, Giles, Southgate the undertaker, King, Bowman, Garrod, Frost, Chaplin, Double, Lockwood, Barfield, Cobb, Smith, Lockwood, Songer and Bumstead. The village Post Office was where the Co-op entrance is now and Mrs King was the postmistress. Then came Scopes, Blair (?), Smith, Cobb, Moss, and Moore. The pork butcher was Mr Hood, from whom we used to buy scraps, pork cheese, etc. Then there was the Bramford Oak, whose landlady was Ada Barfield, and then the bakery, owned by Mr Bowman. Next door was the blacksmith's house and forge, manned by Hayward Plummer, then Lay. Next door to this were Lockwood and Newman. What is now the Post Office used to be the Police Station with PC Parker, then came Rowland, Ruffles, Clover, Tompson and Crooks. Where the bus shelter is now used to be the coal yard, which belonged to Tricker who owned the stores opposite The Angel. Next to Tricker were some more houses with Tunicliffe, Spall – who was a plumber – and Lay who lived in the Chapel House.

Barry Earthy writes:

I was born to parents Ronald and Marjorie Earthy on May 20th 1947 at 4 Runcton Cottages, Bramford. My father was in the Suffolk Regiment and fought in the Middle East.

On 19th July 1951 my sister Wendy was born. We had a happy childhood at Runcton cottages. Several other children lived in the other houses – the Fishers, the Allums, the Hardwicks, the Seadons, and the Abbots. The road that passed our house was then the A1100 but is now the B1113.

We used to cross the field opposite the houses and go down to the river to swim in the River Gipping. Another swimming place was 'deep water' between Bramford Bridge and the waterfall until the river was polluted and all the fish died.

Miss Ethel and Miss Hilda Fiske lived at Runcton Farm, and their nephew Jack and his family lived at Thornbush Hall. At church every Sunday the Fiske family entered by the rear door, had their own pews, and were always first to take communion.

At 5 years old I started Bramford Junior School, and the headmaster at that time was Mr Ellis. In 1957 the family moved to a house in Duckamere, which was our first home with running water and a sink. A few years later the sewer was laid on in the village and so then we had a flush toilet.

I was a newspaper boy for Mrs Saunders who was the

Four generations of the Earthy family at 4 Runcton Cottages, 1947. The baby is Barry Earthy, his father, Ronald Earthy, and his grandmother, Florence Earthy, (who lived at Parish Pond) are standing and his great-grandmother Anna Barfield (Frederick's widow) is seated.

wife of the school caretaker. She supplied papers to part of the village. The morning papers came by Eastern Counties Bus.

At the Bramford Modern School, M. Dosser was headmaster, and Miss Houston the deputy head.

At the age of 15, I joined F.W. Drake at Sproughton to become an apprentice bricklayer, studying for 5 years at the then Ipswich Civic College.

I now have two sons, Scott and Marc, and two grandsons, Joshua and Kaetin.

Justin Reginald Egerton

Much of the following information has been taken from *Early Country Motoring*, by John F. Bridges. Born in 1873, Mr Egerton moved to Bramford in 1935, and until his death in March 1969 he lived with his wife at Tye House in Bramford Tye, a hamlet just over a mile to the west of the village centre.

His love affair with the motor car ran from the turn of the century, when he took part in motor trials as far away as John o'Groats. The English Channel was no barrier to this intrepid motorist, he also drove on the Continent during these very early days.

Justin Egerton with his goats in the 1960s.

We tend to think of speeding motorists only in modern times, but the local constabulary were always having cause to stop Mr Egerton. The early restriction was only 12 miles per hour, and he was fined many times for breaking this and later speed limits.

Eventually, Mr Egerton opened his own garage business, firstly in Northgate Street, Ipswich, before moving to much larger premises not far away, where Crown Pools now stand. By 1950 he had several agencies including Alvis, MG, Riley, Singer, Vauxhall and Wolseley.

A relative who was given a lift by Mr Egerton from Bramford to the Tye used to cling tightly to his seat as a narrow place in the lane was negotiated, Mr Egerton saying that he must get through before anything came the other way. Needless to say, he was breaking the speed limit yet again.

Another love of Mr and Mrs Egerton was their herd of Pedigree Alpine and Anglo-Nubian Goats. These were exhibited at many local shows, including the Suffolk Show. The herd was famous and their kids were purchased by people from all over the world. Mr Egerton had first decided to keep the goats because he was recommended to drink goat's milk, which he found difficult to obtain, as a solution to gastric problems.

Before the Second World War, several local people worked at Tye House, both inside and out, and there was always a party at Christmas time. The tradespeople of Bramford who served Tye House were all invited. The staff and families of the garage in town were not forgotten as another party was held in Ipswich for them.

'Poke' Laffling, c.1960

'Poke' lived in Gipping Cottages, now in Fitzgerald Road, and kept pigs and chickens on the allotment behind his house, which is now the lower half of the school playing-field. He also had a stable on the land in which he kept a chestnut horse. The horse was used to pull a cart on which Poke collected swill to feed to his animals from eateries in Ipswich.

He also hired the field between The Street allotments and the then A1100 road. He would take his horse up Duckamere, which was then an unmade road, to work the land. In the evenings, when the horse needed to go out to grass, Mr Bumpstead, also from Gipping Cottages, would lead it to a meadow beside the railway line, now the picnic-site car park, and leave it out overnight.

Edward Fitzgerald

During the mid-nineteenth century the family of Revd Charlesworth lived in Ship Lane. One of his daughters, Elizabeth, married Edward Byles Cowell who became a professor at Cambridge University (it is rumoured that they met on Bramford Bridge). Their friend, Edward Fitzgerald from Woodbridge,

The house in Ship Lane which Edward Fitzgerald used to visit, later the vicarage, c.1850.

used to visit them in Bramford. He became famous for several translations of the work of a Persian poet entitled 'The Rubaiyat of Omar Khayyam'. It was suspected that Fitzgerald was secretly in love with Elizabeth as he used to send her poems, and in one letter he said: 'I think you should spare me a bit of Bramford… a little piece of green ribbon cut into a leaf pattern which I remember you used to wear this time last year.' He also wrote of Bramford:

In those Meadows far from the World… Before an Iron Railway broke the Heart of that Happy Valley, whose gossip was the Millwheel, and Visitors the Summer Airs that momentarily ruffled the Sleepy Stream that turned it.

He wrote the following about sunsets:

When Winter Skies were tinged with crimson still
Where Thornbush nestles on the quiet hill,
And the live Amber round the setting sun,
Lighting the Labourer home whose Work is done,
Burn'd like a Golden Angel-ground above
The Solitary Home of Peace and love.

Edward Cowell left the village to become a professor at Cambridge University. He and his wife are both buried in Bramford churchyard.

Memories of Malcolm Hood, 1995
Malcolm Hood lived above the pork butcher's and dairy shop in The Street until 1938. He was named after his uncle who died in 1916. His father used to rise at 5.30 every morning to collect the cows from the meadow for milking. The milk then had to be cooled before being transported to Ipswich for delivery straight to the doorstep into the customers' own jugs. For a while his mother produced her own home-made ice-cream from the milk, a real treat in those days. But the ice had to be collected from the Ipswich Ice Company in Turret Lane and brought home in a sack on the bus.

He remembered playing football on the 'Campo', a meadow between The Street and the river. He also enjoyed watching the Bramford team playing in league matches at Broadwater. One of the players, 'Sonny' Rodwell, went on to play for Ipswich Town. There was a bowling-green at The Angel, where he remembered the hunt meeting in the yard, and also the Sproughton Foot Beagles. Other games included tops, hoops and sticks, and swimming in the river, while girls had skipping ropes. When he was a bit older, he also enjoyed playing darts, billiards and cribbage in the Royal British Legion, which was smaller than it is now.

Next to the British Legion was the police cell, opposite the policeman's house on the corner of Ravens Lane. Further down The Street was the blacksmith, then Hayward Plummer who later moved to Offton Limeburners. Then there was Bowman's bakery and the Royal Oak kept by the Misses Barfield. Beyond his father's butcher's shop was the Post Office, kept by the King family, and next to that the yard of Mr Cook the wheelwright. Another Mr Cook was the harness maker, and Mr Mee's boot and shoe repair shop was across the road. There was also Bales the butcher, with Mrs Bales at the cash desk to take the money.

At the south end of The Street was Bramford Cock, again smaller than it is now, and regulars belonged to a Cork Club. This involved being given a small cork to keep in your pocket, which had to be moved between the right and left pockets on alternate weeks. If challenged it was necessary to produce the cork from the correct pocket, and failure to do so would result in a fine. This was a simple but harmless piece of fun of which the youngsters never seem to have tired.

Malcolm Hood's aunt was Mrs Gladys Moore who was born in Bramford on 1 January 1900, she lived there until she died in 1994. Malcolm died in 2003.

Memories of Bert Keeble in the late 1970s
Bert Keeble was born in 1897 in a cottage beside the railway in Ship Lane. At that time a row of cottages stood adjacent to the railway, with a small strip of orchard between them and the line. The cottages were damaged in the fire which destroyed the station in 1912. Before the fire, Bert remembered others who lived there being named Keeble, Pryke, Mrs Cook, Mrs Rattle, as well as his aunt and grandfather. The cottages faced the river with a strip of garden running down towards it. Water came from a well and the water from the ditch was used for pigs and chickens, which were kept by several families. His grandfather worked for Mr Catchpole, the brewery owner who also owned the Royal Oak in The Street.

Bert remembered barges travelling from Ipswich to Bramford Works, but not to Stowmarket. Fisons had three fairly new barges, the names of which he recalled as *Orwell*, *Whale* and *Scorpion*. Packards had more barges which were all named after rivers, such as *Stour* and *Deben*. Only the front barge was powered by steam, but this would have pulled two or three 'dumb' barges. A man and a boy used to be on the front barge and had to lower the chimney to pass under the bridges when the water-level was high. Packards also had a horse which could be used to tow a barge if there was a problem. He remembered phosphates and pyrites from North Africa being unloaded by crane at Packards. Exports were sent all over the world. Packards sent mainly to Europe and Russia, while Fisons sent goods to Australia, New Zealand, South America and Africa.

Bert started school in Bramford at the age of four. In the summer, boys would swim in the river during their lunch break. At the far end of the schoolhouse near the church there were two classes of infants and the teachers were Mrs Rumsey and Miss Peck. Desks stood in tiers so the children at the back of the class had a good view of the church. Older children were taught by Mr Senton, a good quiet teacher, Mr Rumsey, who suffered badly from rheumatism, and Mr Hurry, who was strict but fair. There were school gardens near the lane leading from the school to Vicarage Lane beside the church.

Bert Keeble when he first went away to work in 1912.

Bert and his friends used to go to the house at Riverhill, on Bramford Road, to have tea with the Misses Henderson. He remembered a sunken garden there, and they also had a donkey, a horse and a motor car. Mr Henderson was a school inspector. The hill outside their house was used by delivery vehicles taking loads to Ipswich docks and returning with animal feed, potatoes and maize, and the men who made their horses pull extra heavy loads were rebuked by the sisters, while those who were kind to their animals were rewarded with a sixpence.

After leaving school at the age of 14, Bert worked for a couple of years at a language college in London, before returning to work as a gardener at Sproughton Manor. He would walk there along the towpath beside the River Gipping and through Hazel Wood.

Bert got to know many of the local farmers. He remembered George Fiske from Thornbush, who was also a Justice of the Peace, and his five sons: Harry who farmed at Runcton, Edgar who farmed at Burstall Hall, George who farmed at Playford Hall, Malcolm who farmed at Willisham Hall, and Frank who farmed at Lovetofts Farm in Flowton.

At the age of 16, Bert was asked to form a Scout troop in Bramford, which he did with the help of Harold Warnes from Bramford Lodge whose father bought the uniforms. One of their first entertainments was to put on a play in the Coach House behind the Lodge. Other boys in the troop were Albert Gosling, Jack Gosling, Jim Taylor, Fred Garrod, 'Tooty' Giles, Jim Giles and 'Maury' Hood. They also went camping, sometimes to Dovercourt and other times nearer to home at The Fens beyond Thornbush, where they were provided with food by the Misses Fiske.

By 1914 there were about 25–30 boys in the troop and, at the start of the First World War, some were asked to act as guards for telegraph wires in case of sabotage. At first Bert was stationed in a field beside the road from Stratford St Mary, and then near the river bridge on London Road in Ipswich, where food was often provided by local housewives.

Then a Miss Reeder from Stutton took some of the boys to a depot in Woodbridge Road in her dog-cart. They were issued with clothes and sent out to Shingle Street to watch for the enemy from the coastguard tower. For this they were paid 10s. (50p) a week plus food. He remembered a public house at Shingle Street where the landlady served wonderful meat puddings with vegetables and gravy. Stationed nearby was the First Suffolk Regiment of Cyclists, and Bert used to practice drill with them. Although not quite old enough he decided to join the Army and was sent to France and Palestine during the First World War, where he was wounded several times.

During the Second World War he was in the Bramford Home Guard and remembered there being a suspected German agent living in Ravens Lane, though this turned out to be false.

Bert Keeble died in February 1982 just a few days before his eighty-fifth birthday.

The Gynn and Rowland families.

In 1861 George Gin married Amelia Chinery in Needham Market. They moved to Bramford where 10 out of their 11 children were baptised between 1865 and 1884. George was a farm labourer, and the family lived in what is now Paper Mill Lane, next door to a grocer's shop. The spelling of their name changed over the years to Ginn and finally Gynn.

Their eldest son, Charles William, was born in 1865, and in January 1890 he married Emma Jane Scopes. They also lived in Paper Mill Lane and Charles worked as a lime burner. Their eldest son Frederick was born the same year and they had six more children before Emma died of pneumonia after childbirth in 1906.

A few houses away in Paper Mill Lane lived

Left: *Violet Rowland and her sister Annie, 1910.*

the Rowland family. Thomas Rowland was born in London, but by 1841 had moved to Runting (Runcton) Street, Bramford, where he lived with his grandmother, Mary Rowland. She died in 1893 at the age of 93 and was buried in the churchyard.

Thomas married Lucy Ellen and their first child was born in 1854. They had 11 children in total and William Saul Rowland was born in January 1867. William was a labourer at first and then became an engine driver at the chemical works in Paper Mill Lane. He married Elizabeth Mayhew, a Bramford girl, in 1887. Their daughter, Violet May Rowland, was born in 1890. They lived for a while at Parish Pond before moving to Paper Mill Lane.

Violet Rowland married Frederick Gynn in 1910 and lived in Bramford where their five children were born. Violet sadly died after the birth of her sixth child. Frederick was employed at the chemical works and also served as a volunteer fireman in the village fire service. He lived in Bramford until his death in 1963, when he was buried with his wife in the churchyard.

Their son Leonard went to school in the village, and then worked as a chauffeur for the owners of Gables Farm. He married Dorothy Lewis in 1939 and they moved into Ipswich, as did the other children.

Altogether there are 17 members of the Gynn and Rowland families buried in St Mary's churchyard, though many of the graves are no longer visible.

Memories of Les Beckett

Les recalled the following about the Gipping Valley floods of 1939:

The severe weather conditions of deep melting snow and continuous heavy rain, which caused the floods and isolated Bramford village in January and February 1939 have been documented many times over in the past 60 years or so.

Runcton, where I lived with my parents, brothers and sister, was on the west side of the river, and the Fison, Packard and Prentice Fertilizer Works, where I was employed, was on the east side. It was necessary for me to use the river road crossing near Church Green four times daily.

This story begins as I cycled to work on that dull, wet and fateful afternoon at the end of January when the road bridge – which also carried the gas and water

services – *collapsed into the flood water. The scene that morning of the meadows alongside the River Gipping being underwater was not unusual for the time of year. In the afternoon when I returned to work after my mid-day dinner break, the water at the river bridge was still rising and flowing fast downstream. The flood water had reached an unusually high level and showed signs of submerging the road, which was several feet above the hidden pastures. Close by, the water under the railway bridge was rising rapidly and already too deep to cycle through and so, in order not to get my feet and legs wet, I cycled along the raised boarded platform to pass under the bridge. Throughout the afternoon the flood water continued to rise, swell and spread in the direction of Gables Corner, and the gardens of the houses in Works Lane (Paper Mill Lane).*

The staff at the junior school were worried and concerned for the safety of the children, particularly those whose homes were on the east side of the river. An urgent telephone call immediately highlighted an emergency. A cyclist hurried to Gables Farm to alert David Allum and ask for his help. He hastily placed harness over the back of his shire-horse, Prince, and backed him into the shafts of a high-wheeled farm wagon. Mr Allum climbed onto the wheel hub and quickly pulled himself into the wagon, at the same time nudging Prince into a good moving gait.

The bridge over the swollen river was no more than

Frederick Gynn in his fire service uniform, c.1940.

200 yards away, but by the time the wagon passed under the railway bridge, water was swirling above the horses knees. The pressure of flood water and debris rushing across the hidden road made David's job very difficult in guiding his horse and wagon safely to and fro across the river bridge. Scores of children and teachers were waiting for help at Church Green, many young boys and girls had smiles on their faces as the horse's head came up over the brow of the bridge, but other faces showed worry and anxiety. David turned the horse and wagon while children and teachers moved forward to scramble aboard. The smaller ones were half-lifted and half-bundled onto the wagon floor. Miss Ena Hunt and Miss Salter (the school head) were among the staff who eventually found room on board with a comfortable position. Others too, seeking a safe passage to the rail station side of the river, wedged in the wagon where they could.

Prince, with shoulders embedded deeply in his padded collar, strained every muscle in his huge body as he hauled the heavy human load on its return over the bridge through the ever-deepening flood water. There were sighs of relief from waiting parents as children and teachers reached relative safety at Gables Corner. Small children, seeking attention, looked into the adult faces and excitedly explained the wonderful unexpected adventure they had just experienced. Little did they realise the great danger they and others had encountered that afternoon.

As soon as the wagon was empty David tugged on the rein to turn Prince for another pick-up and at the same time offer transport to those hovering around wondering whether they dare risk crossing the flood waters to Ship Lane. Men and women, some with pushchairs and bicycles hastily climbed aboard. Prince strained and jerked in the wagon shafts to move his high-wheeled vehicle. Splashing again under the railway bridge the flood surged even greater than before, water was now slopping under the horse's body as he moved along. The hump of the bridge over the small stream could no longer be seen.

Nearing the main bridge, Prince was wary of going another step forward, he was unsure of his footing and sensed danger. Mr Allum, standing on the wagon shafts, gave a kind bidding and a flick of the rein to urge Prince forward but there was no response. 'Go on boy,' coaxed David, but again there was no forward movement, the horse stood his ground, he had no intention of crossing the bridge a third time. Evidently troubled, Prince stood firm, he twitched with fear and would not budge, while further urging had no effect. The gathering crowd awaiting rescue on the other side of the river were becoming uneasy, wondering how they would reach home if rescue was abandoned. Those people in the rescue wagon also realised the danger of

being swept away if they did not seek safety. It could have been a matter of life or death had David not made the crucial decision to turn back.

The continuous build up of water coming downstream and bearing against the road and bridge had, over the past 48 hours, been very extensive and had already weakened the bridge foundations. Brickwork was moving out of position and in so doing was no longer able to safely support the weight of the bridge road and steelwork. Within minutes the foundations crumbled and the whole road and bridge structure collapsed and disappeared under the muddy flood water onto the river bed, taking with it the village water and gas supplies. There is no doubt – but we shall never know – that on that cold and rain sodden January afternoon Prince and David may well have saved many lives and averted an even greater village disaster. Prince, the wonderfully intelligent horse, has become a loved part of Bramford folklore.

Rumours were widespread that desolate afternoon at the Fison, Packard and Prentice Ltd Chemical Works. Workmen were becoming concerned as to whether they would be able to reach home at the end of the day. Up-to-date news was scant and no one was foolish enough to wander around outside. One of their lorry drivers came into the yard saying that driving in

Les Beckett at Runcton, c.1930.

Prince and his passengers in the flood in 1939.
(Photo: East Anglian Daily Times)

certain parts of Ipswich was becoming difficult. The view from the high windows of the works warehouses was now one of desolation. Only the tops of a few solitary trees along the river banks could be seen above the swirling water, while the railway track on its embankment ran straight as a pencil to disappear in both directions through the ever rising flood. A telephone message confirmed that the river bridge near St Mary's Church had been washed away by the volume of water surging downstream.

Workers who lived on the other side of the river huddled in groups to discuss ways of reaching home. When Ivan Thorpe sounded the hooter at 5.15p.m. I realised that many employees were not going through the clock office. Curiosity led me to walk through the factory gateway, I looked along the road and there was George Piper's (FPP) lorry loaded with workers and their bicycles. It was too late to join them, we had not cleared away our books and papers in the office. One or two stragglers legged themselves up on a wheel and made themselves room as George drove off. The lorry tail light vanished between the old paper-mill and Pryke's farm and coal yard, in the direction of Claydon where they negotiated safely the low-lying flood water to cross the river bridge.

It was late that night before I finally made it home, having been unable to cross the river near the village, I was forced to travel as far as Stoke Bridge in Ipswich before I could get across on a lorry. Unfortunately I had to leave my bike in Ipswich, which meant I had to return to fetch it next morning, making me late for work.

Within two days the village services had been reconnected and a small wooden bridge slung across the river for foot use and cycles. Another six months passed by before the Army was able to erect a vehicle-carrying Bailey bridge which remained in situ for many years.

Phyllis Cook's School Days

I came from a small family because my father was killed in the first war and my mother had to bring us up on her own. We lived at Works Lane (now Paper Mill Lane) in Bramford, and my mother worked at Fisons. We did pretty well, considering, and she made my school dresses, under which I wore 'stays', and I also had to wear black lace-up boots.

I did well at school, especially at music and singing. I remember the headmaster was Mr Hurry, and another teacher I liked was Mr Woodward. Mrs Stone taught me to play the piano after school and I had to play while the children marched into school for assembly. We had to do exercises in the playground and sometimes it was very cold. Once we put on a display for the parents, when I was dressed as a flower and sat at the front. Suddenly Mr Hurry (who was a bit strict) said 'Come on Phyllis, you can stand up and sing for us.' I had to stand up in front of all those people on my own and I nearly collapsed, but I felt very proud.

There used to be a railway station at Bramford when I was a child, and we used to catch a train once a week to Claydon where we had cookery lessons. After the lesson we took our jam tarts to the Alms Houses where we gave three jam tarts to each lady.

'Ruffy', c.1990.

Memories of 'Ruffy'

Florence was born at Gipping, near Stowmarket, and moved to Bramford when she married her husband, Stanley Ruffles, in 1938 at the age of 21. Not long after this her husband was called up to join the Army and serve in the war, and Ruffy started work at Mann Egerton's in Ipswich.

One night during the war bombs were falling locally so she sheltered at a friend's house. When she returned home her windows were smashed and there was a hole in her bedroom ceiling.

After the war she would regularly cycle to Mendlesham to help her grandmother with the washing. She became the village postwoman and started work at 6a.m. sorting mail and delivering it on her bicycle. One evening in 1969 she was invited to take part in a game of darts at Bramford Cock and she won the match and a prize. From then on she played regularly and won many trophies.

Towards the end of her life she could always be seen at her front window in The Street, where she lived for more than 58 years, knitting toys which she gave for charity fund-raisers.

Robert Southgate's Memories of Bell-ringing

Bell-ringing in Bramford drew in many different people. In 1968 Mervyn Bewley and Buster Crouch joined the ringers. Mervyn was a friend of Kelvin Dakin who was already a ringer but Buster, at that time, was considered the village hooligan. One practice night he came to the churchyard where a group of people had gathered, and was picking a fight with someone. I went down to try and sort it out, and in the process encouraged Buster to come and see what we were doing. We gave him a bell rope to try it, and he found it was not as simple as he thought. I told him he should learn to ring, which he did, and he became a very useful member of the band, always very lively and a lot of fun. Mervyn was also to become a good friend, as was David 'Sid' Johnson who joined that year.

In 1967 the Bramford band came fourth in the Suffolk Guild Striking Competition. The band were, I think, all over the age of 60, and it was commonly thought that only this level of experience could make really good ringers. So we set out to win the competition, which *was to ring 240 changes on six bells in any method you like. The team of Martin, Neville and Roger Whittell, Lawrence Pizzey, Simon Christian and myself was chosen, and we practiced our 240 changes several times at Bramford. The competition was held at Ashbocking in May 1968, and we had just one practice there a few weeks before the event. We arrived accompanied by a band of supporters wearing large rosettes which read 'Bony Bob's Bouncing Bell-ringing Band' [see page 17], which was rather frowned on by a few of the old boys who thought we were not taking the competition seriously. When the scores were read out we had won by having one less fault than what was considered to be the top notch band, which was a surprise to most of the other ringers. This win was not to be a flash in the pan, as in the following year at Woolpit we came first again, which was the first time any team had consecutive wins. This was very satisfying!*

Memories of Irene Dowsett (née Lloyd) and Yvonne Wright (née Rosier)

Both Irene and Yvonne attended Bramford Junior School in Ship Lane where Miss Salter was the head teacher. At that time Mr Hurry was head at the senior school in Duckamere. They had to attend church regularly on Thursday mornings. Each child had a bottle of milk daily, containing one third of a pint, and in winter the crates would stand in front of the open fire to stop the milk from freezing.

Sports days were held in a field behind Vicarage Lane which was normally used by cows so it could be a bit messy, and the children had to wear white plimsolls! On Empire Days they would each wear a white daisy and carry a flag.

Lessons at the junior school were essential subjects only, with an occasional outing in good weather to look at wild flowers. Some of the lessons Irene and Yvonne remembered from the senior school were cookery, art, music and sewing.

As small children they were terrified of 'Old Mother McKenzie' who used to walk around the village pushing a pram. If children misbehaved they were told to 'wait 'til Old Mother McKenzie comes round again'; they thought she would take them away.

During holidays the children would play on the 'Campo'. There would occasionally be a big bonfire there, which Mr Bloomfield from the garage would throw all his old tyres and a supply of sump oil on to make it burn well.

As Girl Guides they were entertained by Miss Loraine at Bramford Hall. The girls were encouraged to obtain their badges by going to the hall to clean the silver and the family shoes. They had very fond memories of Miss Loraine and her Austin Seven car.

One of the most unpleasant memories is that of the night soil cart. Before the days of flushing toilets, each family would have a bucket in the garden privy. A night soil cart came around weekly to empty the

Joseph and Maria Hardwick, William's parents who lived on Church Green. Joseph was the parish sexton.

buckets after dark, which always seemed to coincide with social events at the Victory Hall! Large families had a collection twice weekly. Many people in the village had not seen a flushing toilet until they went into Ipswich to work.

The outbreak of war in 1939 brought soldiers to the village. Bramford Hall was requisitioned by the Army as staff quarters. A weekly dance was held in the Victory Hall, where many local girls learned to dance. A searchlight station, where soldiers were available to talk to local girls informally, was installed in Tye Lane. This was within easy walking distance of the village centre and the arrival of so many new young men in the village caused much excitement and not a little rivalry amongst the girls.

The Hardwick Family

A familiar figure in Bramford in the late-nineteenth and early-twentieth centuries was Joseph Hardwick. He was church clerk and sexton for 34 years up until his retirement in April 1916. On his retirement it was noted that during his tenure of office there had been 1,117 baptisms, 243 marriages and 559 burials.

Joseph was born in Bramford in 1848, the third child of James and Mary Ann (née De'ath) Hardwick and was probably named after his grandfather, Joseph Hardwick, who moved to Bramford with his wife Grace in about 1812. Joseph married Maria Munson at Tattingstone in 1870 and their first home was in Bramford Lane, Ipswich, where their first child, William, was born in 1871. They had moved to Gipping Cottages, Bramford, by April 1873 when their second child, a daughter named Mary Ann, was born. Joseph was appointed church clerk and sexton in 1882 and they moved to the cottage on Church Green where they spent the rest of their lives. They had 15 children, two of whom died soon after birth.

Joseph and Maria's eldest son, William, served in the Army and later worked for the Great Eastern Railway as a railway policeman. As a 'reservist' he was recalled to the Army and sent to South Africa with the 4th Brigade, 1st Durham Light Infantry, to fight in the Boer War. William was killed in action, aged 28 years, near Spion Kopp on 5 February 1900. He wrote to his parents a few days before his final battle, telling them of his determination to fight for his country and for the relief of Ladysmith (see page 79). William left a wife, Eliza, whom he had married in 1896 at Great Blakenham. There is a memorial to Sergeant William Hardwick in Bramford Church, and his widow included a memorial to him on her mother's gravestone in Great Blakenham churchyard.

The Leathers Family

William Leathers came to Bramford from Stowupland, having been born there in 1764. He moved to Bramford following his marriage to Deborah Bearman in 1786. Their son William was baptised at the church the following year. The family continued to live in the village for many generations and in the 1881 Census there were various family members listed as living at the Station House, the west side of The Street, and at Parish Pond.

Robert, the great-grandson of William and Deborah, was born in Bramford in 1852. He married Emily Seaman and they moved to London where he died of smallpox in 1884 aged 32. His youngest son, Frederick, later became a member of the Cabinet and Minister of War Transport in the government of Winston Churchill during the Second World War. His work was rewarded when he was ennobled as Viscount Leathers of Purfleet.

Winifred King's Memories of the King Family

James King set up his wheelwrighting business in Bramford Street during the 1840s, having moved from Reydon where his family had been blacksmiths and carpenters for many generations.

In 1850 he married a local girl, Mary Ann Vesey, whose father David Vesey farmed at Flowton. They had four sons, Harry, William, Frederick and another William (both Williams died at the age of eight months) and a daughter called Ellen. Mary Ann died in 1862 aged 42 years.

James remarried in 1863 to Sophia Wilkinson (or Watkinson) who was born at Saxham. Sophia had two

sons, James and William Henry, and two daughters, Sophia and Anna.

William Henry had saddlery shops in Ipswich and Bramford and eventually took over the Post Office.

By 1860 James was listed as a Post Office Receiver using a small lean-to office built on to his house next to the wheelwrights workshop (where the Co-op is now). He became village postman, wearing the old helmet-type headgear and riding the official PO bicycle. He married Evelynn Webb, cook at Bramford Hall, who came from Basingstoke.

James travelled alone to Basingstoke for the wedding, probably the longest journey he ever made, in 1902; he never went far away again. James and Evelynn lived all their married lives in Cedar Cottage in The Street, where the lane led down to the 'Candy'.

James was hurt in a fall from the PO bike and afterwards occupied himself keeping chickens, breeding spaniels and growing apples and beautiful violets under glass frames – all of which he sold.

Evelynn, or Lily as she was commonly known, was a member of the WI and Mothers' Union. She used to give cookery demonstrations all over Suffolk and was the first to have a gas oven in the village; the gas company presented her with their latest model as a 'thank you'.

They had two children, James Lloyd, my father, and Evelynn May Peace, known mostly as Peggy. James was one of the first Bramford children to pass the scholarship and he attended Stowmarket Grammar School, travelling each day by train.

All went well and the family had high hopes of young Lloyd, as he was called, until the death of a Grenadier Guardsman from the Loraine Family, who was given a military parade and band at his funeral. Being dazzled

The photograph shows the first Post Office in Bramford Street, c.1910. It is situated on the site now occupied by the Co-op.

127

by the uniforms and the excitement of it all, he and a friend ran off to London and joined up.

His mother took both boys' birth certificates up to London (they were only 14 years old) and brought them home. However, Lloyd made such a to-do over wanting to go for a soldier that he was allowed to join up as a drummer boy at 1s.6d. a week. He was to remain in the regiment for 21 years.

Peggy attended secretarial school in Ipswich and worked in the office at Ransomes. She began the Scouts and Cubs in the village, with her cousin, Agnes King, from the Post Office.

Evelynn and James often had a lodger and they took the first District Nurse who was Ida Jacob from Gt Blakenham. She and Lloyd met when he came on leave and married in 1926.

Peggy married Arthur Blunt in 1938 and they had one daughter, Jennifer Lloyd. Ida had three children, James Lloyd, Kenneth Roy and myself, Winifred Joyce.

During the Second World War, we spent a lot of time in Bramford. I have many memories of those days, although I was separated from my parents and later lived for a time with Mr and Mrs Tom Hagland in Limes Avenue, they were happy days.

After the death of William King in 1949, his daughter Olive took over the Post Office, but sadly she only survived him by six years.

The people I remember must be recalled by many who will read this, so I will list a few to bring back those far off days: the Frost family who lived opposite us in The Street; Kathy Sutton and Lily who lived next door; the two Miss Fiskes, one played the organ and Ethel ran the Girls' Friendly Society; Miss Salter, Mr Woolnough and Mrs Shortland at school; Revd Hartford; the Hill family at Copenhagen; Aunt Palmer who lived opposite the Cock Inn; Nellie Banyard who was Aunt May's friend; the Sewells who had a little shop and were sort of cousins; Miss Horrocks who used to cut my hair; the two Miss Ruffles who kept a little shop; Mr Bales, the butcher; Mr Bowman, the baker; Miss Dawe from Limes Avenue and Peter and Pam; Olive King, my father's cousin, who ran the Post Office; Miss Loraine who ran the Brownies.

I remember: concerts in the Victory Hall to raise money possibly for the munitions; emergency exercises which included the Home Guard, Red Cross, Scouts and Guides, WI and whoever, when we were designated as 'pretend casualties'; sitting under the stairs with my grandparents during night-time air raids; being fitted for our gas masks in the Parish Room, and having to keep them with us all the time; going to Ipswich on the bus with all the windows blacked out; my Aunt Mary living at 'Riverhill' when her husband came home from Dunkirk; watching enemy planes

Phillip Pinkney outside his house in The Street during restoration, c.1990.

going over on fire and everyone outside cheering.

There are no more Kings at Bramford but we still visit and get very nostalgic, and perhaps envy the children who are lucky enough to be brought up in the village today.

Robert Clover

Mr Robert Clover died in the 1950s aged 69. He was one of the few remaining hand stone dressers in any of the East Anglian grinding mills. He worked at the firms of Hitchcock and Cooper and, after the war, at Rushbrook's of Bramford. He was a trustee of the Methodist chapel, as well as being a steward and Sunday school superintendent.

Canon Ronald Christian

In 1977 Canon Christian wrote a small article for the community newsletter of his first memories of Bramford. He came to the village in 1956, at a time when the church was still unlocked all night and the key, if needed, could be found under the doormat. This was when everyone knew everyone else. There were no sewers, street lights or playing-field and very little traffic. The night soil cart came round to collect waste from the privies, for which there was a charge of half a crown (12$\frac{1}{2}$ p) per bucket on the rates.

With the arrival of new houses came new 'non-village' people, some of whom fitted well into the community, but increasingly residents travelled out of the village for employment and entertainment, and the character of the village began to change.

Herbert 'Brassy' Hill

Brassy Hill, who was 87 when he died, lived in Loraine Way, Bramford. He was an expert angler and was a member of the Gipping Angling Preservation Society (GAPS). Brassy won almost every trophy belonging to the society and built up a vast knowledge of fishing in the River Gipping. His memory lives on through a senior citizens trophy which he donated to GAPS.

He was also a Fisons employee with long service, having completed 50 years with the company in Bramford and Cliff Quay, Ipswich, before his retirement.

The Pinkney Family

Phillip Pinkney, his wife Dorothy and their children came to live in Bramford in 1951 and from the start participated actively in village life. They renovated Oak Cottage at 6 The Street, replacing the existing standpipe and night-soil closet with hot and cold running water and flushing lavatories. A short time later, Mrs Pinkney's mother bought and came to live in the adjoining 8 and 10 The Street, formerly the Bell Inn. In the late 1960s their son Richard bought Street Farm Cottages from the Loraine estate. He rescued them from dereliction and converted them into a comfortable home for his young family. He and his wife Judith returned to live in Oak Cottage (now 6, 8 and 10 combined) in 1989 where they continue to practice as professional artists.

Philip, Dorothy and Richard Pinkney all served on the Parish Council in the 1970s. Dorothy was a keen member of the Women's Institute and Richard was a founder member of the Bramford Community Council. He was also editor of the BCC's magazine and captained the village cricket team based at the playing-field.

Philip Pinkney was a railway engine driver and cycled to work in Ipswich at all hours, and in all weathers, throughout his working life. He was well known in the village for his service as a councillor and for his collections of gramaphone records, railway memorabilia, bells, swords, brassware and teddy bears, among other things. In his later years, despite his failing eyesight, he could be seen chatting in The Street or making his way to the Co-op to buy a half bottle of 'medicine'. He died in 1995.

Memories of Margaret Warton (née Garner)

I can't remember the exact year, but one Thursday evening during the 1939–45 war, there was an air raid. We were getting ready to go to a whist drive in the Victory Hall when The Street was lit up with a flare that was dropped by a German bomber. A bomb was dropped next to the garage in Ship Lane on the river bridge side. Two men were near at the time, one – the railway stationmaster – ran towards the station and was all right, but Mr Smith ran towards a small wall and was killed by the bomb.

When Bramford Bridge was washed away in 1939 we had time off school until the footbridge was put up. A few years later one of our school chums who was an evacuee with his relatives in Bramford (Bloomfields in Ravens Lane, I think), slipped on a plank on the footbridge, fell into the river and drowned. His name was Peter Leaman and he was about ten years old at the time. Our assistant guider, Winne Lingley, dived in to rescue him but to no avail. A few weeks earlier his mother and brother had been killed in an accident, leaving Pat, his older sister.

One afternoon after school a German bomber was shot down. We watched and cheered as the Spitfires did the Victory Roll! Then we watched the German airman bale out, he was only 18 years old. The Home Guard was called out (or it might have been LDVs) and piled into Eddie Page's van (just like Dad's Army!) to follow one of the parachutes. The airman came down in a field of kale at Sproughton but could speak no English, so the Sproughton rector was fetched to interpret!

Margaret Warton died in 2002.

The wedding of James King and Ida Jacob, 1926. This photograph was taken at the reception at the Victory Hall with local children watching through the playground railings. Left to right, back row: *Best man (either Sewell or Firman), James King (groom's father and postmaster), James Lloyd King in his Guards uniform (groom), William Jacob (bride's father), Lionel Jacob (bride's brother), Ellen Jacob (bride's mother);* front: *bride's grandmother, Evelynn 'Lily' King (groom's mother and postwoman), Evelyn (May or Peggy) King (groom's sister), Ida Winifred Sophia Jacob (bride), Vera Jacob (bride's aunt), Daniel Jacob (bride's grandfather).*

Above: *The village street and pump, which is now the entrance to Gipping Stone Road, c.1900.*

Left: *The house in The Street which was used as the doctors' surgery.*

TEN

❧❀❧

PUBLIC HEALTH

Bramford has always been vulnerable to epidemics. It is certain that a large number of people died in the Black Death during the fourteenth century, perhaps 30–40 per cent of the population.

There is no record of deaths in Bramford until the start of the parish registers in 1553, and from then on it is possible to tell which years had an unusually high numbers of burials. The plague was stated as the cause of death for four people, including Dorcas Woodwarde, 'a maide that lived at our Angell', for the first time in 1666. Local inns were one of the first places to show signs of disease because of sick people travelling through. By the 1670s the cause of many deaths was smallpox. The first to be buried was the son of John Curthoise Esq., one of the better-off families. No doubt richer families travelled more widely and therefore came into contact with diseases more frequently.

There was of course no sewerage system at the time, apart from pits in gardens. As water was drawn from wells in the same gardens, it is no wonder that outbreaks of disease occurred.

Even during the nineteenth and twentieth centuries public health continued to cause concern. In 1895 unsanitary conditions were blamed for an outbreak of dyptheria, with special concern for the ditch that ran behind the houses in The Street, and the following year the Medical Officer of Health reported that the water-supply in the village was inadequate. The only alternative to garden wells was the pump which stood in The Street on the corner of what is now Gipping Stone Road.

By 1911 the local water was still considered to be unfit for drinking, but by 1914 some areas of the village had been connected to a mains water-supply.

The disposal of household waste also caused health problems. Without a collection or recognised tip, most was deposited over hedges and in ditches, or buried in a garden hole. It was not until after the Second World War that a regular collection of household waste was organised by Gipping Rural District Council.

In 1952 it was estimated that the cost of providing a sewerage system was £70,000, but luckily boundary changes meant that a long strip of Bramford Road was taken into Ipswich, thus reducing the cost considerably. However, even as late as 1955, night soil was still being collected by cart from local houses. It was not until 1961 that the majority of houses were connected to the sewers, but there still remained a few outlying farms with their own disposal system.

During the 1950s two doctors attended the village, with surgeries being held in the front room of two houses in The Street, next to the shoe shop of Bob Manning (now Atticus Antiques). There were brass plates outside the houses, one for Dr Staddon and one for Dr Ryan. Later, only one house was used, that of Mrs Worlledge and her son Derek, who was a familiar sight in the village as he was confined to a three-wheeled chair which he would propel around the village with his dog by his side. Patients could wait in Mrs Worlledge's front room until the doctor arrived and then they had to go outside to wait, whatever the weather, while each patient was seen in turn. The family had to wait in the back room until surgery was finished.

When the Worlledge family moved to the Red Cottages in Ship Lane, the surgery was moved to the premises of the British Legion in The Street. Patients waited in an area of the bar set aside for the purpose, and were called into an adjoining storeroom to see the doctor.

In 1970 there was talk about starting a doctors' surgery in the village, but because of the cost involved and the difficulty of providing a suitable building, it was decided to redecorate the room used as a surgery at the British Legion. The local newsagent, Mr Mayes, would take prescriptions to be dispensed for those people who did not have access to a chemist. This service was no longer required when a pharmacy opened in The Street where the Co-op butcher used to be.

By the 1990s the number of nurses and health

visitors who could travel to patients had increased and many families had their own transport, so it was decided that a surgery in the village was not necessary. The pharmacy remains a very useful facility, especially for the residents of Cherryfields.

BRAMFORD BABY CLINIC

The clinic for babies and toddlers was held once a fortnight in the Victory Hall, and was started in the latter years of the Second World War. There were no doctor facilities in the village at this particular time and it was thought prudent to provide nursing services to ensure babies received the best possible start in life.

Young mothers met and used the clinic for social afternoons, as well as for medical and nursing events. Nurse Larner, the District Nurse who lived at 67 The Street, supervised the clinic and visited her patients at home by bicycle in her uniform of navy blue. In the early days Mrs Males and Mrs Barker at the clinic gave valuable practical assistance in keeping an eye on the children as they played with toys on a blanket in the centre of the hall. These ladies were also responsible for the attendance register and the allocation of orange juice, cod-liver oil and dried milk. A lady doctor held monthly sessions in the 'billiard' room, dispensing non-compulsory injections against diphtheria, while at the same time casting a searching eye for a rash or spots. Babies were not particularly happy when leaving the doctor's presence or when introduced to the weighing scales, but tears dispersed quickly. Mums too were grateful for a 'cuppa' to soothe perhaps a throbbing headache.

Following the retirement of the female assistants in 1948, Mrs Peggy Ford (wife of Dennis 'Frip' Ford) became a young mother who availed herself of the service provided by the baby clinic. When her daughter Jennifer reached school age, Peggy continued as resident assistant at the clinic, which had become a regular fortnightly meeting place for the young mothers. Over the years small amounts of money donated by mothers for tea and service accumulated, eventually enabling donations to be made to deserving causes. The funds also covered the cost of Christmas parties for the children and mothers. On such occasions Lily Lewis and Pam Castleton gave invaluable assistance organising the event and providing a present for every child.

When the clinic finally closed, the Director of Nursing Services (Community) within the East Suffolk Health Authority wrote a rewarding and appreciative letter to Peggy thanking her for her loyal and committed service over a period of more than 30 years.

Privies behind Street Farm Cottage in the 1960s.

ELEVEN

ACCIDENTS, TRAGEDY, CRIME AND PUNISHMENT

LOCAL TRAGEDIES

In the days when the lord of the manor was in charge of the people, rules were enforced at the manorial court. More serious crimes were tried at the shire court and, in the case of major crime, such as the so-called Peasants' Revolt, in front of the King's Bench. Some parishes also had village constables elected by parishioners.

Life has not always been easy in Bramford and the parish registers record some accidental deaths. In 1628 John Chambers was killed by a falling tree and in 1670 'Little Hannah Littlewood' died having been kicked by a horse, following which the entry in the register reads 'from sudden death Good Lord deliver us'.

Top-Shop after the fire, 1960s.

Water has been the cause of many deaths over the centuries. In 1657 George, the son of John Gardner, was drowned when he fell into his own well. In 1664 John Mill was drowned at Sproughton Bridge in a 'great flood of waters', in 1669 Robert Wright was killed by the mill-wheel and in 1688 an unknown man drowned at the paper-mill. As recently as 1950 an eight-year-old child, Michael Wallace, drowned in the river while playing on an old boat with some friends.

In February 1661 a violent storm blew down the Parsonage Barn in Vicarage Lane, along with 'seven score oak trees' in Lord Hereford's park, now called Christchurch Park, in Ipswich.

In 1665 the vicar recorded a death which must have been quite sensational at the time:

Old Mother Hillbie was killed, having by accident set her house on fire, she was slaine by it, yet she was not burned to ashes, though all her household stuffe, even the brasse and pewter were consumed, yet the greatest part of her bodie remained a sadd spectacle to behold.

Justices of the Peace, who were appointed to try minor misdemeanours, such as poaching, were much more powerful from the eighteenth century onwards. This was considered unfair by local people as the JP was quite often the person whose game had been poached!

There have certainly been many fires in Bramford over the centuries, as both the mills have seen disastrous blazes at least once. Also the first railway station, a shop and several barns have been destroyed. No doubt there were many more fires in the days when an open fire was the only form of heating. By 1914 the problem had become so widespread that the village decided to purchase its own fire appliance at a cost of £28.12s.6d. The first superintendent was Mr Robert Francis at an annual salary of £1. His helpers were Mr Hazell senr and junr, Thomas Ruffles, R.W. Clover, George Chaplin and Mr Denny. Their first fire was at Bramford Mill in 1917 when it was estimated that they used 60,000 gallons of water to douse the flames. An account was sent to the mill owners, Messrs Cooper and Cooper, for costs incurred, totalling £15.9s.6d. When Mr Francis retired, his post was taken by Mr Charles Giles, and other helpers were A. Sewell, J. Tricker, A. Rodwell, P.C. Parker,

Left: *Fire at Runcton Farm, 1970s.*

Left: *Funeral of Shirley and Arthur Wilson at the Methodist chapel, front page of the* Evening Star *in 1995.*

Above: *PC Jim Thacker with the Hazelwood Trophy for Community Policing, 1993.*

Bramford Fire Engine, c.1920. The names of the men are not known.

C.L. Hibbard, H. Farnish, R.W. Clover, F. Kinsey, A. Hazell, W. Peck, T. Lloyd, Mr Plumber and A.W. Pryke. The fire appliance was finally commissioned for the war effort in 1939, and in return the village received payment of £14.15s.0d.

In April 1932 the Dutch barn at Street Barn Farm, on the corner of what is now Vicarage Lane, was destroyed by fire. It was thought to have been started by a spark from the firebox of a steam-engine threshing machine. Water had to be pumped from the river a quarter of a mile away by Needham Market Fire Brigade. In the 1960s another barn was destroyed by fire at Runcton Farm.

Although the accident did not happen in the village, in 1913 Sydney Keeble, a 32-year-old local man, was killed in a railway tragedy involving the Cromer Express at Colchester. Also on the railway, a three-year-old boy, John Lockwood, was killed near Fisons Works in 1954.

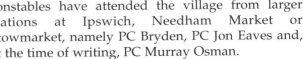

The village lock-up next to the Royal British Legion premises in The Street.

The coming of motor vehicles has unfortunately been the cause of several fatalities. In the 1920s a bus conductor was killed when standing on the top deck of his open-topped bus as it went under the railway bridge; since then only single-decker buses have taken this route.

There have been several accidents along Loraine Way. Probably the first death caused by a motor vehicle was in 1937. Manfred Sheppard was the son of Len and Rose who lived at Runcton. When he was two years old he walked out of the front gate which had been left open by the Co-op delivery man. The horse and cart were out in the road and Manfred walked under the horse into the path of a lorry travelling in the opposite direction.

A tragic event occurred in March 1984 when the body of a seven-day-old baby boy was found dumped at the water meadow between The Grove and the River Gipping. The child was buried in the churchyard at a ceremony attended by many local residents.

An awful tragedy occurred in 1994 when Shirley and Arthur Wilson and, a few days later, Robert Mitchell, were found murdered in their homes. Mr and Mrs Wilson were well known in the village for their work at Cherryfields and the Methodist chapel. Mr Mitchell's son Jason was convicted of the murders.

CRIME AND PUNISHMENT

At some point a village lock-up was built, but no records have survived of this. The Bramford lock-up is still to be found next to the Royal British Legion premises in The Street, although it has not been used for many years and the interior was stripped out some time ago. Ernest Wolton, who was born in 1912 in Paper Mill Lane, Claydon, remembered the lock-up being in use when he was a boy, especially for drunks on a Saturday night.

Some convictions for Bramford people have survived in court records. Charles Hardwick, who moved to the village in about 1830, was sentenced to hard labour in 1857 for stealing an iron trap worth 1s.

Vagrancy was a constant problem throughout the centuries and all parishes were concerned that they did not have to support people unnecessarily. In 1855 Charlotte Hardwick, a widow, was sentenced to 21 days' hard labour for leaving a child chargeable to the parish.

By the 1800s many crimes were punished by transportation, usually to Australia. Bramford residents did not evade this punishment. Between 1843 and 1851, five people were transported for crimes in Bramford, though not all were Bramford residents. In 1843 both William Simpson (aged 41) and Thomas Garrod (aged 20) were convicted for stealing food and transported for life. William Burrows (aged 22) committed burglaries in several parishes including Bramford and was transported for life. Charles Lloyd (aged 37), Bramford-born, was also transported for life for a theft in East Bergholt. George Southgate (aged 27) from Sproughton was transported for seven years for stealing tools at Bramford.

The earliest known Police Station in the village was at the top of Ravens Lane at the building which is now the Post Office. A new station was built in Duckamere in 1950 and was in use until its closure in 1993 when it became a private dwelling.

The policemen who have lived in the village since 1944 are as follows:

PC J.A. James	left in May 1945
PC Wilfred G. Dunnett	1945–49
PC Frederick E. Leeks	1949–55
PC W.E. Moore	1955–58
PC John W. Aldous	1958–64
PC Eric Hopes	1964–66
PC Derek S. Tanner	1966–69
PC Leslie H. Knight	1969–75
PC Anthony Fraser	1975–78
PC Graham Read	1978–80
PC James Thacker	1980–93

Since the closure of the Police Station in Bramford, constables have attended the village from larger stations at Ipswich, Needham Market or Stowmarket, namely PC Bryden, PC Jon Eaves and, at the time of writing, PC Murray Osman.

Above: *The village school which was built in 1860 in Ship Lane.*
Left: *Mr and Mrs Wilfred Hurry, c.1940.*

Below: *Wilfred and Helen Hurry on their wedding day.*

TWELVE

&ᴄ◟◞◠◝◡◟ᴖ

EDUCATION

The following information notes significant events throughout the years regarding schooling in Bramford:

1829 The wife of the vicar, Revd George Naylor, was responsible for the building of the first recorded schoolroom in Ravens Lane. Later used as a reading room and parish room, it was demolished after being badly damaged in the storm of 1987.

1838 The *Ipswich Journal* of 30 June reported:

The children of the Day and Sunday Schools of Bramford, amounting to 100, partook of a plentiful spread of tea, bread and butter, and buns, supplied by a parochial subscription on the day of the Coronation of our Gracious Queen (Victoria), in their spacious School Room when appropriate hymns were recited and sung by the children. The widows of the parish, amounting to 26, were each supplied with a loaf of bread, 2oz of tea and a quarter of a pound of sugar.

1860 The schoolroom with master's house was built in Ship Lane by public subscription on land given by the Broke family.

1873 Another classroom was added. These rooms are now used for the Scouts, Guides, Cubs, etc.

Pupils at Bramford School, c.1900.

1897 A further classroom was added to provide accommodation for a total of 260 children; this is now the Parish Room.

1912 The site was extended and a separate building with two additional classrooms was added, now St Mary's Church Room.

1930 A new school was built in Duckamere for children aged 11 and over. It was called Bramford Area School and later Bramford Modern School. The old building in Ship Lane continued to be used for children aged 5–11.

1968 The senior children transferred to Claydon and the Duckamere buildings were taken over by the junior children who moved there in January 1969.

The earliest surviving log-book for the school begins in August 1862 in which the inspector's report includes the note that in two years the:

... multitude of undisciplined children have been converted into an excellent school, of which discipline could hardly be improved, and the instruction is very satisfactory.

The schoolmistress was Margaret Hammond who ran the school with the aid of two pupil teachers. In 1864 William Dye, who married Margaret Hammond, was appointed headmaster, and by this time there were 164 pupils paying for their education.

In 1873 Abraham Rumsey took over the school, which now had 200 pupils, and a new classroom was added to the end of the building. In 1881 he was living in the schoolmaster's house at the Ship Lane end of the building with his brother and sister. Although crippled with rheumatism and in a Bath chair, he continued at the school with his wife until their retirement in 1922, when Mrs Rumsey was presented with a silver plate for 44 years' service. In 2002 this plate was returned to the village by Olive Thorne, granddaughter of the Rumseys, who lives in Canada. She also returned a dish presented to her grandfather by the Bramford Provident Club in 1894.

Wilfred Hurry was a most popular and respected headmaster. He was born in the village at the paper-mill, now Rushbrook's Mill, in Paper Mill Lane and joined the school as teacher in 1904. He succeeded to the post of headmaster in 1912, transferring to the new senior school in Duckamere in 1930. He should have retired in the late 1930s but stayed on a few extra years because of the outbreak of war. He lived with his family in Holly Cottage on the corner of Duckamere.

When Mr Hurry transferred to the new school, Miss Ellen Salter became the headmistress of the old school in Ship Lane which became the junior school. She served for 16 years including the period of the Second World War which saw evacuees and air-raid shelters in the village.

In 1968 the senior schoolchildren transferred to Claydon Modern School and, following some modifications to the building, the junior children transferred to Duckamere. The headmasters after this were Mr Ellis, Mr Wimpress, Mr Dawson, Mr Nicholls and, at the time of writing, Mr Eden.

THE OLD BRAMFORD JUNIOR SCHOOL (1939–1945)

During the early days of the Second World War, evacuee families arrived from the Essex/London borders and were billeted with local families. The additional children caused overcrowding in the classrooms and desks were huddled together. In the infant building for five- and six-year-olds, some of the little children had to sit on upturned waste-paper baskets.

Before completion of the air-raid shelters, teachers rushed their classes to the lane beside the churchyard. When enemy aircraft dive-bombed overhead, they crouched beneath the hedges for protection. On one occasion, enemy planes machine-gunned the children as they fled across the playground – every child obeyed the command of its teacher that day. Thanks for still being alive were offered in prayer once reaching the dug-out. The air-raid shelters for the junior school were built behind the Victory Hall adjacent to the schoolroom, and those for the senior school were built near Cock Alley on the playing-field behind the school in Duckamere.

The shelters, some 25ft long, had steps leading down at each end. A sack hung at either entrance to shield from the bomb blast. A bucket improvised as a toilet at the foot of the steps. Stalled benches acted as seats and the teacher sat in the centre, with the most nervous children snuggled up to her. The lessons mainly consisted of reciting the times tables, poetry, telling stories or singing songs and hymns. In spite of continuous daily raids and sleepless nights, the standard of learning was extremely good. A hurricane lamp or a torch or two provided light when necessary.

The presentation by her ex-pupils of a seat in Bramford churchyard to Mrs Shortland (Miss Hunt) on her ninetieth birthday, May 1998. She taught at the school from 1930 to 1945. The event was featured on Helen's Heroes *on television. Many ex-pupils attended.* Left to right: *Margaret Warton, 'Miss', Caleta Thomas, being interviewed by Helen McDermott.*

Many of the people from London became homesick and returned to the city, the Blitz and their fate. Some settled in Bramford and still live in the village.

On occasions the children were given days off school in order to help with the war effort. Hips, blackberries and potatoes were gathered. Acorns were collected to feed Mr Fiske's pigs. Girls knitted warm mittens and balaclavas for the troops away from home.

Three teachers, Miss Jewel, Miss Lee and Miss Hunt, married servicemen within a few weeks of each other. Mrs Shortland (Miss Hunt) lost her husband in action a few weeks after her wedding. It brought a huge sadness to the school. Her former pupils who shared her sorrow that day still dearly love Mrs Shortland, who died in 2003, aged 94.

Being a Church school, the vicar, Revd Christopher Harford, gave scripture lessons in the classrooms. The children would also walk in crocodile style to church services.

When the American servicemen came into the area, the children were delighted. The GIs (as they were known) were generous in handing out chocolate, sweets and chewing gum. The chanting was 'got any gum, chum?' as the convoy of lorries carried the men into Ipswich each evening.

Nutritious dinners were served each day by volunteers in the Victory Hall. Dancing lessons also took place there for which black plimsolls were provided. Milk was offered daily and was warmed on the radiators in one-third pint bottles. The British Army stationed at Bramford Hall put on several concerts in the Victory Hall – and very good they were too. Who knows how many of the actors and singers went on to become famous?

It was essential to carry a gas mask at all times.

Senior schoolchildren lined up with their gas masks, c.1940.

They were worn around the neck with a piece of string tied to the cardboard boxes. Some luckier children acquired canvas covers or tin canisters to house the masks. A little light relief came when there was a 'gas mask drill' and the children had to put them on in class; one can imagine that caused quite a bit of laughter!

As the raids subsided and the war was coming to an end, fund-raising began to swell the Welcome Home Boys appeal. Concerts were held by children and adults and a sense of optimism was in the air. Fathers, brothers and uncles gradually returned to their estranged families. Hearts went out to people who could never welcome home their men, but the village will never forget them and their sacrifice.

In spite of being war children, the villagers remember their childhood as wonderful days. You will hear the now 'old' ones saying how lucky they were! There is still a sense of togetherness for those who shared their school days during the Second World War in Bramford.

BRAMFORD AREA MODERN SCHOOL IN THE 1950s

During the 1950s Bramford Area Modern School was attended by pupils from Bramford and the surrounding villages of Sproughton, Burstall, Copdock, Washbrook, Hintlesham, Chattisham and Flowton, who had not passed their eleven-plus examination.

There was an A and B stream for each of the four years and the school staff consisted of the eight class teachers, a woodwork/metalwork teacher (Mr Lowe), a domestic science teacher (Miss Mary

Houston) who also took the girls for games, PE, country dancing and, during the summer months, swimming, and the headmaster (Mr Dosser). They were supported by the school secretary (Mrs Firmin), the school caretaker (Mr Saunders), as well as the school cooks.

In the mid-1950s the class teachers were Miss Olive Messenger (class 1A and girls' 'craftwork'), Mrs Dorothy Hitchcock (class 1B and girls' needlework), Mr Parr (class 2A and art), Miss Pamela Bowling (class 2B and music), Mr Keyte (class 3A and boys' science), Mr Cooper (class 3B and boys' 'rural science' (gardening) and boys' games, PE and swimming), Mr Brian Humby (class 4A and geography), and Mr Thompson (class 4B and English literature).

Transport to school was on foot or by bicycle but for those pupils from the distant villages who did not own a bicycle, Suffolk County Council provided one on loan, together with waterproof cape and leggings. However, during the 'sugar beet campaign' from

The 'new' school in Duckamere, c.1945.

Class of five- and six-year-olds, c.1950. Left to right, back row: *Edward Cobbold, John Squirrell, Angela Grindy, Jennifer Dosser, Adrian ?, Brian Locksmith, Stuart Prike, Margaret Elmer, Jill Fisher, Peter Scott (?), Lewis Hood;* third row: *John Davis, Janet Garrard, Joy Bloomfield, Jean Daldry, Jill Southgate, Rosemary Hitchcock, Leon Fiddler;* second row: *Lorna Spurling, Ann ?, ?, Miss Salter, Winifred Robinson, Helen Bradbrook, Margaret Turner;* front: *Colin Pipe, Kenneth Fish (?), ?, Samuel Langford.*

The schoolchildren were encouraged to be self sufficient, the boys to grow vegetables (right) and the girls to cook and make jam (above).

In 2002 the pupils at Bramford Junior School made a calendar. The children born in each month of the year were photographed together.

Below: *The official opening of the hut for the playgroup in 1972. (Copyright East Anglian Daily Times)*

mid-October to mid-February a school bus was provided for road safety reasons for pupils from Copdock, Washbrook, Hintlesham and Chattisham, although many pupils still had quite a distance to travel to the pick-up points of the school bus.

During the winter months, netball and football matches were played against teams from other secondary modern schools in the area (e.g. Holbrook, Stowmarket). Every summer the best athletes from Bramford Secondary Modern would represent the school at the Schools Area Athletics meeting held at Stowmarket.

THE PLAYGROUP

Bramford Playgroup has been a place of happy memories for most of the village children over the years. It was in January 1969 that Mrs Elizabeth Jackson became concerned by the lack of facilities for young children in the village, and she was instrumental in forming an enthusiastic band of volunteers to start planning and fund-raising for a playgroup. So it was in 1969 that the first Bramford Playgroup began in the Victory Hall with just a few children, supervised by Jean Smith. Interest soon grew and numbers increased to 24 and 'opening hours' were extended.

Loren Butler at playgroup, 1994.

The playgroup, as a non-profit-making organisation, was run by a committee made up mainly of parents of playgroup children, but regular fundraising involving many more people in the village was essential to maintain the operation. In 1971 the playgroup, now running five sessions a week, began looking for their own permanent premises. Frustration and disappointment followed as attempts were made to raise a loan, but finally the big breakthrough came. Bramford V.C. Primary School provided the land and the group approached East Suffolk County Council for a mortgage to purchase the building. Instead, the County Council agreed to provide a prefabricated classroom, which it rented to the playgroup.

And so, 4 September 1972 was a real 'red letter' day in the history of the playgroup and the building was officially opened by Miss Fitzjohn of the East Suffolk Education Department, who had worked so hard on behalf of the playgroup during the negotiations. Also in 1972 a Bramford Mother and Toddler Group was formed, which met one afternoon a week.

In 1985 the Manpower Services Commission built a wooden fort in the garden, which was very popular with the children. This was demolished in 1994 as some of the timbers had begun to rot and it was thought to be unsafe.

During the 1980s and 1990s playschool was very

well attended and ran eight sessions a week with approximately 16 children in each, each child having three or four sessions.

In 1996 the building was painted on the outside with Noah's Ark and the animals by Mrs Williams, one of the mothers.

In 1997 the 'Voucher Scheme' was introduced whereby the Government paid some fees. This was the beginning of big changes. All four-year-olds were being funded and the Bramford Primary School decided to open a nursery school for all children who were aged four at the beginning of the school year. This took several children away from playschool and numbers dropped. It was decided that the playschool should be run to enable all four-year-olds to come every morning if required, and three-year-olds as many as four afternoons each week.

Then came the government's minimum wage legislation and so all supervisors and helpers had to be paid the minimum wage. Now all supervisors have to have an NVQ certificate, which meant many hours of study and college attendance.

And so, from humble beginnings, run by mums for the benefit of Bramford children, the village now has a playschool which is virtually controlled by the County Council, where the supervisors have to work to a curriculum and daily records are kept of the children's behaviour and ability, with regular visits by Ofsted.

Many happy hours have been spent at playschool. There is always an annual outing, either by train to Felixstowe, a zoo visit, or the favourite, Bourne Park – a wonderful venue in the 1980s and 1990s. Then came Playworld at Stowmarket, which of course is an ideal place where the weather doesn't matter. Nativity plays have always been performed for the benefit of relatives. Visits to Mrs Redman at Offton to see new lambs have been popular for many years, and every year there is a Christmas party.

Sylvia Harvey has had 25 happy years at playgroup. Other supervisors include: Mesdames Pearson, Plant, Playle, Lapworth, Williams, Renton, Hardingham, Wardley, Rice, Ward, Steward, Gibson, Crooks, Davis, Sago, Hunwicks, Farncombe, Chenery, Welham, Cordle and Carrol. Mrs Steward was on the original fund-raising committee and has always been associated with playschool, for several years running the mother and toddler group. The supervisors in 2003 are Mrs Smith and Mrs Challis.

There are many other Bramford mums who have been associated with playschool, either as helpers at sessions, chairmen or committee members, all far too numerous to mention.

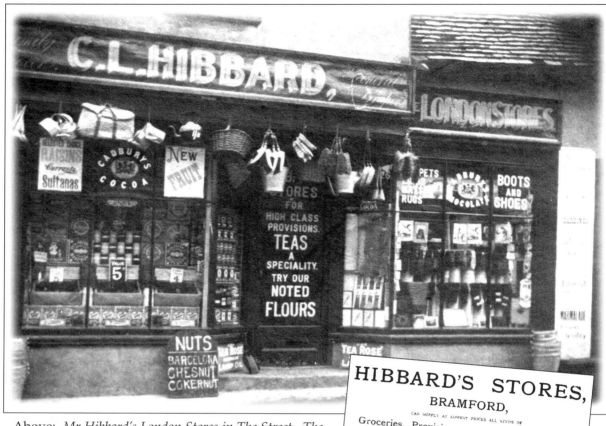

HIBBARD'S STORES,
BRAMFORD,
CAN SUPPLY AT LOWEST PRICES ALL KINDS OF
Groceries, Provisions, Draperies, Hardware,
Wall Papers, Rugs, Carpets, Linoleums.
PATENT MEDICINES and METHYLATED SPIRIT.
Noted for BREAD and PASTRY FLOURS.
We have a large stock of BOOTS and SHOES to select from.
COALS and COKE at lowest prices.

Above: *Mr Hibbard's London Stores in The Street. The advertisement (right) dates from c.1920 and shows that the store sold almost everything.*

Pallant's butcher's shop in The Street, where the chemist is now.

THIRTEEN

SHOPS AND PUBS

VILLAGE SHOPS

In 2003 Bramford still has a good range of shops despite many smaller outlets having come and gone, many being almost forgotten in the mists of time.

In the *Postal and Commercial Directory of Suffolk* published in 1864, there were listed: two grocers, Benjamin Baxter and Edward Haward (who was also a draper); one baker, Mrs Rachel Bowman; three boot- and shoemakers, James Chamberlain, Isaac Giles, and Thomas Mays; two butchers, George Hardy and Thomas Pallant; and one general store kept by Mrs Eliza Lewis.

Kelly's Directory of 1900 listed that there were still two grocers and drapers in the village, Frederick Bovill and Walter Tricker. Walter was now also supplying coal and corn from his premises, Commerce House. The bakery was still in the hands of the Bowman family and two boot- and shoemakers, Albert Mee and Walter Taylor, were operating. John and Henry Pallant were the butchers, as well as Charles Hood who was a pork butcher. Bramford had two general stores kept by Charles Chittock and Thomas Scopes. The *Directory* also recorded the new addition of a Post Office, kept by William King.

In *Kelly's Directory* of 1922 there was Walter Tricker's shop, which was described as a grocery. The bakers had expanded to become Bowman & Sons, Bernard Haste was the butcher and Mrs Hood was the pork butcher. Miss Green had a tobacco shop, Albert Mee was the only bootmaker, and general stores were kept by Charles Hibbard, Arthur Page and the Misses Ruffles – Happy and Violet.

By 1937 there had been a tendency to move from specialised shops to general stores. The tobacconist had been replaced by a newsagent and there were eight small shops, most of which were along the Bramford Road in what is now Ipswich, together with a fried-fish shop. However, Bales the butcher and Hood the pork butcher were still in the village (the latter became a pottery studio in the 1970s).

By the 1930s two grocery and sweet shops had opened in Paper Mill Lane – Humes and Daniels – presumably to serve the expansion of new houses and bungalows in that area. Another grocer's shop was started by Mr Sewell in a shed behind his house in Duckamere to take advantage of the school there; it closed in 1957.

The shop at 636 Bramford Road in Ipswich, which used to be in Bramford Parish. Left to right, back: Janet Francis and her cousin Cora Garnham; front: Jackie Steel and Gillian Steel.

Above: *Top Shop before the fire.*

Left: *Charles Hibbard, c.1930.*

Below: *Bowman's Bakery in The Street, later Fish's, now a dwelling. The advert (right) dates from 1942.*

THIS SPACE IS SMALL
BUT
BOWMAN'S BREAD
NEEDS LITTLE ADVERTISEMENT.
Established 130 Years.

Many of these small shops were in the front room of houses. In 1958 the following shops existed in Bramford:

R. Fish, baker, The Street

A.R. Bales, butcher, The Street

H.E. Page, grocery, etc., The Street

J. Page, wool, drapery and toys, Town House, The Street

A. Wilkins, grocery, confectionery and hardware, Commerce House, The Street (also known as Top Shop)

A.R. & W.E. Rayner, cycle repairs, distemper, hardware and ironmonger, The Street, where the present Post Office is, formerly the Police Station

M. Francis, wool shop, Mill Lane

R.G. Manning, shoe repairs, The Street

Daniels Stores, groceries and sweets, Paper Mill Lane

Home Stores, Paper Mill Lane

Mr Herbert Holder's barber shop was situated between The Angel and Bullen Lane. He was nicknamed 'Cut-a-customer', because if waiting boys got too noisy he would call out 'Be quiet, or you'll make me cut a customer.'

Several of the former shops used to deliver goods to surrounding villages. Bales the butcher had a van which was at one time driven by Mrs Doris Bewley, now a resident in Cherryfields. The bakery, first

AS NATIONALLY ADVERTISED - - -
just right . .
JOHN WHITE
FOOTWEAR
Appointed Retailer
R. G. MANNING
BRAMFORD
Repairs a Speciality
Leather, Rubber or Crepe at Moderate Charges

An advert for R.G. Manning's of Bramford, 1954.

Bowmans and later Mr and Mrs Fish, Commerce House, and Mr Page the grocer, also delivered. At the time of writing the village is very fortunate to have a mobile fish van owned by Mr Neal Dawes. He took over Whites Sea Fish from his father-in-law, and has parked his van in the yard of the Cock every Thursday morning for the past 10–12 years.

The village newsagents, until recently run by Mr and Mrs Wilkinson and before that the Mayes family, is next door to the Cock. They are also agents for the lottery. A little further up The Street is the Green Cross Pharmacy, proprietor Mr Glyn Mitchell, where prescriptions are dispensed, health items sold, and photographs developed. Mr Hollins took over the former boot and shoe repairers of R.G. Manning, and turned it into an upholsterer's and bygones shop.

Left: *Another local advert dating from 1954.*

Grocer and Provision Merchant
For Quality and Prompt Attention
F. G. COOK
"Home Stores," Paper Mill Lane, BRAMFORD

Bramford Street, 1930s. On the left is the shop of Albert Mee, shoemaker, on the right is the first Post Office, and beyond that the pork butcher, the Royal Oak, the bakery and the forge.

Left: *Herbert Holder, hairdresser, next to The Angel, c.1950.*

Above: *Wilkinson's newsagents, The Street.*

M. FRANCIS,
THE WOOL SHOP,
BRAMFORD.
Wools ▾ Haberdashery ▾ Stationery

Above: *Bramford Post Office on the corner of Ravens Lane, formerly the Police Station.*

Left: *West End Carpets in The Street, previously the Spar shop, one of the oldest buildings in Bramford.*

Left: An advert for a local builder, 1954.

About a 20-minute walk north of the village centre is Dairy Farm Nursery, rose centre, and a very recently opened farm shop selling fresh fruit and vegetables. Also on sale are home-made cakes, savoury pies and preserves, as well as numerous gifts. Lorraine Wright started the venture in 1996 and is planning to open a vegetable delivery service.

Turning left into Gipping Stone Road the electrical contractors are in premises which were used as a greengrocers in the 1970s. Next door is Doreen and Terry Lillie's fish-and-chip bar which opens Tuesday to Saturday.

Back in The Street, opposite Gipping Stone Road, is the Co-op selling almost everything in the household line and including both greengrocery and butchery departments.

There are not many country villages that can boast a ladies' hair stylist but Bramford has Jane's Hair Fashions. There are some gentlemen only too pleased to have a short back and sides attended to by the ladies' stylists! From 1967 to 1972, before the advent of lengthy locks for gentlemen, Barry Baxter used an upstairs part of the building as a gentlemen's barber.

Adjoining the hair stylist's is West End Carpets. This building housed a small Spar supermarket in the 1970s and '80s. Before that the further end of the property was a tiny greengrocer's and sweet shop owned by the Ruffles family, which closed around 1955–60.

The last shop in The Street, further up on the same side as the Co-op, is the village Post Office, which was once the Police Station. In the early 1950s a new station was built in Duckamere and the old building was converted into a hardware and ironmonger's shop, owned by A.R. & W.E. Rayner, who also repaired bicycles. The occupant of the Post Office in 2003 is the postmistress Sue Withell. In spite of its small size, it sells stationery, many household items, haberdashery, and is also an agent for dry cleaning.

Other businesses include two car dealers in the village and another at the White Elm in Paper Mill Lane, Scott's Fertilizers (formerly Fisons), Rushbrook's Mill which makes sports turf products, a roofing company, plus fencing and gate makers, and several small builders.

BRAMFORD PUBS

The riddle below is often recited by older Bramford residents but in fact only tells half the story of the rich history of drinking establishments in this ancient village:

Where is it?

> *The Cock doesn't crow,*
> *The Bell doesn't ring,*
> *The Oak doesn't grow*
> *and The Angel doesn't sing.*

(or the local version)

> *The Elm that never grew,*
> *The Cock that never crew,*
> *The Angel that never flew.*

Answer: Bramford

Historians suggest that the total number of pubs in Bramford, past and present, could be as high as nine. In fact, five of them were, amazingly, located within a radius of just 700 yards in Bramford Street and Ship Lane.

So, let us take an historic walk through Bramford starting at the north end, turning off the old Roman road, now the B1113, into Bramford Street. Some 300 yards on the right, at 79 The Street, is The Angel Inn which can be traced back to at least 1608. Still a very popular tavern today, The Angel was at one time set in 12 acres of land with a vast array of stables, barns and allotments. It can be seen in a very early postcard *(see page 4)*. The Angel was home to the village bowls team, where the old pavilion still remains, and is also, according to tenant Kevin Brown, the home of three ghosts! At the end of the nineteenth century the landlord was Henry Palmer. The Angel still provides good food and comfortable accommodation.

An advert dating from 1954.

Above: *The Ship Inn, now three dwellings, 2002.*

Left: *The former Bell Inn, now two dwellings, 2002.*

Right: *The Royal Oak, now a dwelling, 2002.*

Bramford Cock in the 1930s with the Cyclists Rest shed. (From the Gillson Collection SROI JI 6/37)

A few yards down from The Angel on the left, at 68 The Street, is Royal Oak House which has been a private dwelling since the early 1960s, but prior to this was a public house called the Royal Oak. The pub is just about visible in an old photograph *(see page 147)*. According to early directories Emma Barfield was the landlady in 1926 and continued in that role until the late 1940s when her daughter Ada had a brief spell in charge. Ada was followed by William Garrod and Frederick James and then, around 1960, Francis Partridge made the short journey across the road from The Angel where he had been landlord since 1940. Many local residents have fond memories of the Royal Oak.

Continuing another 100 yards on the same side one comes across Numbers 6–10 The Street, the oldest group of houses in the village. This was once the home of the Bell Inn, which was developed from a fifteenth-century medieval open-hall house. Advertised in 1799 as a former public house, it is many years since the doors were open to the public, although the owner, Richard Pinkney, has uncovered many artifacts during alterations. These include copper coins dating back to the 1790s, oyster shells, clay pipes from the late 1600s and gaming coins from the late 1700s.

Directly opposite the former Bell is the second of the two public houses surviving to this day, the Cock. Built in 1604, the timber-framed tavern has been at the heart of the village for generations. One of the earliest photographs featuring the Cock was taken during the funeral procession of Captain Loraine. Featured in the photograph is a (green) shelter attached to the pub that was only recently demolished to make way for the new conservatory. In the early-twentieth century it was known as the Cyclists Rest. The lean-to shelter was used in earlier days to house the indoor quoits competitions. During the

Susanna Page and Prince in front of the White Elm, Paper Mill Lane, 1920s.

1950s Bramford were Suffolk Quoits Champions for six years running. The timber from the green shelter lives on however, forming part of a kitchen/dining-room floor in the home of the sister of landlord Bill Stoddart. It is thought that many of the ancient beams used in the construction of the pub can be traced back to the old barges.

The pub also housed its own butcher's shop in years gone by. Like The Angel, it is supposedly home to a ghost which has been seen three times by the landlord. The ghost, George, can possibly be traced back to a suicide at the pub more than half a century ago.

According to local directories the landlady in 1844 was Rebecca Wiggen followed by Pearl Hardy (1856), Abraham Dale (1874), Thomas Woollard (1884) and Charles 'Tom' Lloyd (1926). These were followed by George Reeve (1938) and his son Charles, in 1940, before Frederick Page took over between 1943 and 1962. The pub stayed in the same family for the next 18 years when the daughter of Frederick Page, Peggy, together with her husband Tom Wardley, were licensees. Their retirement was marked by a party and the presentation of a clock.

On entering Ship Lane there is a timber-framed house which stands on the corner of Church Green; this used to be the Ship Inn. Built in 1499, possibly as a guildhall, the fine pink building is a well-loved Bramford landmark. The earliest reference to it as a pub was in 1709; this continued until 1788.

Further down Ship Lane one makes a left-hand turn into Paper Mill Lane in order to locate the final known pub in Bramford, the White Elm. Bramford resident Dennis Page of Paper Mill Lane has strong connections with the tavern that closed its doors for the final time in 1978. His grandparents, Susanna and Arthur Page, were landlords in the 1930s and 1940s. This couple were followed by Herbert Giles (1943), Arthur Rose (1947–56), and Reg Fox. The old pub is now the home of a flat-roofing company and a second-hand car sales business.

Records suggest that there were more pubs in Bramford. One which was definitely in existence was at 667 Norwich Road, and was known as The Crown. Demolished in 1990, the Whitton pub was formerly in the parish of Bramford. The earliest record of the former Cobbold pub is 1756.

Records show that there was a public house called The Bull in existence in 1778 and a further reference was made in 1619 to The Princes Arms, but the sites of these are not known.

The Angel, Bramford, 2002.

Aerial view of the main area of housing looking south, with The Street at the top-right corner, the river top left and Acton Road along the bottom.

Aerial view of The Street looking east, with Gables Corner and Paper Mill Lane at the top, in front the railway, then the river and church, with The Street running across the picture and the Cherryfields complex in the near foreground. (These two photographs are reproduced with permission of Suffolk County Council Education Advisory Service.)

FOURTEEN

❦

INTO THE TWENTY-FIRST CENTURY

Over the centuries Bramford has changed enormously. It was once a purely agricultural village, which then became a moderately industrial community and subsequently a dormitory village for Ipswich. Very few inhabitants now earn a living in the community and, as transport becomes more convenient, workers are travelling further and further afield.

Ipswich is creeping ever closer to the village, with just one field and the A14 trunk road now separating the two communities. It seemed possible at one stage that the village would be lost completely. In the 1960s a plan was drawn up to extend Ipswich by 250,000 inhabitants to the south and west, which would have absorbed all the small villages in the area. Bramford would have become a satellite town of 60,000. As might be expected, opposition to this was very strong and, following two crowded meetings in the village hall, Bramford's case was fought by Alec Pryke and others at the inquiry, and the scheme was eventually dropped.

In the early 1970s the Boundary Commission proposed that Bramford should be included in the new Ipswich District. Once again the village fought to retain its identity and won.

At the time of writing Bramford is still a thriving community in spite of the fact that Ipswich is creeping ever closer. There are still many leisure

Neville Barrett and Bud taking advantage of some winter sunshine at the millennium sundial and seats.

Above: *The millennium banners in Bramford Church and the people involved with their production and installation. Left to right, back row: Jean Dedman, Margaret Warton, Joy and Ian 'Bill' Barrett, Olive Godbold, Pat Jarman, John Wilding; middle: Wynne Browes, Mary Oakes, Stella Alderton, Margaret Dakin; front: Kayleigh Chinery, Stephanie Keeble.*

Above: *The millennium banner. Left to right: Beryl Sims, Evelyn Boast, Daphne Ellis, Pat Wright, Sylvia Harvey, Gloria Baxter, Don Golding.*

Aerial view of Bramford Church beside the River Gipping.

groups, both sporting and more sedentary. The shops are having to work hard to compete with the ever-enlarging supermarkets nearby.

The arrival of the new millennium did not go unmarked in Bramford. A small committee decided that the most appropriate symbol would be a sundial, which has been erected on the village green incorporating the village sign, which was erected in 1977 to celebrate the Queen's Silver Jubilee. The funds were obtained in various ways. Many residents sponsored a brick, the seats were kindly donated by the family of the late Mrs Kathy Sparrow in her memory, Mr John Williams, County Councillor, kindly obtained a grant, and there were also talks and raffles. However, the bulk of the money was raised from two concerts produced by Bridget Harvey in the Loraine Victory Hall. All the performers were present or past residents of Bramford, and it was amazing to see the range of talent in the village. The first half consisted of songs from shows and comedy sketches and the second half took the form of an old-time music hall. Perhaps the most unforgettable act was performed by local policeman Jim Thacker, dressed in a nightgown and cap and a wig of blond curls, holding a candle, singing:

Jim Thacker on stage at the variety concert, 2001.

My mother said, 'Always look under the bed,
before you blow the candle out,
see if there's a man about.'
I always do, you can make a bet,
but it's never been my luck to find a man there yet!

Two banners were also produced with squares representing each group in the village. Even the children at the playgroup each contributed a few stitches towards their square. The banners hang in St Mary's Church.

A team of hardy volunteers planted 2,000 daffodil bulbs on grass verges around the village, some at Gables Corner opposite Paper Mill Lane, some at the junction of Fiztgerald Road and Loraine Way, and others on a traffic island at Parish Pond. Unfortunately this last site has since been altered by improvements to the junction and not many bulbs appear to have survived.

2003 ONWARDS

The people of Bramford have a great deal for which to be thankful. The village is a thriving community despite not having much in the way of employment. The Blue Circle cement works lying a couple of miles north of the village has closed, as have the beet sugar factory south of the village, and Scotts fertilizer company in Paper Mill Lane. However, there is plenty of employment available in Ipswich and even London is within commuting distance.

Bramford has an adequate bus service, though it could always be improved. There are a number of social events regularly taking place in the village, of both indoor and outdoor varieties. The school and activities for young people are flourishing, though no doubt they would like more. There are now strict rules about adult supervision making it difficult to set up youth activities.

Plans are under way to improve facilities at the playing-field, and a hard surface has been installed for skateboarding. Discussions are also taking place about the refurbishment or replacement of the Loraine Victory Hall. To ensure that Bramford provides the facilities required by its residents, a village questionnaire is being prepared, which will be delivered to each household. The answers will help formulate a Parish Plan. Leisure groups and residents will also be consulted.

Perhaps the greatest treasure are the water meadows *(see page 6)*, a haven for wild flowers and birds, and lovely for people and dogs too! They will not be built on in the foreseeable future as they still flood regularly. The meadows are an area of natural beauty and attract walkers and fishermen. They form part of the Gipping Valley Footpath along the old tow-path from Ipswich to Stowmarket.

Further up the valley to the north, some of the old gravel workings were transformed into a water park with fishing and quiet water sports in the 1980s. Just recently a golf range has been added, with plans to extend to a full-size golf course.

Bramford has been in existence for over 2,000 years and, with the support of its residents, both present and future, the authors hope that it will continue to thrive and retain its individual character.

SUBSCRIBERS

William Arthur Abbott

Beverley D. Aldous, Bramford, Suffolk

Arthur W. Allen, Bullen Close, Bramford

Mr and Mrs G. Allum, Ipswich, Suffolk

Mr Len Allum, formerly of Bramford

Colin and Averil Ault, Fraser Road, Bramford

Jean Austin (née Hardwick)

David J.S. Bailey, Bramford, Suffolk

Don Balmforth, Bramford, Suffolk

E.J. Banks

Alison Bardwell, Bramford, Suffolk

Mrs Gloria and Mr Barry Baxter, Bramford, Suffolk

Lee Baxter, Bramford, Suffolk

Ron Baxter, Bramford, Suffolk

Ryan Baxter, Bramford, Suffolk

Andy and Jan Beckett, Bramford, Suffolk

John Beckett, Oadby, Leicestershire

Leslie Beckett

Ernest S. Bennett, Ipswich, Suffolk

Jack Benstead, Bramford, Suffolk

Doris Bewley, Bramford, Suffolk

Mr and Mrs E. Black, Bramford, Suffolk

Brian Blomfield, Sproughton, Suffolk

Ray Bloomfield, Ipswich, Suffolk

Bernard V.G. Blowers, Bramford

William H. Blowers, Bramford, Suffolk

Abi Borrett, Bramford, Suffolk

Karen and Paul Botwright, Royal Oak House, Bramford

Margaret and Helen (née) Bradbrook, Bramford

Hilda I. Brady, Suffolk

Kerry and Karen Briggs, Bramford, Suffolk

Rita Brink (née Drane), USA

Daren, Louise, Anna-Louise and Holly Broadway, Bramford

Mr Pat Broadway, Bramford

Pat and David Brooke, Bramford, Suffolk

Wynne Browes, Ipswich

Evelyn Brown, Ipswich, Suffolk

Mrs Jean P. Brown

Pauline and Steve Brown, Bramford

John N. Bugg, Ipswich, Suffolk

David and Lynn Bullock, Bramford, Suffolk

Anne Bumstead McGee, Sevenoaks

John Bumstead, Mistley

Peter Bumstead, Ipswich

Maureen Burrows (née Hardwick)

Mr and Mrs F. and P.D. Burton

The Cairns Family, Papermill Lane, Bramford

F.G. Chandler

Melvyn Chaplin, Lewes, Sussex (Page Family of Bramford)

David Chappell, Bramford, Suffolk

Keith and Pat Charman, Bramford, Suffolk

Charlie and Wendy Clarke, Bramford, Suffolk

Jean Ann and Peter Clarke

Roy J. Clover, Bramford, Suffolk

Barry J. Coleman, Bramford, Suffolk

Alan W.S. Cooper, Ipswich, Suffolk

Paul Crane, Bramford, Suffolk

Roy Victor George Cross, born 1928 Ravens Lane, lived 29 years The Street, Bramford

Raymond J. Crouch, Bramford, Suffolk

Tony Cudmore, Bramford, Suffolk

Adrian Cunningham, Brussels, Belgium

D.M. Curran
Margaret R. Dakin, Bramford, Suffolk
Sheila M. Daldry, Ipswich, Suffolk
Joyce E.J. Davey (née Gynn), late Bramford, Suffolk
Basil G. Dedman, Bramford, Suffolk
The Revd Canon Roger Dedman, Priest in Charge, Bramford
Lilian J. Dodds, Offton, Suffolk
Mrs B. Drinkwater
Keith Driver, Ipswich
Miss Anthea M. Durose, Grove House, Bramford
Michael B. Earthy, Ipswich, Suffolk
Barry J. Earthy and S.M. Heath, Bramford
Robert Ellis, Laxfield
John and Val Ellis, Bramford
Peter Ellis, Capel St Mary, Suffolk
Charles E. Ely, Bramford, Suffolk
Ron Everitt, Bramford, Suffolk
Adrian T. Fowler, Bramford, Suffolk
Ronald Fowler, Bramford, Suffolk
Anthony D. Fox, Bramford, Suffolk
Mrs Audrey Francis, Bramford, Suffolk
Brian E. and Valerie J. Francis, Bramford, Suffolk
Mrs Tracey Freeman, Somersham, Suffolk
Jill Freestone, Ipswich
Charles B. Frost
B.A. Game, Bramford, Suffolk
Margaret A. Gant, Bramford, Suffolk
Elsie and John Gardiner, Ringshall, Suffolk
Kerrie Gardiner, Needham Market, Suffolk
Michael Gardiner, Ringshall, Suffolk
Eric and Margaret Garnham, Bramford
Mr and Mrs C. Garrod, Bramford, Suffolk
Dane Garrod, Abingdon
Robert S. Garwood, Bramford, Suffolk
Fred Gee, ex Fisons Horticulture
Patricia A. Gilbert, Bramford, Suffolk
John A. Godfrey, Ipswich, Suffolk
Don and Doreen Golding, Bramford, Suffolk
Ian Golding, Ashfield, Suffolk
Susan K. Goodall, Bramford, Suffolk
Mr and Mrs G.T. Goodchild, Bramford
Sonia P. Goodson, Bramford, Suffolk
Phyllis M. Gould, Ipswich, Suffolk

Derek S. Green, Bramford, Suffolk
Mrs J. Gregory
Steve Gulyas, Bramford, Suffolk
John W. Gynn, Ipswich, Suffolk
Louise E. Gynn, Ipswich, Suffolk
R.L. Hammond, Lower Somersham, Suffolk
Margaret R. and Raymond P. Hardwick, Bramford, Suffolk
Mr and Mrs Peter Hart
Mr and Mrs T.W. Harvey, Bramford
Sheila M. Herd, Bramford, Suffolk
Miss Megan L. Hicks
Christian Hill, Romsey, Hampshire
Steve Holden, Bramford, Suffolk
Mr and Mrs I.J. Hood, Great Blakenham, Suffolk
Margaret A. Hood, Bramford, Suffolk
George C. Huggett, Dunmow, Essex
Rob, Emma and Joshua Hughes, Bramford, Suffolk
Mr Peter and Mrs Janet Jackaman, Bramford, Suffolk
Stan Jackaman, Bramford
Elizabeth Jackson, Caversham, Berkshire
Patricia A. Jarman, Bramford, Suffolk
Kenneth Jay
Mary E. Jolly, Ipswich, Suffolk
Morag and Graham Jones, Bramford, Suffolk
Herman Kearney, Tara, East Bergholt
Dorothy J. Keeble
John F. Keeble, Bramford, Suffolk
Nigel F. Keeble, Bramford, Suffolk
Judy Kemish, Bramford, Suffolk
Eileen and John Kettley, descendants of Songer family, Bramford
James L. King, Victoria, Canada
P. Kingham
Les, Jenny, Frances and Lee Knight
Samuel Langford, Ipswich, Suffolk
Mr David and Mrs Julie Last
Cecil and Jenny Laughlin and Family, Bramford, Suffolk
June Laws (née Norman), Bramford
Derek Lay, Barham, Suffolk
J.M. Lay, Peterborough, Cambridgeshire
Trevor and Beryl Lay, Bramford
The Viscount Leathers, Bury St Edmunds

The Lee Family, Bramford, Suffolk
Bert W. Leech
Doreen and Terry Lilley, Bramford, Suffolk
Emma L. Lilley, Bramford, Suffolk
Lee Lilley, Bramford, Suffolk
Mr S. and Mrs P. Lilley, Bramford, Suffolk
Maurice (Monty) Lockwood, Ipswich
Peter S. Lockwood, Little Blakenham
R. and M. Lockwood, Bramford, Suffolk
Mr and Mrs T.W. London, Ipswich, Suffolk
Joyce Manning, Bramford, Suffolk
Alec Marsh, Bramford, Suffolk
Sue Maskell, Bramford
Keith and Valerie Mather, Paper Mill Farm,
    Bramford
Sophie, Charlotte, and Oliver Mawson,
    Tara and Kieran Risby, Paper Mill Lane
David W. Mayhew, Bramford, Suffolk
Hazel and Derek Mayhew, Bramford
Peter and Margaret Mayhew
Ian, Karen, Erin and Daniel McAllister,
    Bramford, Suffolk
Mr and Mrs T.J. McCusker, Bramford,
    Suffolk
Michael D.H. McErleane, Bramford, Suffolk
Samuel A. McGinty, Bramford
Wendy McGinty (née Earthy), Bramford
Mr David Meadows, late mother's name
    née Tricker, Bramford
Joan W. Mills, Bramford, Suffolk
D. and P. Murton, Bramford, Suffolk
Mr and Mrs Richard Nash, Bramford,
    Suffolk
David Neville, Richmond
Colin G. Newman, Ipswich, Suffolk
Tony I. Newman, Bramford, Suffolk
Julie D. Nicholls, Bramford, Suffolk
Juliet Oldring, Ipswich, Suffolk
Mr Dennis R. Page, Bramford, Suffolk
Peter and Doris Page, Bramford, Ipswich
Mr Colin Payne, Bramford, Suffolk
Raymond D. Payne, Stowmarket, Suffolk
Stuart Pearson
Basil M.J. and Zena C. Peck, Bramford
Kevin J. and Lucy E. Peck, Bramford
Richard (Dick) Pegg, Capel St Mary, Suffolk
Bernard Keith and Pamela Beatrice Petch,
    Bramford, Suffolk

Elizabeth Pettman, Woodbridge, Suffolk
Freda Phillips, Ipswich
Capt. R.N. Phillips, Little Blakenham,
    Suffolk
Richard Pinkney, Bramford
Brian James Plant, Bramford, Suffolk
Derek A.J. Porter, Bramford, Suffolk
Trevor and Angela Potter, Bramford,
    Suffolk
Lilian C. Power, Bridge House, Bramford
Dorothy Pryke, Bramford, Suffolk
Frederick W. Pryke, Somersham, Suffolk
Ingrid Pryor (née Haward), Bishops
    Stortford, Hertfordshire
Bernard J. and Maureen V. Purbrick,
    Bramford, Suffolk
J. Alan Purdham
Mrs Joan B. Pyke, Ipswich, Suffolk
Christine and Graham Ranson, Bramford,
    Suffolk
A.F. Raymond
The Razzell Family, Bramford, Suffolk
Janet Read, Bramford, Suffolk
Mr B. Reader, Bramford, Ipswich, Suffolk
Stuart and Tina Reid and Sons, Bramford
The Renton Family, Bramford, Suffolk
Joy Rhodes and Nick Day, Ipswich
S. and J. Rhodes, Bramford
The Rink Family, Bramford, Suffolk
Sandrina Risbridger, Bramford, Suffolk
K. Robin, Bramford
Trevor R. Rowe, Bramford, Suffolk
Mervyn Russen, Employee at Bramford
    Works for 36 years
Richard and Jane Sago, Bramford
Arvin Sareen, Bramford, Suffolk
Beryl Savidge, Ipswich
Mrs Jennifer Peggy Sayer (née Ford)
Brian Scarlett, Bramford, Suffolk
Evelyn L. Scopes, Bramford, Suffolk
Robert J. Scruby, Bramford, Suffolk
Roy J. Scruby, Bramford, Suffolk
Margaret K. Self, Tonbridge, Kent
Jim Shipp, Bramford, Suffolk
Jim and Maureen Sillett, Bramford Hall
    West Wing
Irving and Vivienne Silverwood, Bramford,
    Suffolk

Olive C.E. Simpson
Chris and Beryl Sims, Bramford
Robert and Susan Skinner, Flowton, Suffolk
Freda Slade and Isaura Riley (née Slade),
    Ipswich, Suffolk
Claire M. Smith, Bramford, Suffolk
David E. Smith, Ipswich, Suffolk
Kirsty J. Smith, Bramford, Suffolk
Richard W. Smith, Ipswich
Susan and John Smith, Bramford, Suffolk
Jenny A. Smith (née Brown), Bramford,
    Suffolk
Revd Edwin J. Softley
Mrs J. Southgate, Pittsburgh, Pennsylvania,
    USA
Mr Colin Sparrow
Jacqueline and Bill Sparrow, Bramford,
    Suffolk
Jayne Sparrow, Bramford, Suffolk
Patricia J. Sporne, Little Blakenham, Suffolk
Frank Squirrell, Kesgrave, Suffolk
John A. Squirrell, Rushmere St Andrew,
    Ipswich, Suffolk

P. and J. Stannard, Bramford, Suffolk
Rosemary and Richard Steward, Bramford
James and Lisa Studd, Barham
Mr F.R. and L.J. Summers, and Janet
Brenda Sutton (née Gynn), Ipswich, Suffolk
Arthur Taber, Bramford
Mr and Mrs Taber, Bramford, Suffolk
Angela, Andrew, and Carla Tarini,
    Bramford
Sam and James Templeman-Webb,
    Bramford
Jim and Carol Thacker, Bramford, Suffolk
Caleta Thomas, Ipswich
Ms Olive Thorne, Edmonton, Alberta,
    Canada
Wendy K. Thrower, Bramford, Suffolk
Richard Thurlow, Ipswich
May P. Tibble, Bramford, Suffolk
Rose Tooke, Bramford, Suffolk
Dr David Travis, Bramford, Suffolk
Paul and Helen Tricker, Bramford, Suffolk
Paul and Rose Turnell, Bramford, Suffolk
Whitmore, Joanne and Tony, Ipswich

Community Histories

The Book of Addiscombe • Canning and Clyde Road Residents Association and Friends
The Book of Addiscombe, Vol. II • Canning and Clyde Road Residents Association and Friends
The Book of Axminster with Kilmington • Les Berry and Gerald Gosling
The Book of Bampton • Caroline Seward
The Book of Barnstaple • Avril Stone
The Book of Barnstaple, Vol. II • Avril Stone
The Book of The Bedwyns • Bedwyn History Society
The Book of Bickington • Stuart Hands
Blandford Forum: A Millennium Portrait • Blandford Forum Town Council
The Book of Bramford • Bramford Local History Group
The Book of Breage & Germoe • Stephen Polglase
The Book of Bridestowe • D. Richard Cann
The Book of Bridport • Rodney Legg
The Book of Brixham • Frank Pearce
The Book of Buckfastleigh • Sandra Coleman
The Book of Buckland Monachorum & Yelverton • Pauline Hamilton-Leggett
The Book of Carharrack • Carharrack Old Cornwall Society
The Book of Carshalton • Stella Wilks and Gordon Rookledge
The Parish Book of Cerne Abbas • Vivian and Patricia Vale
The Book of Chagford • Iain Rice
The Book of Chapel-en-le-Frith • Mike Smith
The Book of Chittlehamholt with Warkleigh & Satterleigh • Richard Lethbridge
The Book of Chittlehampton • Various
The Book of Colney Heath • Bryan Lilley
The Book of Constantine • Moore and Trethowan
The Book of Cornwood and Lutton • Compiled by the People of the Parish
The Book of Creech St Michael • June Small
The Book of Cullompton • Compiled by the People of the Parish
The Book of Dawlish • Frank Pearce
The Book of Dulverton, Brushford, Bury & Exebridge • Dulverton and District Civic Society
The Book of Dunster • Hilary Binding
The Book of Edale • Gordon Miller
The Ellacombe Book • Sydney R. Langmead
The Book of Exmouth • W.H. Pascoe
The Book of Grampound with Creed • Bane and Oliver
The Book of Hayling Island & Langstone • Peter Rogers
The Book of Helston • Jenkin with Carter
The Book of Hemyock • Clist and Dracott
The Book of Herne Hill • Patricia Jenkyns
The Book of Hethersett • Hethersett Society Research Group
The Book of High Bickington • Avril Stone
The Book of Ilsington • Dick Wills
The Book of Kingskerswell • Carsewella Local History Group
The Book of Lamerton • Ann Cole and Friends
Lanner, A Cornish Mining Parish • Sharron Schwartz and Roger Parker
The Book of Leigh & Bransford • Malcolm Scott
The Book of Litcham with Lexham & Mileham • Litcham Historical and Amenity Society
The Book of Loddiswell • Loddiswell Parish History Group
The New Book of Lostwithiel • Barbara Fraser
The Book of Lulworth • Rodney Legg
The Book of Lustleigh • Joe Crowdy

The Book of Lyme Regis • Rodney Legg
The Book of Manaton • Compiled by the People of the Parish
The Book of Markyate • Markyate Local History Society
The Book of Mawnan • Mawnan Local History Group
The Book of Meavy • Pauline Hemery
The Book of Minehead with Alcombe • Binding and Stevens
The Book of Morchard Bishop • Jeff Kingaby
The Book of Newdigate • John Callcut
The Book of Nidderdale • Nidderdale Museum Society
The Book of Northlew with Ashbury • Northlew History Group
The Book of North Newton • J.C. and K.C. Robins
The Book of North Tawton • Baker, Hoare and Shields
The Book of Nynehead • Nynehead & District History Society
The Book of Okehampton • Roy and Ursula Radford
The Book of Paignton • Frank Pearce
The Book of Penge, Anerley & Crystal Palace • Peter Abbott
The Book of Peter Tavy with Cudlipptown • Peter Tavy Heritage Group
The Book of Pimperne • Jean Coull
The Book of Plymtree • Tony Eames
The Book of Porlock • Dennis Corner
Postbridge – The Heart of Dartmoor • Reg Bellamy
The Book of Priddy • Albert Thompson
The Book of Princetown • Dr Gardner-Thorpe
The Book of Rattery • By the People of the Parish
The Book of St Day • Joseph Mills and Paul Annear
The Book of Sampford Courtenay with Honeychurch • Stephanie Pouya
The Book of Sculthorpe • Gary Windeler
The Book of Seaton • Ted Gosling
The Book of Sidmouth • Ted Gosling and Sheila Luxton
The Book of Silverton • Silverton Local History Society
The Book of South Molton • Jonathan Edmunds
The Book of South Stoke with Midford • Edited by Robert Parfitt
South Tawton & South Zeal with Sticklepath • Roy and Ursula Radford
The Book of Sparkwell with Hemerdon & Lee Mill • Pam James
The Book of Staverton • Pete Lavis
The Book of Stithians • Stithians Parish History Group
The Book of Stogumber, Monksilver, Nettlecombe & Elworthy • Maurice and Joyce Chidgey
The Book of Studland • Rodney Legg
The Book of Swanage • Rodney Legg
The Book of Tavistock • Gerry Woodcock
The Book of Thorley • Sylvia McDonald and Bill Hardy
The Book of Torbay • Frank Pearce
The Book of Watchet • Compiled by David Banks
The Book of West Huntspill • By the People of the Parish
Widecombe-in-the-Moor • Stephen Woods
Widecombe – Uncle Tom Cobley & All • Stephen Woods
The Book of Williton • Michael Williams
The Book of Witheridge • Peter and Freda Tout and John Usmar
The Book of Withycombe • Chris Boyles
Woodbury: The Twentieth Century Revisited • Roger Stokes
The Book of Woolmer Green • Compiled by the People of the Parish

For details of any of the above titles or if you are interested in writing your own history, please contact: Commissioning Editor, Community Histories, Halsgrove House, Lower Moor Way, Tiverton Business Park, Tiverton, Devon EX16 6SS, England; email: naomic@halsgrove.com